## ALSO BY CLIFF FARRELL:

TREACHERY TRAIL

DEATH TRAP ON THE PLATTE

THE GUNS ON JUDGMENT DAY

COMANCH'

CROSSFIRE

BUCKO

RETURN OF THE LONG RIDERS

RIDE THE WILD COUNTRY

THE WALKING HILLS

THE TRAIL OF THE TATTERED STAR

RIDE THE WILD TRAIL

THE LEAN RIDER

FORT DECEPTION

SANTA FE BOSS

OWLHOOT TRAIL

PATCHSADDLE DRIVE

SHOOT-OUT AT SIOUX WELLS

TERROR IN EAGLE BASIN

# THE MIGHTY LAND

# THE MIGHTY LAND

By Cliff Farrell

1975

DOUBLEDAY & COMPANY, INC.

GARDEN CITY, NEW YORK

*Library of Congress Cataloging in Publication Data*

Farrell, Cliff.
  The mighty land.

  Bibliography: p. 193
  Includes index.
  1. Frontier and pioneer life—The West.  2. The West—History—1848–
1950.  I. Title.
F591.F37      917.8′03′2
ISBN 0-385-09759-X
Library of Congress Catalog Card Number 74–12685

# Contents

# THE MIGHTY LAND

CHAPTER 1

# THE WONDERS OF THE LAND

From the Shining Mountains the view of The Mighty Land is stupendous. It's like sitting on top of the world with everything slanting off in all directions around you.

For instance, if you have been gazing southward from this exalted viewpoint at the right time you might have seen the buffalo emerging in an endless stream from the misty caverns on the Staked Plain of Texas, far, far away beyond the ragged green thread that is the course of the Arkansas River. At least that's where the Indians believed the buffalo came from in an inexhaustible supply.

Turning northward there might have been on display such a marvel as the "putrefied" glass mountain where Jim Bridger's rifle bullets bounce back to terrify him as he shoots at game that seems near at hand, but is actually miles away on the other side of the transparent ridge.

Quite a distance to the west you peer over the peaks of the high California mountains and watch James Marshall gaze excitedly at a handful of gravel that he has picked up from the bed of a stream.

Nearer at hand, in that same direction, the sun reflects on the surface of Great Salt Lake in its arid lonely basin, awaiting the coming of the Mormons, who will convert its wastes into a land of milk and honey.

But it is to the east that you gaze, spellbound, for a long, silent time. You are seeing the vast showplace of The Mighty Land.

These are the Great Plains. They stretch all the way to the Mississippi River, an endless carpet of lush prairie and gray-green buffalo country—silent, overwhelming. At first it seems deserted.

To the north lies the crooked break in the Plains that is the Missouri River on its way to join the Mississippi in the greening country to the east. To the south, if you peer closely, you can make out the faint trace of a yellow thread that winds southward, crosses the Arkansas, and heads toward Mexico. That was made by the wheels and hoofs that carry the Santa Fe traders in their loaded wagons toward Spanish territory.

Midway between the Missouri and the Arkansas lies the network of another great stream. Its branches and veins originate at your feet in the snows of the Shining Mountains.

What you are seeing is the Platte River in its wide valley. Meandering willfully eastward, it is a mere thread in places. In others it is a mile wide and an inch deep as the saying goes. It is looked down on with scorn by the raftsmen and steamboat pilots on its deeper neighbors north and south, but, nevertheless, it is the artery of the Great Plains. It carries the pulse beat of The Mighty Land.

As you gaze, you discover that the Platte is paralleled by another yellow thread similar to the Santa Fe Trail, but much longer, much wider, more pronounced on the face of the land. The Great Trail, the Oregon Trail, the California Trail, the Great Medicine Road. These are some of the names it bears. It is all the same pathway.

You now begin to detect movement in that majestic sweep of country eastward. Those dark swaths that cover immense sections of the treeless plains, and which you at first thought were the shadows of moving clouds, turn out to be buffalo in enormous herds, grazing in their eternal drift north and south. Along the yellow thread that roughly follows the winding Platte, you detect dust—more movement. You make out wagons, with tilts that are as white as sails in the sun. The Great Parade through The Mighty Land is there before you.

First come the buffalo and the Indian. Very much the buffalo, very much the Indian. They possessed The Mighty Land in the beginning. The buffalo were there by the millions, the Indian by the thousands when the first explorers ventured up from Spanish territory or westward from Canada and gave the high Rockies the name Shining Mountains. At a time of day when the sun is right, the peaks swim like silver castles in the sky, and beckon men on, daring them to match their strength against the allure of the ridges.

A few survivors of the once-mighty herds are still around, carefully preserved. The Indian also continues to exist on the Plains, but at the white man's tolerance. He is hemmed in on reservations, still trying to adjust to the ways of the hordes that have swamped him.

Next come the Mountain Men in their buckskins and foofaraw, riding their mules, with their Indian wives on foot, leading the pack animals. They are the vanguard of the Great Parade. They are the trumpeters sounding the near doom of the buffalo and the Indian.

You see Kit Carson and his men ride up from Taos with their mule strings. They camp on the South Platte and damn it to perdition, for it always seems to be high when they want to ford. They finally make it across, and head for the mountains to float their trap sticks in the beaver streams. They return in the spring, bearded and gaunt, their numbers fewer, their animals loaded with plews. They head for Bent's Ford on the Arkansas to sell the pelts and then to move on to Taos and Santa Fe, where they will fatten up and dance with the señoritas.

Marcus Whitman's wagon party creaks into view, en route to the Oregon country where they aim to Christianize the tribes. Jim Bridger rests his stock along the Platte for a day or two, bound for the Black Fork on the fringe of the Ute country, and to map out Bridger's Road. John C. Frémont rides by, accompanied by Carson, and continues up the South Platte on one of his empire-building journeys.

The ranks of the columns in the Great Parade swell, the pace quickens. Ox wagons lurch into view, accompanied by determined stampeders who talk of Oregon and free land. The dust from Mormon handcarts drifts in the wind. Drums and bugles sound and troops appear. Forts begin to spring up along the main Platte. The dust billows higher into the sky. A mighty armada is sailing into view over the horizon. Here come the forty-niners in their prairie schooners. They cruise endlessly by in the greatest gold rush of all time. This excitement barely begins to subside when the Pikes Peakers come stampeding over the skyline, bound for the new strikes in the nearby Rocky Mountains.

Pony Express riders make running dismounts at the rude sod or rock or log huts that are swing stations along the route, transfer the mail *mochilas* to fresh mounts, and are on their way to the next strong point. Overland stagecoaches come off the trail at the relays with six- and eight-horse teams lathered, often with Sioux or Cheyenne arrows jutting from animals and vehicles.

The Army builds Fort Sedgwick in the heart of the hostile land up the South Platte. Wild Bill Hickok rides in to scout for the cavalry. Ben Holladay, the stagecoaching tycoon, rushes over the Great Medicine Road in his plush, red-leathered private coach, with a pretty woman at his side, en route, hell-for-leather to Salt Lake, Denver, or whatever.

Bugles sound again. A band strikes up. The tune is "Garry Owen." George Armstrong Custer, that most controversial of military figures, is on his way up the Platte at the head of a contingent of the 7th Cavalry. New orders turn him back and detour him into waters even deeper than any he has encountered in the past in his amazing career.

Another, with long hair like Custer, fringe on the buckskin jacket streaming in the breeze, causes every head to turn, especially the feminine heads, as he rides by on the streets of Denver or Cheyenne. William Frederick Cody—Buffalo Bill—who was to hobnob with kings, and die in poverty, starts and ends his career in The Mighty Land.

The list of those who march in the Great Parade seems endless. There goes Jules Benti, founder of one of the first frontier trading posts on the South Platte, for whom the little present-day community of Julesburg, Colorado, was named. And Joseph Slade, the gunman, who cut off Jules's ears and used them as watch fobs. Ned Buntline, the fictioneer, appears. Horace Greeley alights from a dust-caked Overland stage on his "Go west, young man" trip. Wyatt Earp swamped for a bull-team freighter bound for Salt Lake, his renown as a gun marshal still in the future.

Steam whistles wail. Jack Casement and his terriers push steel rails up the Platte Valley. Gamblers, percentage girls, gunmen, pickpockets, and footpads swarm off flatcars and begin setting up their temporary saloons and brothels. Hell on Wheels has arrived with its peripatetic carnival of sin and frolic. General Grenville M. Dodge, chief engineer of Union Pacific construction, strolls by in his frock coat and silk hat, accompanied by a coterie of eastern bankers and their ladies, who gape at the sights and pretend to be horrified.

They all parade along the Great Trail. Famous names, romantic names, notorious names. Heroes and thugs, brave men and cowards, lawmen and desperadoes. They are a part of the Plains, part of The Mighty Land, as much a part of it as the incredible sunsets that glow over this land of great distances, rugged bluffs, and erratic streams. This is a land where the wind moves free, the sky is finger-tip close, and there is always wine-fire in one's blood.

And yet, in this sublime country, where red men and white men fought and tortured and pillaged, there is still no real peace. Over the graves of many who passed by in the Great Parade the debate grows more and more fierce, even as their bones turn to dust. Their detractors slash more and more savagely, their defenders stand all the more firm. Cody is derided, defended. Hickok is denounced, praised. Earp is castigated, glamorized. And Custer! Over his grave the battle really rages.

The hand of man lies heavily on The Mighty Land now. Great checkerboards that are fields of wheat and corn have replaced the gray-green sweep of the buffalo grass and the grama. Denver, on the benches of the Shining Mountains, has its million inhabitants, and its traffic problems. The haze of industry and of Union Pacific diesels hovers over Omaha and Council Bluffs to the east. Cheyenne is a state capital. Salt Lake City sprawls near the lake with its broad boulevards and green lawns. Traffic speeds across The Mighty Land on wide interstate highways.

The old days are gone. Forever, the white man says. Not so, believes the Indian. He yearns for the days the old ones have told about in tales handed down. He hopes that the day when a man rode as free as that same Plains wind will return. The days when the great buffalo herds were the monarchs of The Mighty Land. Ah, the buffalo!

CHAPTER 2

## THE MIGHTY HERDS

The American buffalo is believed to have been the most numerous of any species of mammal to appear on the planet. The fork of the Platte in central Nebraska where the north and south branches join was the heartland of the buffalo country. It was quite a domain. It stretched from Mexico almost to the Land of the Little Sticks in upper Canada. But it was in the valleys of the Missouri, the Platte, and the Arkansas that the buffalo were found in herds whose extent staggered the descriptive powers of viewers.

The buffalo are gone from the Plains, at least for the present, although there is a school of thought which believes that if the big, final, world shoot-out ever comes, it will be some of these short-horned, clumsy beasts that will ride through the cataclysm and preserve the species.

They are a hardy breed. The big Sharps .50 rifle almost did them in after they had conquered the calamities of nature and disease for centuries. But they weathered that. Like the Indian, they now subsist on reservations—and wait.

What manner of creature is this beast? At first glance, and even a second look, he seems to be one of the most awkwardly proportioned animals on four legs. He stands about as tall as a man at the hump, and considerably less at his hindquarters, which seems pitifully inadequate for the rest of him. His hide scales off in patches when he is shedding, so that he appears to have fallen out of a rag bag. In winter, he sports a beautiful, glossy, fur robe.

He seems clumsily defenseless, but he has been known to put

grizzlies to route. He has been clocked at thirty-five miles per hour when he is in a hurry. When he settles into a running pace he can keep it up for a dozen miles or more and has been known to distance three relays of horses. He has survived blizzards that left ranchers wiped out by the hundreds. He can rustle for a living where even sheep can't make it.

Purists insist on referring to him as the American bison. We will continue to call him the buffalo. Daniel Boone helped hunt down the last buffalo in Kentucky. That was before the Revolutionary War in the Dark and Bloody ground around Boonesboro and Lexington.

Still earlier, explorers came upon the great, shaggy animals as far east as where the Pentagon now stands on the Potomac River. The Conquistadores sent back to Spain descriptions of the weird, humpbacked beasts they encountered in Mexico. But their real birthright was the Plains. It is said none were ever seen west of the Pecos River in the southwest, and their numbers were few beyond the continental divide and in the Salt Lake Basin. The Plains was their habitat.

Some researchers say that, at their peak, there were forty million buffalo on the continent. This is certainly a very conservative figure. It is true their numbers had been reduced somewhat before the white man appeared. The red man, no conservationist, who lived for the day and was unconcerned about the morrow, slew indiscriminately, one method being to stampede herds over the brinks of cliffs. Even so, handicapped as he was by lack of other weapons, any effect he had on the number of animals in existence must certainly have been minor and probably was a blessing in helping retain the balance between the buffalo and its means of subsistence.

When French-Canadian traders moved in, placing muskets and gunpowder in the hands of the tribes, the killing was stepped up. Great caravans of two-wheeled ox carts carried "flints," as hunters called the dried hides, to shipping points in Canada. Europe began wearing buffalo-fur overcoats and using buffalo leather. British troopers in the Crimean war wore shoes shod from the hide of the buffalo, although its spongy quality made this use questionable.

Then came the men armed with the big .50s. The Union Pacific, the Kansas Pacific, and the Santa Fe remained solvent on the profits from carrying trainloads of trophies of the slaughter eastward.

These were hides, mainly, but pickled and smoked buffalo tongue and meat were also prized on eastern tables. Coyotes, which were called prairie wolves in those days, lived high and waxed fat, for they weren't particular whether the carcasses were pickled or smoked as long as they were left by the thousands by the hunters for their sampling.

The railroads also made money in passenger traffic, transporting hunters to the herds—not only the businesslike commercial hide hunters, but also the trophy nimrods. The latter came from far and near, armed to the teeth, breathing fire and brimstone, ready to shoot at anything that moved.

Came the Englishman in tweeds, laced leggings, and Scotch-reddened nose, and speaking a language that immediately branded him as an object of ridicule. Some were lords and earls, with wealth that they invested in cattle ranching after the buffalo were gone. Some turned out to be pretty hairy customers who ran more than one would-be western bad man up a tree and showed native cattlemen a thing or two about grading up a beef herd.

Came German barons, Russian dukes, French counts, and Italian nobles. Also commoners. All thirsting to down a buffalo, or maybe a dozen or more. Came the American sportsman by the thousands for the same purpose.

One of the most colorful of the hunters, and certainly the most publicized at the time, was the son of the Czar of all the Russias, the Grand Duke Alexis. Another elite sportsman was the Earl of Dunraven. Both the Grand Duke and the Earl had Buffalo Bill Cody as a guide.

Who was America's most famous hunter? Famous, not skillful. That title probably must go to Theodore Roosevelt. His forte was not pursuit of the buffalo. He came to the Plains a little late for that, although there were still some to be had. But there was abundance of other game.

A man of great mental, physical, and personal qualities, Teddy Roosevelt was a tireless exponent of the chase. He loved the zest of it. He loved the outdoors. In his view, the hunt brought out all the manly qualities that he believed were essential to the individual, and to the nation. His writings in his sedentary years echo his longing to return to the scenes of the past, to know again the thrill of the chase. He gloried in roughing it, and yearned to enjoy again the tang of campfire smoke and the spice of pine forests. He

was America's most ardent pursuer of game for the sake of sport
alone.

Not so the professional buffalo hide-taker. Despite the inroads
of the Indians and the French-Canadians, the great herds were
still virtually untouched when he stepped on the scene, a Sharps
rifle over his shoulder, a skinning knife at his belt, a jug of whisky
on his mule.

Traveler after traveler, hunter after hunter, in the region from
the valley of the Platte south to the breaks of the Brazos River in
Texas have left records of sights that might lead one to conclude
that they, also, must have been carrying a jug with them.

Drunk or sober, the accounts are so uniform they evidently were
on the side of caution, even in a time when exaggeration and the
telling of tall tales was an art.

Theodore Roosevelt, who came upon the scene just too late to
see the mighty herds, much to his regret, talked to many older
hunters who were there when. He quotes a friend, Clarence King,
who estimated a herd that was moving north in western Kansas in
1862 as covering an area seventy miles by thirty miles in extent.
Mr. King arrived at this figure after riding through the gathering,
which, like all buffalo herds, was not a solid mass but consisted
of bands of various sizes grazing at reasonable distances from each
other.

Roosevelt quotes another friend, General W. H. Walker, of Virginia, who was caught in the path of a buffalo stampede some ten
years earlier. While hunting a mile or two from the Arkansas
River, he heard that ominous sound so dear to writers of western
fiction. It was the deep, growling, distant rumble that might at
first be mistaken for thunder.

It was not thunder. It was the real thing, a buffalo stampede.
General Walker was not the first to describe that sound, nor the
last. Many who heard it did not live to tell about it.

Walker, in a race for life, reached the pinnacle of a small bluff
along the river around which the mass of beasts rumbled. From
his vantage point he could see the brown flood rolling endlessly
over the horizon and flowing toward and around him. The stampede rushed down the cutbanks into the Arkansas, converting
water into mud and froth, ascended the opposite low bluffs, and
continued northward across the prairie. The sheet of oncoming
flesh continued to emerge over the horizon to the south as though

on an endless belt, thunder past beneath a growing fog of dust, cross the river and sweep northward. Walker managed to find an opening and returned to his hunting camp, which was out of the path of the stampede.

Darkness came and there was no apparent decrease in the tumult. Not long before dawn, the uproar ended. Silence returned over the prairie. When daybreak strengthened, Walker returned to his vantage point on the bluff and gazed southward from whence the stampede had come. He expected to view an empty prairie. Behold! The land was carpeted by buffalo, which were grazing peacefully in the dawn, and were drifting in from the south. Events like that, no doubt, led the Indians to believe there never would be an end to the supply of buffalo.

The animals drifted in such great numbers during a terrible blizzard in November 1871, that the garrison at Fort Dodge fired artillery into the masses to prevent them from crushing the buildings and corrals of the fort.

Billy Dixon, famed buffalo hunter, rode up the Arkansas after the storm had ended, hoping to sight targets for his Sharps. About to give up, he came upon an area that looked as though a giant roller had passed by. Grass and brush were flattened for miles. He followed this mighty swath and came to the rim of higher ground. He halted his horse, staring unbelievingly. As far as his vision carried in the clear air, the Plain was a mass of buffalo. Hide-taking was easy in the days that followed for Dixon and for the other hunters who came hurrying out from Dodge and Griffin and Harker when the news got around.

Roosevelt's brother, Elliot, at the age of seventeen, and a cousin, John Roosevelt, were caught on open prairie on the Staked Plain by a stampede in 1877 and saved their lives by opening fire with their rifles, succeeding in splitting the herd at the last moment.

However, it was just one thing after another for Elliot and John. Their narrow squeak in the stampede became a secondary event two days later when they escaped a Comanche war party by an eyelash. Buffalo hunters in a neighboring camp were jumped and left dead and wounded by the Comanches. The two Roosevelts lost their horses and reached Fort Griffin on foot days later, feet blistered, bellies touching their backbones.

The men of the 10th Cavalry didn't miss this sort of thrill either.

They were caught in one of those earth-shakers while patrolling against the Cheyennes out of Fort Wallace, in Kansas. Homer W. Wheeler, later to become a colonel, who was scouting for the outfit at the time, told about it in his book *Buffalo Days*.

The sound was first mistaken for that of an oncoming thunderstorm. When the truth dawned, the guns of the company managed to divert the stampede so that it passed a hundred yards from the troopers. But the buffalo wrecked two of the company's three wagons. All of the mules took off for parts unknown and few of them were ever seen again.

All these happenings took place when the buffalo was still king of prairie and plain. For ages he had grazed the land, generation after generation, decade after decade. His natural enemies were insignificant. Wolves and coyotes cut off a calf here and there or filled their bellies on the still-living flesh of mired beasts or decrepit bulls that had been driven from the herd. Buzzards, ravens, crows, and magpies darted in to claim their shares.

The horse Indians fed on the buffalo, built their lodges and clothed themselves from his hide, used his gall and spleen to protect them from scurvy, depended on his intestines and bladder for water bags and other purposes, his sinews for thread, his horns, hoofs and bones for ornaments and many other uses. They followed the buffalo, bound to it like slaves. They could not have existed as nomads without the great beast of the Plains. Still, their demands for a livelihood had little effect on the great mass of animals that speckled the land.

Disease was sometimes a formidable factor. Rinderpest and other plagues decimated some of the herds at intervals, but the buffalo shook off these losses and refilled its ranks. An epidemic swept through the herds as late as 1862, but it passed and the animals soon seemed as numerous as before.

But his near doom was at hand. An enemy more impersonal than pestilence, as relentless as nature itself, had stepped on the scene. The boom of the big .50 Sharps was heard in the land.

Soon, thousands of hides were stacked on the levees at St. Louis, brought by steamboats down the Missouri or by wagon all the way from the Platte Valley. Memphis became a hide center also, a receiving point for the Arkansas and Red River country.

The guns of the hunters provisioned the cookshacks of the construction crews as the railroads built westward. Bill Cody and

Wild Bill Hickok made money as meat providers for the men who were pushing the Kansas Pacific to Hays City. Jack Casement and his Irish terriers ate buffalo beef as they spiked down Union Pacific rails in the Platte Valley. Sledge swingers and gandy dancers ate hump ribs while they marched A.T. & S.F. steel across the Kansas prairie toward Dodge and on into New Mexico.

The Sharps buffalo rifle threw a slug from a bottle-shaped cartridge. Its impact was like the blow of a mallet. Hunters who knew their business could run up scores of fifty to sixty animals from a single stand, their bag being limited only by the danger of ruining their guns from overheating.

Billy Dixon, the buffalo hunter, is quoted in a book of his life, written by his wife, Olive Dixon, as saying that the gunfire could be heard hour after hour, as though a battle was being fought along a line from Dodge City on the Arkansas River to Granada on the high Colorado plains.

Hundreds of men, out of work when the Santa Fe ran out of money and stopped construction for a time in Colorado, turned to hide and meat hunting as a means of livelihood, and the slaughter increased. Rath & Wright, traders, shipped two hundred thousand hides out of Dodge the first season they were in business.

Trading stores at Dodge and North Platte and Julesburg, and other places along the Platte and the Arkansas and the Red, sold powder by the keg and lead by the mule load to hunters, and reaped a second profit on the hides that were brought in.

Enormous warehouses sprang up at Grand Island, Sidney, and Cheyenne. They held thousands of hides waiting shipment. No traveler downwind from any of these communities needed directions, come storm or blackness of night, as how to reach shelter. He followed his nose.

On the Plains the situation was worse, what with the skinned carcasses left to rot in the blazing summer sun. Even coyotes and the ravens avoided the horror, for there was always fresh meat elsewhere, in clearer atmosphere, on which to gorge as the skinning crews moved onward, following the herds, with the rifles of the hunters playing a relentless drum-fire.

The buffalo was on his way to the same fate as that of the passenger pigeon, whose flights once darkened the midwest skies. The fate that other species have suffered.

It seems that a man with a weapon in his hand must use that

device on *something*. In the cave man days, clubs whacking on skulls was the pastime. Then came the maces, lances, and whatnot, along with bows and arrows, and then the crossbow. Finally, gunpowder increased the distance from which a hunter could strike down a quarry without much risk to himself—as long as the target could not shoot back.

Hand the average person a firecracker and he will likely not rest until he ignites it beneath the chair of some unsuspecting soul. Hand another a firearm and he's *got* to shoot at something or suffer the agony of sheer frustration. Witness the bullet-torn highway signs on back roads, the damage to insulators on telephone poles in areas where the nimrod, finding no deer to bag, nor even a rabbit or a ground squirrel to exterminate, simply has to shoot that beautiful gun. How many times in our wanderings on dim wheel-track back roads in desert or mountains have we come to road signs that were intended to tell us the right way home only to find all information destroyed?

I was riding with a friend in a car on a dusty back road through the timber in Oregon not far from the old pioneer town of Jackson when a bobcat ran across the trail in front of us. This was at midday, a rare occasion for viewing these elusive, nocturnal animals.

The bob, and it was a beauty in size and pelt, vanished into the brush, making a considerable racket in the dry underfooting. My friend, who is quite a hunter, almost literally tore his hair. "If only I'd have thought to have fetched my gun along!" he lamented. "I'd sure have taken care of that cat."

"Why?" I asked. "You've already got some nice bob pelts at home."

My friend eyed me. "Why—why, that cat, he kills things," he said.

This same man told about coming upon an ancient, half-blind black bear in the back country. "That time I did have my gun along," he said with satisfaction. "It took only two shots. That fella never knew what hit him."

"What did you do with it?" I asked. "The carcass?"

He stared at me as though I had gone out of my mind. "Do with it? Now just what could I do with a stinking old bear?"

A mighty slayer of bears was one General Wade Hampton, who operated in pioneer Mississippi. Theodore Roosevelt recorded that the general slew at least five hundred of these animals during a hunting career before the Civil War. He did not achieve this record without help. He used as many as forty hounds to bring his prey to bay so that it could be dispatched.

The grizzly, for which California was chiefly named the Bear State, has been extinct for half a century in the Golden State. The fate of the passenger pigeon is well known, along with the battle to save the trumpeter swan, the whooping crane, the California condor, and many other less publicized species, both awing and on foot.

Conservationists are concerned about the prairie chicken, which only a generation or so ago was abundant in the sagebrush on the Plains, fearing it also is on its way to extinction. The Eskimo curlew, which once migrated across America by the millions, is believed to be extinct along with the passenger pigeon. Pot hunters with volley guns slew them by the hundreds of thousands. Finally, the guns could find no more targets.

But it was the buffalo, above all other game, that fired the killing urge to the boiling point. Nearly all accounts left by travelers of the California and Oregon Trails tell of the impatience with which the prairie and plain was scanned each day as they marched westward and approached the "Coast of Nebraska," as the Platte Valley was known. Finally would come the hoarse, excited shout: "Buffalo! Buffalo!"

Often, at this outpost to the great herds farther on, the game would be a lone, aged animal, or a small band of a few cows and calves. A journal kept by forty-niners Vincent Geiger and Wakeman Bryarly tells of the "loud huzzas" that came from the men of their wagon party when a buffalo was sighted. All hands left the wagons to join in the pursuit until the animal fell dead, perforated by many slugs. The journal added that the quarry proved to be none too fat.

When the quarry became more numerous the killing often became more wanton. This was one of the main grievances of the Indians in their peace parleys with the Army. But it was not always slaughter for the mere thrill of killing. Buffalo meat was a common sight, hanging from the bows of prairie schooners to cure in the dry Plains air. It was a valuable addition to the larders of the stampeders.

Buffalo meat retains its magic appeal to this day. The sound of that word—buffalo—seems to bring a mental picture of savory hump ribs roasting over an open fire, of mountain men feasting on barbecued quarters at Brown's Hole and the Green River rendezvous, of succulent steaks sizzling in skillets over campfires as dusk moves in from the pine forest.

Even the thought of it whets the appetite. The reality was almost as delectable. There are stories of two or three mountain men, who had been on lean rations for a spell, taking care of an entire young buffalo at a single sitting. It was said that a hungry Sioux could almost perform that feat alone if he put his mind—or his stomach—to it in earnest. Buffalo meat seems to have the magic quality of digesting easily, and of being very nourishing without pushing a consumer to the need of bicarbonate.

Susan Shelby Magoffin, bride of the famed Santa Fe trader Samuel Magoffin, who is believed to have been the first white woman to travel the trail to New Mexico, stirs the appetite of readers of her diary with a few words about fine fat meat being stretched on ropes to dry during a stop on the Kansas prairie in order to fill the larder before pushing on south where game might not be as abundant. Soup made from hump ribs she found on a par with any competition from eastern chefs, and she expressed a young, pretty woman's fear of putting on weight on such a diet.

However, she worried about her husband when he was off on a buffalo hunt out of sight of camp, not entirely because of the Indian danger, but because of the hazards of the chase itself. She imagined him lying, bones broken or stunned after his horse had fallen, with angry animals charging to finish him off. In fact, one of Sam Magoffin's companions returned from such a hunt with a badly injured head, proving she had reason to be apprehensive.

That was meat hunting in the best sense of the word, of course. Santa Fe traders were businessmen and they rarely slew game for the mere sake of watching the beast crumple and fall to the long-distance magic of their fire sticks. But, later on, passengers riding Kansas Pacific and Union Pacific and Santa Fe trains were hoisting windows and shooting at anything that moved in range or out of range as their coaches rattled across prairie or plain. The K.P. offered ten-dollar excursions out of Leavenworth and Lawrence to hunters, and practically guaranteed they would find buffalo to kill.

Prairie dogs, sage hens, jack rabbits were fair game when better targets were not available. The canny coyote soon learned to give the thundering monsters that rumbled across the land a wide berth.

Antelope, which ran in bands of thousands, were picked off on the hop and left dead, or dying, for "goat meat" was held in low regard when buffalo beef was likely to be available. The buffalo was the grand prize. Fortunate was the passenger who could boast when he alighted at North Platte, shook the train grime from his hat, and headed for the nearest saloon, that *his* arrival had been delayed by a big herd crossing the tracks down the way and that he and fellow marksmen had killed maybe a hundred critters, all of which were left to stink in the sun, of course, what with the train already behind schedule.

The real slaughter reached its peak in the seventies. Buffalo meat, both fresh, salted, and smoked, was shipped east by the hundreds of thousands of pounds. Refrigerator cars came into use, in turn creating big icehouses at the loading points. Pickled tongues were on the menus of every restaurant of any consequence in the East, were carried in stock by butcher shops, and were standard fare on the free lunch counters in the better saloons.

The hide business gave the railroads a source of revenue that tided them over the rough early days, and almost ruined them when the supply ran out. It has been estimated that two million buffalo were killed in 1871 and that one St. Louis dealer alone bought a quarter of a million hides that year.

The handwriting was on the wall. The old belief that the supply was inexhaustible was crumbling. The voices of the conservationists were heard in the land. But other voices were louder. Some of the northern Plains states passed laws to control buffalo hunting. Such efforts failed in Kansas, where the herds still ranged in big numbers. The economy of the newly settled country depended on the buffalo, with the majority of the population engaged in hunting down the great beasts or handling the hides and meat for shipment.

A live buffalo was of no use whatever to the railroads. A nuisance in fact. When the buffalo wasn't blocking trains with his lumbering drift north or south across the right of way, or getting hit by locomotives that often came out second best in the collisions, he was ruining telegraph communications by using the poles as back-scratchers to rid himself of ticks. After the passing of an itching herd of buffalo, the telegraph line often appeared as though it had been in the path of a cyclone. And then there were often windowpanes or window frames in the cars to repair from bullet holes placed there by armchair hunters who were too excited to be exactly sure what was in their sights when pulling the trigger aboard a jolting coach.

Furthermore, men wearing tall-crowned, wide-brimmed hats and big spurs were appearing at the ends of steel, driving with them herds of Texas Longhorns. Shipping beef eastward opened a new source of revenue for the railroads. Texas cows and bulls also began to stock the northern Plains, which could not support both buffalo and cow. The day of the trail town, the Texas trail hand, the gun marshal of legendary skill, dawned with the sunset of the American buffalo.

But probably the greatest weight of all in the scales against the buffalo was the United States Army, at least that portion of it that manned the lonely and often-besieged forts on the frontier. "Kill a buffalo and you have one less Indian to fight," said one general, William Tecumseh Sherman by name. "Wipe out their commissary and you've won the war," said another. "The buffalo is the Indian's grocery store. Destroy it."

For once, the Army was right. With the dwindling of the buffalo herds the power of the Indian weakened, although other factors contributed to the fading. The appalling truth dawned so abruptly that the men who had slaughtered the animals could not believe it. Buffalo were becoming scarce.

Before the 1880s arrived it was about over from the Platte down to the Staked Plain from which the buffalo were supposed to emerge in an endless river. Hunters began traveling far, day after day, passing over places where they had made their stands only a year or two in the past. The skulls and ribs, white as ghosts, lay on the prairie to attest to their marksmanship and ruthlessness. But that was all. Where had all the live buffalo gone? Surely, the big herds must be around somewhere.

What scattered small bands were left had grown elusive, but they were hunted down and wiped out even though the slayers knew that a priceless heritage was being destroyed, a heritage that had given majesty and wild beauty to a mighty world. Still they could not stay their hands.

It was a mania. Kill! Kill! Kill! The Indians were subdued. Custer and his men lay in their graves. Cody was a circus man.

Billy Dixon had turned to ranching. Hickok was dead. Dodge City had been tamed.

Still they trailed the survivors of the host that had reigned over the Plains. Then the news came that it was not yet over. Up north, in Montana and Dakota, there were still buffalo by the thousands. It had not been worth while to work that country in the past because of the cost of hauling hides through the Sioux and Cheyenne hunting grounds to the Union Pacific—a cost both in scalps and money.

But the Northern Pacific had built through. Thousands of hunters, experts in the art of mass slaughter, marched north. That was in 1880–81. Within a few years it was about over up there also. The story was the same as on the lower Plains. Where the devil had they gone? Surely, there must still be lots of them somewhere! Why, they had been here by the thousands only yesterday!

Maybe they had drifted farther north. But hunters who ventured great distances into the Canadian plains found no trace of their quarry, only deserted wallows.

They were gone. Off into the blue. Into the land from which no hunter, no buffalo would ever return. The great herds had been obliterated.

It couldn't be true! The minds of men refused to grasp the harsh fact, refused to accept the guilt. Buffalo was still the big game, the obsession. Someone was trying to cheat the hunters of their right to kill. They relentlessly pursued the survivors which had managed to tough it out by scattering into the deep canyons and brush-matted ravines of the Black Hills and the Rockies. Some had taken refuge in the badlands of the Dakotas.

Peril had made these creatures wary. Trackers believed they were more fleet of foot than in the past, of better eyesight, and more dangerous when brought to bay. Climatic conditions, particularly the hard winters of the upper Plains, had made these survivors particularly valuable as trophies because of the richness and dark texture of their pelts and the magnificence of their heads. Many hunters believed these were a distinct species and named them mountain buffalo, or sometimes wood buffalo. This, of course, was not the fact. The buffalo of the Staked Plain, of the Kansas prairie, came often in dun, and even in so pale a hue they were almost white. They may have been heavier of belly and haunch than the buffalo of the north, which endured more severe winters and probably were more agile because of lack of girth, but they were all one and the same as to species.

Theodore Roosevelt was not immune to the fever of the final hunt. A few survivors of the great northern herd hung on in the Dakota badlands when he was ranching there in the 1880s. The tracks of a band of half a dozen were discovered in the fall of 1889, and Roosevelt set off with his party, trailed them down, and slew the bull in the group. In one of his books on hunting in the West he tells with obvious relish of the tense wait, rifle in hand, for the bull to move into the open for a clear shot. The shot came, the buffalo fell. In this case, however, the cows and calves were allowed to escape into the canyons unharmed.

By that time the great hide sheds along the Union Pacific, and along the Santa Fe and the Kansas Pacific, had stood empty for so many summers that even the stink had faded and were no longer much of an offense even downwind.

Indeed, there were not too many noses to be offended, for, with the revenue from the buffalo gone, the Plains had fallen on hard times. The wave of settlers that had swept into the country after the Indians had been subdued had crested and subsided. Homesteaders who had bet the government they could grub out a living on the dry, hostile Plains during the hot summers and bitter winters, where even the buffalo had scrabbled for existence, were fleeing east, ragged, discouraged—busted.

The dance halls at Dodge, at Cheyenne, at Hays City, rarely resounded to the thrum of a banjo or the clump of a sodbuster's boot heel. They awakened only when the trail drives came through, and even these were beginning to dwindle. The music was generally some doleful tune, such as "Mother Machree," or "The Cowboy's Meditation." The majority of the saloons, always the last to leave a sinking town, were boarded up. On the Kansas and Nebraska prairies, the story was the same. Homesteaders' deserted shacks began to lean with the wind and stare with vacant eyes at the withered stubs of corn around whose roots the eternal breeze was blowing away the disturbed soil.

But the buffalo had left one heritage. His bones. The era of the bone pickers began. The pennies of profit from gathering the whitened skeletons of the mighty beasts kept body and soul together for the majority of those who had hung on through the lean years when hard money was as scarce, almost, as a live buffalo.

The railroads began carrying trainloads of bones to the crushers in the fertilizer plants. Skulls, ribs, thighbones, brought in by wagonloads, filled the warehouses once more and stood in great ricks along the tracks at the shipping points.

Among the bone pickers were many of the men who had left the carcasses to the sun, wind, and the coyotes. Even a buffalo hunter had to swallow his pride when he was starving. He had one advantage over the sodbusters. After the pickings became slim close to the settlements, he knew the best places to look for the shine of white skulls and ribs in the vast land along the Platte, the Republican, the Arkansas. He knew because that was where he had made his stands and had slain them.

One bone-buying firm estimated it had purchased the skeletons of nearly six million buffalo during the decade when the pickers were burning off the prairie long grass so that the skulls and ribs could be located.

The nation, at least that segment of it that concerned itself with such things, suddenly awakened to the realization that what had been considered an impossibility had become a chilling reality. The buffalo was nearly extinct. A hurried, and not very accurate estimate showed that less than three hundred animals survived in public zoos, and that probably less than a thousand existed in a wild state. These latter were still being hunted.

Efforts of W. T. Hornaday, taxidermist for the U. S. Museum of Natural History, reversed the tide. He is credited with being responsible for creating reserves for herds in Yellowstone and other national parks.

They are nurtured now in reserves in both the United States and Canada, and on private holdings, and their numbers have grown into the thousands, so that danger of complete extermination seems remote, barring unknown disease. Buffalo meat even appears often in markets over the country alongside displays of dinner beef.

They need fences or other protection for existence. Just as do the Indians, apparently. The proud Indians.

CHAPTER 3

WHO OWNS THIS LAND?

In the beginning, the Indians tolerated the French-Canadian trappers who came into their hunting grounds, and who often married into their tribes. But, when the more belligerent mountain men started coming up from the south, from Taos and Santa Fe, the red men began to fight the invaders. From the beautiful vistas of South Park in the Rockies to the Blackfoot country on the upper Mississippi, red men and white men died, and the hatred grew. The war spread to the Ute country, to the bleak stretches along the Salt River in Apache land, to the fish-eating tribes of the Pacific Coast.

The antagonisms, the treacheries, the cruelties, multiplied until they culminated in the great Indian war on the Plains. It ended when the Indian, like the buffalo, were in danger of being exterminated. They were forced to accept defeat or face obliteration.

It began far back in the continent's history. The Pilgrims had their innings of war against the tribes in New England, fighting with their flare-muzzled muskets. Indian also fought Indian. They allied with the French or British, swinging from side to side as the occasion suited them.

Before the coming of the white man, the powerful Iroquois League ruled the frontier from the northeast coast to the Ohio River. The Sioux, whose original home was east of the Mississippi, could not stand before the might of the eastern tribes. They fled to the Plains and became horse Indians, buffalo Indians rather, their fighting power strengthened by having the greatest commissary

ever to be at the hand of primitive man. They became a scourge
to all the other western tribes and to white settlers. They were an
arrow in the flank of the Army. They would run no farther. There
they made their last stand, and there some of them now still stand,
trying to adjust their way of life to that of the white flood around
them.

War was always an important part of the Indian scheme of life.
It was his pastime, his way of proving his manhood, his demonstra-
tion of superiority over weaker neighbors. Tribes fought tribes,
the stronger raided and massacred weaker villages, seizing loot
and women.

Some commentators believed that if the white man had not
appeared on the scene when he did, the Iroquoian nations would
have eventually wiped out all other tribes on the continent. Then,
no doubt, they would have fought among themselves until only
one tribe remained. The word Mohawk was already a term for
terror when the first crude white settlements were established in
upper New York State.

The white man brought not only his guns and other refinements
of civilization but also his own long list of national feuds and
rivalries between nations that were a part of his struggle for power
and territory.

The white's struggled for control of the New World, and the
Indian was caught up in it. The white man's ways fascinated the
Indian and also bewildered him. He could understand why French
fought English and why French or English fought the Spanish, and
why the Spanish seemed to fight everybody, but he could never
quite understand why, unlike the tribes, towns or states did not
fight each other.

At times the Indian fought alongside the white man in his national rivalries, often for sheer love of fighting. More often he
fought both white man and his own hereditary foes. These tribal
feuds continued until toward the end, when Sioux, Cheyenne,
Arapahoe, and others finally tried to unite, too late, against a
common foe.

The tribal feuds had been handed down in lore and legend that
was passed on from generation to generation by the old ones. The
foes went at each other with spears, knives, teeth, rocks, or whatever else was handy. Those who were defeated took to their heels,
leaving their lodges to be plundered and burned, their wives to be

ravished and taken into slavery, their children to be made menials of their conquerors. There might be a better day to fight. There were more women available who could produce children to replace the lost ones. When traditional opponents were not around they fought among themselves, family against family, in the villages. Often, the larger villages formed their own groups of Indian police to prevent such strife.

The picture of the primitive American Indian, as painted by the pen of James Fenimore Cooper, is often the image in the minds of scholars. Cooper's view was that the Indian was a sort of Tarzan, noble, handsome, and magnanimous toward foes, living in a sort of pristine luxury.

We listened to an educated man who had enjoyed Cooper's writings, but who had happened to come upon a copy of *The Oregon Trail* by Francis Parkman. This is a genuine classic by a man who traveled the Sioux country and lived among the Indians in the 1840s. My acquaintance scoffed at Parkman's book, seeming to believe that it was fiction and nonsense. He refused to believe that the Indian, as Parkman described him, was a savage, not far removed from the Stone Age, existing in squalor and filth, indifferent to personal pain and misery and still more indifferent to the sufferings of others.

Although some of the eastern Indians had reached a somewhat higher way of life, the situation as Parkman had related was especially cruelly true of the Plains tribes. It is said that the white man taught the Indian to scalp enemies, dead or alive. If so, the tribesman needed no teaching in other arts, such as that of torturing captives. Nor did the white man need instruction when bent on vengeance.

It is on this point—torture and inhumanity—that there was no meeting of the minds, and no forgiveness, especially by the whites. Whichever side instigated the practice of torture, it was carried on by both races, and was the basis of the long, shocking list of treacheries, murders, rapine, and massacre that is a part of the story of the settlement of this continent.

It evoked such phrases as, "The only good Indian is a dead Indian." "Nits breed lice." This latter remark is attributed to an Army general who condoned the killing of Indian children by the troops.

It began in the east where the Mohawks and the Senecas in-

flicted every imaginable pain on their captives. Then came the
Dark and Bloody ground of Kentucky, where names such as
Daniel Boone, Simon Kenton, and George Rogers Clark became
known to history. Also the names of Simon Girty, the renegade,
Colonel Henry Hamilton, at Detroit, the British hair buyer of
Kentucky scalps, and others.

Whites and reds raided and counter-raided across the Ohio
River, stained with blood the waters of the Muskingum, the Miami,
the Scioto. Simon Kenton, captured by the Delawares, was tortured in a dozen villages, forced to run the gantlet many times
while squaws and children beat him and fired gunpowder into his
flesh. Simon Girty watched such atrocities and refused to help captives who were forced to march, chained, within scorching reach of
roaring fires.

Peaceful Dunkards, who had settled in the Ohio wilderness to
escape religious persecution in the colonies, were massacred by
Indians on the Muskingum River. On another occasion, ninety
Christian Moravian Indians, including women and children, were
lured into their places of worship by white woodsmen and slaughtered with mauls and axes. A marble shaft marks the place of the
first atrocity at Salem, Ohio. A state park where log cabins were
built in many frontier styles now stands as a memorial to the
Moravian Indians at Schoenbrunn, Ohio.

And what were the crimes of the Dunkards and the Quaker
Moravians? They insisted on remaining neutral in the strife between the Ohio tribes and the Kentuckians. They wanted only to
live in peace. For this they were treacherously slain.

After the eastern tribes were overcome by the onrush of population, the hatreds—and the torturing and murdering—moved beyond the Father of Waters. It became the turn of settlers on the
Texas frontier to be struck down as they worked in their corn-
fields or slept in their rude cabins.

This time the name of the terror was Comanch'. Or Kiowa. Or
'Pache. The spearheads that skewered many of the victims were
heavy broad-bladed implements—the weapons of the Comanche
buffalo hunters on the Llano Estacado. The arrows that pierced
men and women and babies on the Plains were bound to the
shafts with buffalo sinew.

But the fighting was about the same. Men were tortured. White
children were hurled aloft and caught on spear points. Indian

children were hunted down like mice and slain. "Nits breed lice." White women were ravished, then impaled on pointed posts. Squaws trapped in burning lodges were wounded when they tried to escape, then thrown back into the flames. An eye for an eye, a life for a life, a cruelty for a cruelty.

White man go away! This is my hunting ground!

Red man get out! This is now my land!

The Comanche and the Kiowa were relentlessly pushed back. Kit Carson, wearing the insignia of an Army colonel, led a campaign against the Navajos, and gave them such a defeat in spectacular Canyon de Chelly they never returned to the warpath.

The battle line moved farther into the Southwest. Apaches fought it out there. This was where that classic—the six-horse stagecoach, racing at wild speed, pursued by bronze-skinned men on wild Indian ponies—came to full flower. It was lived out in real life. Stein's Station and old Dragoon on the Butterfield route are ruins now, and the Apache Pass road is rarely traveled, but even the mention of those places brings visions of dramatic and dangerous days of the West that is no more.

Among names that still flame in the story of the Southwest are those of Mangas Coloradas, Cochise, Vittorio, Geronimo.

Geronimo! That was a word with which to inspire terror over hundreds of miles of territory. Years later, it was shouted by American fighting men in World War II as they charged ashore in bloody island battles in the Pacific. Another word whose meaning is almost universally known is Apache. Apache! It harks of wildness and adventure. It appeals to the imagination. The gangsters in the bistros of Paris adopted that term as their symbol.

The fighting Apache, in real life, was a short-legged, flat-nosed savage, as grim and gnarled as the land in which he lived—and as pitiless. His garb resembled that of Mongolian herders. He did not know he would be a romantic figure in the eyes of the world. He was a product of his harsh environment, and it took many years, many lives, before he was subdued. His best warriors and chiefs were to know confinement in lands as far away as Florida. Other chiefs were to die rather than submit to loss of freedom.

When the Apache laid aside his bow and arrow and the rifle he had taken from burned ranches or stagecoaches, the war in the Southwest was over. There was no longer the sobbing of women, nor the smell of scorching flesh of captives tied to the wheels of burning Concords. There were no longer stony-eyed Apaches being herded at bayonet point into cars on the Santa Fe Railroad at Flagstaff, believing they were to be moved to a new and better hunting ground when it reality they were on their way to dark cells.

But it was in the war on the Plains that the course of empire was decided, a nation was conquered, and a new world power was created. The real Plains war began early in the 1860s. The hundreds who had died before that, been scalped, terrorized, been on the receiving end of arrows, knives, spears, and musket bullets, along with other items, would dispute this vehemently, no doubt, if they could speak.

Many wagon trains had been wiped out before 1860, many graves had been dug, many treaties had been broken, and many squaws had gashed their breasts and chopped off fingers to mourn slain braves. Many whites had sworn blood vendettas against all red men, vowing they would slay ten for one to avenge lost friends or relatives.

Those were the preliminary skirmishes. Powwows were held, promises made, peace pipes smoked, threats voiced, solemn warnings exchanged. It all was finally decided by violence.

The military moved in to protect the frontier while the Civil War was raging. These units were usually volunteer militia companies from the prairie states, which fought their own war apart from the conflagration that raged in the east.

The Indians were fully aware of the big war, and it was about the only thing they ever did fully understand about the white man. To them, it was apparent that it was a fight for domination between tribes—an event they had long been awaiting.

They were accused by the federal government of taking advantage of the situation. Attacks along the Overland Trail increased. Wagon trains—and travel along the trail in those days was enormous—were forced to combine and move in such cumbersome caravans for the sake of safety that they were plagued by problems of forage and sanitation at the campsites. The thin forces of the military were inadequate to meet the demands for protection.

On the other hand, the Confederates made the same accusation. The Texas border became nearly deserted as Comanches and Kiowa stepped up their raids on settlers.

But, it was on the Plains where the big fighting was done.

Sioux, Cheyenne, and Arapahoe had gazed at first with amazement and then a rather sour amusement at the creeping columns of wo-haws and Goddamns and blast-your-hides that had started as a trickle in the early days of the Oregon Trail, then had swelled to a torrent suddenly in '49.

At first, the tribes had regarded this phenomena as only a temporary irritation that would eventually go away, and would be no more than a legend among medicine men and finger paintings on the walls of lodges. Young warriors found raiding wagon trains both a sport, a training for battle with hereditary foes, and a means of acquiring quick wealth. They held the view that this windfall must be taken advantage of before it vanished.

This belief was strengthened during the fifties, for the bulk of the California rush had passed by and a great part of the traffic on the trail began to flow back on itself—eastward. Thousands who had fought their way to California in '49 and '50 were returning home, the majority broke and disillusioned, a few laden with gold. The Indians breathed easier. Soon all white men would have gone back from whence they had come. Apparently the trail had been only a small thorn in the flesh after all. The medicine man and the prophets had been right. The white man was too weak, too timid, to fend for himself in the land where the Indian hunted the great buffalo.

Then came the Pikes Peak stampede. The columns of oxen and canvas-covered wagons once more came lurching up the Platte and up the Smoky Hill River, right across the great buffalo hunting grounds.

The tolerant, amused scorn faded. A small, icy sensation began to form in the breasts of the wiser chiefs. They felt unclean. They had seen pestilence and calamity before. Years earlier, the trappers, who took squaws as wives, had brought epidemics that had swept through the tribes, causing great grief and misery. The Mandans had been nearly wiped out by smallpox. The Blackfoot were no longer to be feared, for disease had accomplished what the Sioux had never been able to achieve. Decimation. Many Indians carried pockmarks as proof they had endured this white men's scourge and conquered it.

They had seen other plagues. They had seen grasshoppers darken the sky and leave the land eaten down to bare soil so that they had to travel many days to find game. They had seen lean years when the Great Spirit had turned its face from them, keeping the buffalo out of sight of their hunting parties. Great blizzards had buried them in their lodges, and some of their people had frozen to death.

All those things had been part of their existence in the past. This scourge was different. This time the invasion did not end. It was not only gold stampeders who were driving the wo-haws now. Habitations began to spring up along the Platte. White men's lodges, built of logs, pierced with loopholes for defense. Wagons, instead of lumbering on over the horizon and out of sight, were pulling off the trail and staying. Forts were strengthened and garrisoned at old trading posts such as Kearney, Laramie, and Julesburg.

Game began to be scarce along the river where it had been abundant in the past. It got so, after the spring and fall drift of the herds, buffalo were rarely to be found between the forks of the Platte and the mountains. The Sioux hunting parties had to range far afield from the Platte into the Plains, where there was no wood, only buffalo chips for the cookfires, and only the cutbanks of dry streams to temper the fury of the blizzards.

The killings of the invaders, the tortures, the ambushes, and the treacheries increased, hardening in the fires of mutual hatred.

The powwows continued, spurred by orders from distant Washington, which was up to its neck in the greater flood of gore that had started at Bull Run, and was to flow at places like Shiloh, Vicksburg, Chickamauga, Gettysburg, and in the Wilderness. Treaties were made which both sides interpreted from their own viewpoints, which meant that neither really intended to abide by them.

The powder barrel that touched off the red holocaust was the Sand Creek massacre. It started at Denver City, which had been created by the "buster" rush of '59. A wild frontier town. A roaring mining camp. A rough-and-ready, man-for-breakfast town sitting on the knee of the Rockies. A town where things happened, where men made the biggest fortunes, built the biggest opera houses, patronized the most elaborate bawdy parlors, played poker for the biggest stakes, and went broke in the most spectacular fashions.

Denver was swept by fire in '62, its countryside was picked bare by the great grasshopper plagues of '64 and '65. Cherry Creek rose in its wrath and nearly flooded it off the map. It had its organized outlaw bands, its robber barons, its lynchings and gunfights. Its vigilantes.

It was a frantic town, leaping from one pinnacle of excitement to another. It was open to every rumor and alarm. Above all, it lived in terror of the Indians, and with some reason. Wagon trains were being attacked on the trail between Denver and Julesburg. Stagecoaches were being waylaid and the passengers massacred.

Although there were some twenty-five thousand citizens in Colorado Territory, of which Denver was the mainspring, the town was set on a hair trigger, ready to go up like a rocket. Still demoralized by the Cherry Creek flood, it was sent into a senseless panic one night when some addlebrained person rode through the streets screeching, "The Indians are coming!"

Women and children fled in nightdress to the doubtful shelter of business buildings. General pandemonium lasted for hours until the Denverites became convinced it had been a false alarm.

Shortly after, a rancher twenty miles down the South Platte was killed, along with his wife and children. This deed was laid to Roman Nose and his Cheyennes. The mutilated bodies were brought into Denver and exhibited.

That was the last straw. The tribes were warned by the territorial governor. The chiefs heeded. More than four hundred Cheyennes came into Fort Lyon, on the upper Arkansas River.

The Cheyennes surrendered and left to camp on Sand Creek, a long march from Fort Lyon. There they were joined by other Cheyennes and Arapahoes until there were some eight hundred in the encampment including many women and children.

During the night, Colonel John M. Chivington, commander of the 3rd Regiment of Colorado Volunteer Cavalry, led his men secretly upon the camp, their approach silenced by heavy snow. Surrounding the lodges, which were strung out on the frozen flats below the bluffs where the troopers crouched, they waited until daybreak gave them light enough to shoot at targets.

Scencs followed that various researchers have described, some true, no doubt, some based on dubious hearsay. Such as: Chief White Antelope of the Cheyennes, hands raised in surrender, being shot down as he walked toward Chivington; Chief Left Hand folding his arms scornfully, facing the fusillade until he died. Old

men, women, and children being picked off as they tried to surrender, the women baring themselves to prove their sex. Others
died as they clawed at the frozen earth in a futile attempt to find
shelter from the bullets.

Mutilation of the dead, and even some of the wounded Indians,
is described. Ears and sexual parts of Indians, both male and female, were in possession of many of Chivington's men when they
returned to Denver, it is said.

Chivington, who was a presiding church elder, boasted that
no prisoners were taken. He was formally thanked by the Territorial Legislature. However, when the enormity of the affair
stirred the nation to angry protest, he was court-martialed. And
acquitted. He later served in Denver as coroner.

Billy Dixon, the buffalo hunter, visited the Sand Creek battlefield six years after the massacre and found the area still littered
with human bones. The slaughter has gone down in the records
as one of the most brutal offenses by white men against the Indians, ranking in infamy with the Wounded Knee affair years
later.

But whatever Chivington accomplished or did not accomplish at
Sand Creek, he sealed the doom of many more than he slaughtered
there. The spark had been applied to the full powder keg. He
succeeded in bringing about a happening the Army had been trying for years to avert by bribes, subterfuge, and promises. At
last, the great Sioux Nation, the fierce Cheyennes, and the grim
Arapahoes cast aside their tribal feuds and united in a common
cause against the invaders of their hunting grounds, against the
Army that sought to pen them on reservations, against the whole
locust swarm that was upon them.

Soon, all that remained of stage stations and ranches along the
Platte from Denver to the forks and from the forks to Fort
Laramie were the ashes and the scalped bodies of men and women
who had been unable to reach the forts in time. All stage schedules
were abandoned.

Then came Julesburg's turn, leading to some of the most spectacular events of the war on the Plains. Julesburg? It is a small,
peaceful farming and ranching community on the South Platte in
the northeast corner of Colorado. Tiny then, and tiny now, it is
virtually unknown, but its history is colorful. In fact the present-
day hamlet is Julesburg Number 4. It was moved twice from its

original location to accommodate the Union Pacific and economic demands. On another occasion it was burned by the Indians, a happening that makes it unique among Plains communities.

It had been a Pony Express station, a Western Union telegraph point, an Overland Stage station, and later on one of the notorious "Hell on Wheels" that followed the westward course of the Union Pacific.

Julesburg's real emergence into the history of the Plains began on January 7, 1865. On this frigid day, when the coming of the railroad was still only a dream, Indians began appearing in considerable numbers near the sod and log-built settlement on the fringe of the frozen South Platte. Townsfolk and nearby ranchers and homesteaders, with screeching warriors at their heels, fled toward Fort Sedgwick, two miles from the town. Some did not make it. The survivors joined the garrison on the firing steps and made ready to fight to the end.

The commanding officer made the mistake of ordering sixty troopers out to engage the hostiles. It was an error that was to be repeated many times during the war on the Plains by officers who had not learned to respect the Indian's fighting prowess and his ability at the game of ambush. Forty-five of the soldiers managed to make it back to the fort alive. The others were killed and their bodies mutilated in sight of the garrison. The small number of Indians they believed they had been sent to engage had suddenly multiplied until they had found themselves facing hundreds of foes.

From the fort, the defenders watched the Indians loot Julesburg. In the unpredictable way of the tribesmen, they did not burn the town that time. They rode away across the ice of the Platte, vanishing into the snow-covered Plains with their booty. But they were to return soon.

In the meantime, General R. B. Mitchell, commander of the campaign on the Plains, with all his forts along the Platte under siege, with the trail blocked and wagon trains immobilized, the prairie schooners drawn up in the interlocking frontier circles at camps along the road, decided to strike at the Indians with a new weapon. He ordered prairie and plain burned off.

That was the big he-dog of all prairie fires. It was set by the Army on a five-hundred-mile line from Denver to Fort Kearney. The season was mid-winter, but the weather had been unusually dry. The long grass on the prairie burned furiously, and so did the short grass on the high Plains. The flames swept as far south as the Staked Plain of Texas.

However, the majority of the Indians had been north of the Platte when the blaze was set, and not much damage was done there. The other tribesmen, with hundreds of square miles around them stripped of game and devoid of feed for their ponies, moved north of the river also. These had been mainly peaceful Indians who had refrained from forcing the issue with the Army. Now, their bellies lean, their fury whetted, they joined in the fight.

A week after the big blaze, the Indians returned to little Julesburg. This time they set fire to the deserted settlement. Eugene Ware, then a lieutenant in the 7th Iowa Cavalry, was not only an eyewitness to the burning of Julesburg, but came within a hairsbreadth of losing his own scalp. One of the most articulate writers of the frontier, he has left an account of this and other events in which he participated in his book *The Indian War of 1864*, edited by Clyde C. Walton.

Ware's outfit is not to be confused with the regular Army 7th of Custer. The Iowa 7th was one of the militia units commissioned to guard the settlements along the Platte. Ware held little admiration for the Indians. He took issue with those who denounced Chivington, and even approved of the Sand Creek massacre. His only complaint was that there were about fifteen hundred warriors who did not get killed, Ware's figures.

Ware had seen Indians shoot arrows down the throats of chickens, pinning the living fowls to the ground where they died in agony to the vast amusement of their torturers. He had watched helplessly from across the flooded Platte as Indians attacked a settler's wagon and murdered two men. He had watched the scalps being brandished tauntingly, the slayers being out of rifle range and safe from retaliation.

He had been present at a parley at Fort McPherson down the Platte during which General Mitchell had arrogantly ordered Spotted Tail and his Sioux to stay clear of the Platte Valley, which had been their prized hunting ground. This was tantamount to a declaration of war.

It had been intended as a peace parley, but all the officers present, including Ware, had pistols concealed on them, just in case. Ware was sure the Sioux in the parley room had guns and knives hidden beneath their blankets. Such was the trust each side had in the other.

Mitchell's ultimatum, of course, received the only reply a proud chief like Spotted Tail could offer. Refusal—a verbal brandishing of the tomahawk. That parley resulted in the red man stepping up the attacks on ranches and ambushing stagecoaches. Then had come Chivington's march on Sand Creek.

Ware's lack of affection for the red men was not softened, no doubt, when he figured in his race for life through the smoke of burning Julesburg with some of the same warriors whose escape from Chivington he had deprecated shooting at him. His plight with its elements of high drama and comic relief, ended in a genuine cliff-hanger.

Ware was on his way back to Fort Sedgwick from a mission at the time, at the head of fifteen troopers. They were escorting two stagecoaches and had with them a wheeled howitzer. Ware and his command sighted Indians in scattered numbers near the river as they neared the town, but low bluffs concealed the true situation. Ware even traded a few shots with an Indian across the river.

Still unaware they were riding toward hundreds of Sioux, Cheyennes, and Arapahoes, painted for war and thirsty for scalps, the cavalcade continued on its way, evidently placing its faith in the howitzer's power to deter hostiles.

Then a fearsome discovery gave the contingent a pause. The priming wire, which was a necessity for arming the shells for the howitzer, had been lost. By this time they could see Indians driving off cattle from ranches across the frozen river. Despite this evidence that they were in the presence of more opponents than they had anticipated, they spent half an hour chopping down a telegraph pole and cutting off a length of wire to form a makeshift primer. Then, dutifully, they spent more time stretching wire so that the telegraph line could be spliced, although it, no doubt, had been cut in a half a dozen places ahead and back of them.

Smoke was sighted beyond the bluffs that still hid Julesburg. Scouting ahead, their real plight dawned. Indians by the hundreds were swarming around the settlement, which was burning. The stage station and its huge supply of hay was also on fire. Indians were crossing the river on the ice.

Believing they had been sighted and that they would only be overtaken if they tried to turn back, they loaded the howitzer with canister and made a dash for Fort Sedgwick beyond the burning town.

Smoke from the haystacks lay heavily over the scene. The Indians were so taken aback by the sight of the contingent racing toward them at full speed, with the howitzer bounding over the terrain, stagecoaches lurching wildly, drivers using whip and voice, that they hesitated to attack, probably believing that this presaged the arrival of a larger force.

They finally began closing in when Ware's contingent was still nearly a mile from the fort. Ware and his troopers drew sabers and continued charging. They were sighted at the fort where the gunners began lobbing shells. They paused long enough to fire a round from their own howitzer.

The Indians must have decided they were dealing with mad-men, for the guns at the fort were bearing almost directly on the troopers' path to safety. The Indians gave way. The imperiled group reached the fort safely. Inside, they joined their comrades of F Company and some three score civilians and watched Julesburg burn.

Some years earlier, the Sioux had slain more than a thousand settlers and soldiers in Minnesota in an uprising that was secretly planned and carried out with the utmost savagery. It ended with the rounding up of the hard core of the Sioux leaders. Three hundred of them were sentenced to be hanged, but President Abraham Lincoln pardoned all but thirty-eight, who were positively identified as murderers. These were executed on a single scaffold on February 26, 1863.

But the basic cause was the belief that the Indian must be exterminated and that he was not to be trusted. It was war to the end. A sad and bitter story. Custer destroyed Black Kettle's village on the Washita. In 1877 there was the epic of Chief Joseph and his Nez Percé in their desperate attempt to flee to Canada and join Sitting Bull. And the grim flight of a band of Northern Cheyenne who had been exiled to Indian Territory, now Oklahoma, and tried to return to their hunting grounds. They left a trail of blood for hundreds of miles, some of it in snow. This was in the late fall of 1878.

There had been countless other fights, murders, and treacheries. In the summer of 1873 Captain Jack, the Modoc, had slain the men of a peace commission as they talked under a flag of truce during the Lava Beds War in California. Comanches and Kiowa raided the Texas frontier, leaving burning cabins and the screams of torture victims behind them as they rode back to the Staked Plain. Apaches scourged the settlers in the Southwest. Custer was wiped out on the Little Bighorn on June 25, 1876. Crazy Horse, the Sioux, was bayoneted to death by a soldier when he tried to escape confinement at Fort Robinson, Nebraska.

But it was the Sand Creek affair in November 1864 that had set the Plains ablaze and placed the Army on the defensive for years. The forts along the Bozeman Trail were under virtual siege in the late 1860s, especially Fort Phil Kearny, which was surrounded by hostiles almost continually during its two years of existence. This fort was named for a Civil War hero, other than the Kearney of the Platte River fort. Killings and scalpings of soldiers and woodcutters were almost daily occurrences around the beleaguered post.

It culminated on December 21, 1866, when Captain William J. Fetterman was lured by Red Cloud into pursuing a small band of hostiles which had attacked the wood train. Fetterman and eighty-one men galloped over a knoll north of the fort and none returned. Like Custer later on, Fetterman had found himself facing overwhelming numbers of hostiles. For this, Fetterman has been excoriated by Army review courts and some historians, who label him as incompetent and inexperienced. He was accused of disobeying the orders of his commander, Colonel Henry B. Carrington, who testified that he cautioned Fetterman not to pursue the Sioux.

Brigadier General William H. Bisbee, who said he was an officer at the fort at the time and saw Fetterman and his command ride away to their deaths, angrily denied this in writing about the tragedy after his retirement. He stated that Fetterman was a brave, disciplined soldier with whom he, Bisbee, had campaigned through four years of the Civil War. Bisbee implied that Fetterman received no such caution from Carrington. He evidently had no liking for the commanding officer, for he said that after the massacre Carrington was sent to another post where there were more dress parades and no Indians with which to contend.

The Fetterman disaster hardened the Army's purpose on the Plains. A week after the massacre General Sherman, commander of the armed forces in the West, sent a message to General U. S.

Grant which said: "We must proceed with vindictive earnestness against the Sioux, even to their extermination—men, women and children. Nothing else will reach the root of the case."

It was a grim purpose and one that took considerable doing. The Sioux were fighting men. Also the Cheyennes. The Army had several advantages the greater part of the time: technology, better food, superior weapons and horses, although there were fights in which the red man was the better armed. Often he was better led. Fetterman was not the only officer whose conduct has been condemned. There was Custer at the Little Bighorn, and his staff, of course. The actions of both Captain Frederick W. Benteen and Major Marcus Reno in that affair have been a typographical football that has been kicked around by researchers for nearly a century. Reno's name was officially cleared of any suspicion of misconduct after a lapse of most of that century.

In the same year that Fetterman and his command were wiped out, the mourning and the wailing and gashing of breasts was shifted to the lodges of Red Cloud's people. It started out something like the Fetterman affair.

Some thirty-two soldiers, under command of Captain James Powell, were moving out to save the horses of the wood column which were in danger of being cut off from Fort Phil Kearny by Red Cloud's warriors. In the classic manner of Indian strategy, Powell and his men found themselves surrounded by overwhelming numbers of Sioux who were anxious to repeat the Fetterman wipe-out. The Indians had odds twenty to one in their favor, but they, not Powell, were the ones who found themselves in a trap—a trap set by modern mechanical superiority.

Powell and his detachment barricaded themselves back of wagon boxes and hunkered down. The fight has gone down in annals as the Wagon Box battle. It took place on August 2, 1867.

The Sioux charged. The flower of Red Cloud's warriors withered under a steady hail of bullets that came from the besieged force. The breech-loading, repeating rifle had arrived on the frontier, giving a man many times his former fire power. The killing had become easier to achieve, the slaughter greater.

The repeater had been used by some Union outfits during the latter stages of the Civil War. Its virtues had been instantly recognized by the men in the ranks. Possession of the weapon became something to be hoped for, but rarely realized, for the War

Department continued to favor the old single-shot weapon. Why change? It had served its purpose for many years, had it not?

The Confederates not only respected the repeater—the damned gun "thet you load in the mawnin' an' shoot it all day," but made it their especial object of capture in fierce forays against Union forces so equipped.

The lesson Red Cloud learned from the repeater went down in tribal lore as "the bad medicine fight with the white men." The Indians had been brave. Too brave. They had charged again and again into the face of the leaden scythe that mowed them down.

One chronicler of Indian history says the Indians themselves afterward admitted that eleven hundred of their number died in the Wagon Box fight. Another puts the figure at fifteen hundred.

Now, just a moment. Eleven hundred? Fifteen hundred? The consensus is that enthusiasm for drama got the better of these researchers. The Sioux lost heavily in the Wagon Box fight, but each defender would have had to down three dozen Indians to have reached even the total of eleven hundred dead.

Red Cloud should have realized his cause was hopeless when he suffered a dire setback a few weeks earlier in what is known as the Hayfield fight. And from the same cause—superior fire power. Evidently he did not believe his own eyes at the Hayfield fight and moved on to the greater disaster at Wagon Box.

The Hayfield battle took place near Fort C. F. Smith on the Bighorn River north of Fort Phil Kearny. Some twenty civilians in the haying crew, along with nineteen cavalrymen and a young lieutenant, were besieged in a hayfield. The civilians were armed with Henry and Spencer breech-loaders, the soldiers with the new Springfields.

This fight went on all day, a testament to the bravery and determination of the Sioux. The firing could be heard at the fort, but its commander is said to have claimed afterward that he heard only a few distant shots. He did not send out help until late in the day. Then, the major leading the two relief companies is accused of wanting to turn tail and run when he came in sight of the battle. However, a junior officer is said to have prevailed on him to move in, and the besieged men were saved. Many Indians had been slain, and the defenders' losses were slight.

This, along with the Wagon Box disaster, no matter how greatly Red Cloud's losses may have been exaggerated, ended that chief's active participation in the war against the Army. He and his villages stood aside and let more belligerent Sioux carry on the fight.

There was that other famous Indian-Army battle on the Arickaree River in northeast Colorado, known as the Beecher Island fight, which has been dramatized in fiction, history, and motion pictures. It lasted nine days and had all the elements of action so dear to Hollywood—falling horses, falling men, heroism, and sacrifice. It took place in September 1868 and is named for Lieutenant Frederick H. Beecher, who was killed during the battle. He was the nephew of Henry Ward Beecher, the noted clergyman of Brooklyn, New York.

Fifty-one army scouts, under command of Major George Forsyth, were surrounded by what some survivors said were eight hundred Sioux and Cheyennes under the Cheyenne Roman Nose. Twenty-one of the Army men were killed or wounded. The company doctor was killed, and Major Forsyth sustained a severe leg wound.

Through the heroism of scouts, who crept through the Indian lines at night and made their way for miles on foot through hostile country, the siege was lifted by Colonel L. H. Carpenter with troops of the 10th Negro Cavalry. The Indians, who suffered heavy losses, and were exhausted and out of supplies, gave up the fight when reinforcements appeared and faded away into the Plains.

There were to be many other fights, the majority so minor their stories are buried in War Department files. But men, both red and white, died in them, and women mourned for them. Only the big ones are remembered. Indians would wipe out Custer and his command on the Little Bighorn, and, in turn, would be cut down some years later by Gatling guns at Wounded Knee. Well into the present century, ranchers and farmers in isolated areas of the West feared and distrusted the red man. A flare-up came in 1905 in southern Utah, not far from Monument Valley, which is now a tourist attraction. But it did not amount to much more than false rumors and a scare among ranchers.

However, the gap of understanding has narrowed but little. To this day the Indian still fights for his land, but mainly in the courts, although he sometimes tries force. He remains stony-eyed toward white tourists, although they are often his best source of revenue. He once owned the land over which they walk and ride, scattering empty beer cans and picnic plates. He feels he was robbed of his heritage. He feels that the whites are here only because they are stronger.

Although antagonism and resentment on the part of the Indian and indifference and suspicion on the part of the whites form the big picture, there have been many exceptions to the rule. There is the legend of Pocahontas, the Indian princess who saved John Smith from death by throwing herself on him when he was about to be clubbed to death by her father's people. She later married John Rolfe, went to England, and there succumbed to the white man's scourge—smallpox. Many whites married Indians and lived happily.

There is the story of the yellow-haired Plains idol, Custer, having loved a young Indian girl and fathering a son by her. The majority of trappers took Indian wives. That, no doubt, was partly due to the fact that an Indian girl could set up a lodge in a blizzard, have a fire and a meal going while the master of the house was finishing his second drink of Taos lightning after a hard day on the trap lines.

Santa Fe traders married Indian women, and these traders were often leading men in their professions, educated and of considerable means, who mingled with the best circles in both St. Louis and in Santa Fe. Some of them were equally at home in a drawing room or at a fandango where the señoritas of Santa Fe or Chihuahua flirted with them over black lace fans, smoked cigarillos, and danced with the grace of panthers. In other words, these chaps had been around. Yet they married Arapahoe or Cheyenne or Crow women.

William Bent, who with his partner had built the famous frontier trading post on the Arkansas, married Owl Woman, the daughter of a chief. She was keeper of the sacred medicine that the Cheyenne people guarded jealously. Their son Charles was in Black Kettle's village when Chivington's militia from Denver staged the slaughter on that bleak, wintry morning. Charles Bent survived the massacre. He and his brother George led the tribes in many reprisals against his half brothers, the whites.

Army officers married Indian women, but were almost invariably cashiered, or induced to resign. Kit Carson is listed in Stanley Vestal's biography as having first married an Arapahoe girl, who died, and then a Cheyenne woman from whom he was summarily divorced under Indian law when she drove him from their lodge. Many fine and leading citizens of the West, particularly in Oklahoma, are proud of their tribal heritage, and justly so.

However, in the majority of instances, the old gulf remains. Theodore Roosevelt, a man of great vision and generally tolerant views, was not soft in his opinions of the Indian when he wrote his brilliant and lengthy *Winning of the West*. In speaking of the wars along the middle border in 1771, he castigates the tribes, especially the Delawares, who had a way of winning the confidence of settlers, then falling upon their unsuspecting victims, torturing and murdering the men, committing unspeakable outrages against the women who had fed them in their kitchens.

It was this trait, above all, that went beyond the understanding of the white man. Not that he was above treachery. Far from it. The Cheyennes at Sand Creek had believed the white man was their friend. So had many other tribesmen who found themselves being mowed down by rifle or cannon fire.

Roosevelt tells of an incident at Vincennes in the pioneer days of the Ohio and Indiana country when a settler was ambushed and scalped in his cornfield. The man lived, but his neighbors in Vincennes, enraged, seized a friendly, innocent Indian who was in the town on a peaceful mission, dragged him to the blockhouse, where he was shot and scalped by the wife of the original victim.

As a result, the French settlers, who far outnumbered the Americans, ordered the latter to leave Vincennes. Several hundred Indians came down from Canada to attack the Americans, who retreated to their stockade and held them off. That was the way it went as the strife moved west. A scalp for a scalp, an eye for an eye, a grave for a grave.

Custer's men, after destroying Black Kettle's village on the Washita, a matter into which we will go more fully later, found an eight-year-old white girl who had become demented because of torture and rape by young braves. A young boy captive is said to have been disemboweled by squaws. This was in what some researchers say was a peaceful village.

W. E. Webb, a member of a party of fossil-hunting scientists in the frontier days, relates a conversation with General Phil Sheridan at Fort Hays, and tells how "Little Phil's" eyes glittered angrily as he described to Webb the cruelties that had been inflicted on settlers. The general told the scientist about the most recent outrage, in which the wife of a granger had been found with a rusty sword driven both through her body and that of the unborn infant she was carrying. The woman had been still alive when found, but died after hours of agony. The sword had been twisted in the wound by her torturers.

Eugene Ware, he of the dash through the smoke of burning Julesburg, dwelt on his view that the Sioux males were of feminine appearance as to facial features, and that their women tended toward harsh masculinity as they aged. He evidently did not take into account that this might have been due to the hard life the squaws led.

He described Spotted Tail, the noted war chief, as looking like a woman. It was his belief that none of the warriors could stand up to any soldier in his command in a test of strength. He made only one exception, a big Mandan Indian, who was present at the Fort McPherson parley and to whom he accorded some grudging respect.

His views were distinctly not shared by many other military men who agreed that an armed, fully trained Indian warrior was as formidable an opponent as they cared to face. The mounted Indian fighter has been described by army experts as the best light cavalryman the world has seen.

Ware had many grievances against the Indians. In addition to those already mentioned, he suffered another humiliation at their hands. He was stationed at Fort Laramie, along with units of the 11th Ohio Cavalry on a day when a detachment returned from a scouting trip, reporting it had sighted no Indians and were sure none were within many miles of the fort. They turned their tired horses loose so that the animals could roll on the sandy parade ground. A party of mounted Indians appeared from nowhere at full gallop, raced down the parade grounds, waving blankets and firing guns. They stampeded the cavalry horses and vanished with them into the Plains.

It all had happened so quickly scarcely a shot was fired by the soldiers. The cavalry organized hot pursuit, with Ware in the chase. All that was accomplished in a two-day ride was to wear out Army saddle stock so that the animals were not worth much afterward. Some of the troopers had to walk back, leading drooping horses. Ware chalked up another score against the noble red man.

However, by the early 1880s it was about over. The great chiefs were dead or in prison. Sitting Bull had demeaned himself by traveling with Buffalo Bill's circus. Santank, the great Kiowa chief, arrested for murder, was killed, like Crazy Horse, in an attempt to escape. Roman Nose, Cochise, were dead.

Everywhere the war fires were burning low. They had fought the fight, year after year, winning small victories here, losing the big ones there. They had thought that exterminating Custer would convince the white man this land was theirs forever.

Instead, the white man had kept coming. It was not the vanishing of the buffalo that had crushed them, nor the "Yellowlegs," as they called the cavalry, nor the slogging foot soldiers, who seemed to live on dust, profanity, and whisky.

What did them in were the spidery, canvas-topped wagons, with sunbonnets and petticoats fluttering under the bows, with phlegmatic men in run-down boots, and barefoot urchins driving milk cattle in the cow columns. The wagons never seemed to quit crawling over the horizons, the plows they unloaded never stopped tearing up the buffalo grass. The soddies and dugouts they built never stopped spreading farther and farther across the country.

The Indians were forced to the reservation. These were places of white men's choosing, usually what white men considered worthless land. Young, hotspur braves kept jumping the reservations to stage raids. Many were arrested as common criminals, tried and hung or sent to prison.

Bitter, uneasy peace came. The raids dwindled to minor incidents. Then, in 1889, far to the west, a Piute medicine man had a vision. He said he saw the buffalo returning, and the extermination of the white man. He had seen the wild horses running free on the Plains again in great bands, furnishing the tribes with mounts on which to hunt and roam.

To make this come true it was necessary to dance at each rising of the new moon and continue until the spirits appeared. The ghost dancing spread eastward to the Plains. The Sioux began to dance. The Cheyenne emerged from his apathy and danced. So did the Arapahoe, the Ute, the Kiowa.

The craze reached its height in 1890 in the lodges of Sitting Bull's Uncpapa Sioux at the Standing Rock Agency in North Dakota. On December 15, the reservation agent made the error of sending Sioux police to arrest the chief, branding him as the ringleader of the Messiah craze. Shooting broke out among the excited Indians. When the smoke cleared, Sitting Bull lay dead, slain by his own people.

With the passing of the medicine man and the chief who is credited by many researchers with having directed the Sioux's greatest victory, the Messiah craze died.

On a bitter wintry day, two weeks later, the men of the 7th Cavalry, heirs to the grudge of the Little Bighorn, surrounded a Sioux encampment at a snow-covered field in the badlands, a place called Wounded Knee. Again a shot was fired, and a general battle broke out. The troopers opened with carbines and Gatling guns. When it was over, 150 Indians, men, women, and children, lay dead, along with 25 soldiers. The cavalrymen carried 75 wounded from the field, some who had been hit by their comrades' crossfire. One more snow had been dyed crimson by Indian blood and white blood.

That was about the last of it. The proud Sioux, the fierce Cheyenne, the grim Kiowa, the tough Arapahoe, the wily Apache, had bowed to the inevitable.

But the fires are still far from dead. Wounded Knee came into front-page prominence once more after a lapse of more than eighty years. Citing a list of grievances, Sioux Indians moved in and seized control of buildings on the reservation, and held them by force for many days until a compromise was reached, a compromise that apparently has not satisfied either side. Gunplay broke out in this affair, but casualties were not serious, although at times all the elements of the original Wounded Knee lurked in the situation. In a similar incident, Indians seized the abandoned Alcatraz prison in San Francisco Bay, holding it for days, demanding a better deal for their people until a compromise was again reached. Other tribes are pressing their claims.

Too many of the tribesmen still live in poverty and squalor. This despite the efforts of charitable groups to lighten their plight. This is not true of all Indians, of course. In the Painted Desert some of the Navajo ride fine horses and wear necklaces and armbands of heavy silver, studded with turquoise. They haughtily ignore passing tourists. They own many ponies, and their children tend flocks of sheep. They sell wool and lambs at Flagstaff and Gallup. Many live comfortably in modern houses built near the old mud hogans where they had been born. Their habitat is a fantastic land of buttes, fantastic canyons, fantastic colors. They live in the lap of stunning beauty.

In Oklahoma many Indians became rich on land that was believed worthless when it was set aside as a reservation. Many have become leading citizens of the state and ask no favors of any men in business matters in which they can take care of themselves.

The Palm Springs Indians of California own a section of land in the heart of that plush community which has the potential of becoming the most valuable development of that nature in the West. The Jicarilla Apaches, eighteen hundred strong, have financed a movie production costing two million dollars, advancing the cash from their tribal fund, which comes from gas and oil that the white man was not aware of when he allotted reservation. The movie? A western, of course.

But the majority do not own oil wells or fast horses or valuable property. What jewelry they might have once possessed has been pawned at Gallup long since. In the back reaches they exist in mud hogans, depending on the missionaries for food. In places like Standing Rock and Pine Bluff on the Plains they fight a losing battle trying to subsist on land where their forefathers slew the buffalo. They listen to tales handed down from the great days of the tribe—tales of the golden era before the wagons with the white sails came lurching over the horizon.

CHAPTER 4

# THE GREAT TRAILS

First, the creatures made the trails—the elk, the erratic antelope, the deer, and above all, the ponderous buffalo. Through the ages animals cut the paths, following the easiest routes over the long swells in the plains and the breaks in the bluffs. Water was the key to survival on the Plains, and these paths always led to water. So it was in the beginning, so it is to this day.

The game trails were followed by the Indian when he appeared on the scene. He traveled on foot at first, and then mounted, after the Conquistadores introduced the horse to the New World. He followed these trails in search of game, to visit friends, to migrate. Enemies lay in wait along these routes to ambush him. He crouched under cover at strategic points to slay his foes, rocks in his hands, or crude spears with stone heads, or with arrows after he had learned the art of the bowstring. And, finally, with firearms.

The trails usually followed the general course of the streams. The main arteries in the buffalo country were the Missouri, the Arkansas, the Red River of the south, and, principally, the Platte, whose south fork led into the mountains, the north fork leading the way to the continental divide.

First of the great paths was the Santa Fe Trail, over which heavy wagons lurched, carrying trade goods to and from the settlements in New Mexico and Chihuahua. Contrary to the natural law of following the course of streams, the Santa Fe route traveled for considerable distance at right angles to those arteries. The wagons moved across what is now the great Kansas wheat country, depending on cross-creeks and springs and rainfall. These were sufficient. Water, except for the short cut that the more daring used south of the Arkansas River to Wagon Mound, was not a problem.

The Arkansas was the principal watercourse that lay athwart their path. It offered a sort of perplexing choice to the captains of the caravans. When they reached a point not far from where Dodge City was to stand, they had to make a decision. They had the option of fording the river and cutting directly across the blank space on the map through dangerous Indian country where finding water was a gamble or they could continue on up the river past Bent's Fort and reach New Mexico over Raton Pass on Dick Wootton's toll road.

This route was much longer, and the lift over the Raton was far from child's play. But it avoided the hunting grounds of the Southern Cheyenne, the Comanche, and occasional plunder parties of Apaches and Navajos. It also avoided the long waterless stretch beyond the Cimarron River, which itself sometimes turned out to be dry in its upper reaches.

The route by way of the Cimarron, which was followed by the more hardy traders, was one of the many journeys in the Southwest that the Spanish termed *El Jornada.* This expression was usually reserved for long, dry marches. The Cimarron route was occasionally referred to as *El Jornada del Muerte,* the journey of death. There were several "journeys of death" in the Southwest, but the one below Santa Fe on the long haul to Chihuahua now holds the title exclusively, at least on the maps of today. However, trappers and early explorers, who traveled both paths, regarded the terrible trip in summer across the blazing Colorado River and Mojave Deserts on the Spanish Trail between Santa Fe and Los Angeles as a very real *Jornada del Muerte,* and the one most deserving of the name.

The Santa Fe Trail was deep-cut for years by the wagons. Even so, its busiest year, 1843, according to Gregg's *Commerce of the Prairie,* saw less than half a million dollars in goods going down the trail, along with 350 persons.

Meanwhile, fur companies and independent trappers were pushing into the Plains and the Rocky Mountains. Some were going as far as the Oregon country and California, laying the groundwork for those areas to become states. The Missouri River was the "trail" at first, used principally by the fur companies until they realized it was much easier to travel overland by pack.

Lewis and Clark had followed the Missouri to the mountains on their way to the Pacific Coast in their historic trip, toiling upstream with keelboat against the current until they took to land in western Montana. In a nation that was stream-minded and boat-minded, they instinctively chose the tougher way to travel up a mighty river that challenges taming even to this day.

But it was the Platte River that was destined to offer the mightiest path of empire of them all—by land. Its valley saw the greatest migration in the continent's history. In fact, the mass of humans, taking with them their livestock, their customs, vices, and virtues, that moved westward over the Oregon and California Trails was a phenomena never equaled in recorded history. The emigrants were not driven to migrate by famine, pestilence, war, or persecution. They went of their own free will in search of wealth, happiness, and free land.

John C. Frémont, castigated as a schemer and an ambitious adventurer by his critics, probably did as much as any person to open the West to settlement. The maps he made on his first trip over the continental divide at South Pass showed that wagons could cross the mountains, and that it was possible to reach the Pacific on wheels. He had followed the headwaters of the North Platte to prove that point.

That wagon travel was feasible on the Plains had been demonstrated earlier by fur company men. In 1830, ten mule-drawn wagons carried ten tons of trade goods without much difficulty to the trappers' rendezvous in Wind River Valley.

Marcus Whitman and his small party of missionaries pushed across South Pass with wagons in 1836 with the first white women to cross the continental divide. The Whitmans reached the Oregon country and the news of their journey electrified the nation. The Oregon Trail was open.

Narcissa Whitman and Elizabeth Spalding accompanied their husbands on the trip. Mrs. Spalding, a young bride at the time, became revered among the Nez Percé Indians for her work. Narcissa Whitman's star was dark. She lost a child by drowning and she and her husband were murdered in Oregon by Cayuse Indians, for whom they had labored years to help.

In spite of the Whitman tragedy Oregon was a dream word in

the East, synonymous with that of a paradise where a man could have his own land for practically nothing, and grow crops on virgin soil in a green, rain-watered land.

The Oregon migration reached its peak in 1843. In that year somewhere around a thousand hardy souls forded the Platte, crossed South Pass, and toiled through the sagebrush along the wild, hostile rim of the Snake River, which led them to the Columbia River and on to Mecca.

This trickle up the Platte River trail continued. Then came the Mormons, bound for the Great Basin where they were to make the desert bloom by hard work and devotion. Brigham Young followed his scouting parties with the first group of settlers in 1847, heading for the promised land with 72 wagons, 143 men, 3 women, 2 children, 93 horses, and livestock and chickens.

The main Mormon migration followed in 1848. That was also an influx that has not ended to this day. New adherents to the Church of the Latter-day Saints are still arriving in the inland empire the immigrants created.

In the early days they came by wagon, saddleback, and handcart. The handcart migration of the Mormons is one of the amazing feats of pioneering. Men, women, and children pulled heavily laden, two-wheeled carts the eighteen hundred miles from the Missouri border across the Plains, over South Pass, over the high Wyoming plain past Bridger's Fort, down Echo Canyon, up the mighty flank of the snow-crowned Wasatch range, down Parley's Canyon until it opened to command the vista of the basin at the point where Brigham Young is said to have uttered the famous words, "This is the place."

Following the Mormons came the stampede of '49. Endless fleets of great wagons, their white tilts glinting in the sun, appeared on the "Coast of Nebraska." There the stampeders had their first sight of the Platte Valley. Along with that view came the realization they were leaving behind all with which they were familiar and entering a new way of life, a new world. This was where homesickness really began.

Many wagons bore inscriptions daubed on canvas with paint or axle grease:

*Californy, Here We Come!*
*Hangtown or Bust!*
*We're on Our Way to See the Elephant!*

Voices sang wistful songs of home to the tinkle of banjos.

*Oh, the gal, the gal, the purty little gal,*
  *The gal I left behind me . . .*

The white sails never stopped rising over the rim of the world to the east, growing bigger and bigger as they approached along the Platte. As they came nearer, the creak of wheels and the screech of hubs on axles became a weird chorus. Voices could be heard and the words became distinguishable:

"Haw, damn yore mangy hides! Haw, I say!"

"Whoa, you short-eared jack rabbits, afore I git really riled an' tan yore rumps real good!"

"You mean we got to *cross* thet river, Paw? We'll all drown fer sure. I never should have listened to you 'bout such a crazy thing to do like movin' to Californy! The good Lord have mercy on us all!"

"Whar's thet damned jug o'corn, Henry? I don't want you to drap an' bust it like you done when you got tanked at Fort Kearney with them soldier boys."

"O-o-o-h, I'm on my way to Californy with a banjo on my knee!" Plunkety, plunk.

"Maw, you keep them blasted young'ns in the wagon. First thing we know some thievin' Injun will steal one o' them tads, an' then what'll we do? Keep thet shotgun handy. Fill any copperskin full o' lead if'n he gits too close. You hear me now? I cain't watch them brats an' mind them cattle if'n I'm goin' to keep this here wagon on the trail, now kin I?"

The voices come closer. The great tilts loom higher in the sky, the squawking of penned chickens, the bleating of leashed milk goats, and the snuffling of oxen, gaunted to muscle and loose hide join in cacophony. The Indians have a name for the oxen. They are Goddamns, for that seems to be what the bearded, nerve-strained men in hide boots, hickory shirts, and striped breeches always call them. Caravans powered by horses and mules usually traveled separately because they moved faster than the bull trains.

Indians? There always seemed to be scores of them hanging around the Platte fords. The diaries of some forty-niners assert there were beautiful young squaws among them, but also noted that the majority, men and women, were "half-naked, dirty and disgusting."

It might be pointed out that the bulk of the stampeders were young. It was a young man's game, this forty-niner stampede, and the average age was in the early twenties. By the time they had traveled as far as the Platte ford they had not seen anything feminine in some time.

The ships of the prairie swirled and circled in hostile seas at the river. If the travelers were lucky, they arrived when the crossing was feasible. True, the Platte was never described as deep at the fords, but there were many times when men and stock could not stand against the current. That was after storms upstream or heat spells in the high snow fields of the Rockies to the west, had made the Platte a savage opponent as dangerous as the Indians. The graves began to multiply on both sides of the ford, dug secretly at night and blotted out by driving the stock over them the next morning.

The first ford on the South Platte was downstream from Julesburg, about where Brule, Nebraska, now stands. Later, it was moved a short distance above Julesburg to what was called the upper crossing or Mormon ford, for the Saints had abandoned the route on the north bank of the river and had adopted the upper crossing as the safest.

Many stampeders did not make it to either crossing. The trail along the Platte was strewn with abandoned wagons tilted drunkenly on broken axles or collapsed wheels or shattered reaches. Their owners were making their way back to St. Joe or Independence as best they could.

Valuable furniture and personal belongings began to litter the trail. Items hard to pass up became commonplace. Chairs, bedsteads, chests, heirlooms that had been considered indispensable at the start, stood abandoned in the sun and rain as the need to lighten wagons became paramount.

Indian squaws adorned themselves in hoop skirts, bustles, or lace-bottomed drawers and paraded topless while their men strutted in mutton-legged sleeves and feather-boa scarves. Anvils because of their weight, literally became a dime a dozen, being among the first items to be found expendable in the sandy going on the Coast of Nebraska.

Some wagon travelers, unable to bring themselves to passing up these windfalls, brought about their own ruin by overloading their wagons with this easy plunder, which broke down their stock farther along the trail.

Thousands, more prudent, ignored temptation and profited by it. Well-organized companies had semi-military codes of procedure. Each member was required to meet minimum standards. Some of the qualifications for joining the better companies included: wagons of well-seasoned lumber with watertight beds that could be raised from the bolsters in fording streams; lumber must be of three-quarter-inch stock, braced with iron and with strong supports so that it would withstand the rigors of steep ascents and descents; tire felloes must be equipped with bolts so that wheels could be tightened to hubs and rims in the dryness of the Plains; a supply of extra hickory bows must be carried, as well as spokes and felloes for repairs; each wagon must be drawn by four yoke of oxen that had been toughened and seasoned; provisions called for a minimum per person of one hundred pounds of flour, one hundred of bacon, thirty of sugar, as well as such staples as coffee, tea, salt, pepper, and dried fruit. The rule of thumb for everything was that, be it food, tools, ammunition, or personal belongings, it must be worth a dollar a pound to be worth taking.

Once the Platte was crossed, the graves became even more numerous. The numbers who marched across the Plains in the gold rush seem incredible. Vincent Geiger noted in his diary that when he and his party arrived at Fort Kearny on May 28, 1849, some 2,500 wagons were already ahead of them. At least 200 more passed the fort that day. Geiger's company sold their flour and bacon to lighten the wagons and abandoned other articles such as picks and hobbles. However, they did not hesitate to buy a quantity of whisky there. Firewater was considered a necessity.

Speaking of brands of water, the Platte carried its share of mud when it was on the rise in those days and continued the habit to the present. It rates among many rivers that are described as too thick to drink and too thin to plow. It has its normal, peaceful spells, of course, when it subsides to a rippling stream, moving along in the folds of its wide, unmade bed, but no poet or song writer has ever been inspired to form odes to the azure Platte.

Men, laboring to keep wagons moving in the muddy ford, floundered into holes over their depths and found themselves unable to rise to the surface. Their boots, their pockets, their belts, had become traps that had filled with mud and sand. And so they drowned. In a single week seven stampeders lost their lives at the North Platte ford during the '49 rush. The lower crossing, near the site of Julesburg, took its heavy toll also.

It was not only the California-bound stampeders who met death at the Platte. Texas trail drivers should have learned the lesson before they reached the river with their Longhorns, for they had seen some of their comrades drown in the sand-laden floods of the Red and the Arkansas. But the Platte exacted its price nevertheless. Many Texans were buried along its shores.

Not only drownings took toll of the forty-niners. In fact it was one of the lesser killers of the trail in spite of the terrors it inspired in the minds of the stampeders. The greater executioner was cholera. This deadly plague was to harass travelers on the trail until the railroad was built. It not only affected the forty-niners, it spread to the Indians, who were less equipped to resist it. Tribes were decimated, entire villages wiped out.

Every chronicle of the trail seems to proclaim the dread in which this disease was held. Cholera is said to have entered the country by way of New Orleans and was spread through the nation on the steamboat arteries.

The forty-niners, beset by nerve and physical strain, and by fear—fear of Indians and of the vast, wild country through which they traveled and, not least of all, by homesickness, were particularly susceptible to the malady.

The cholera began cutting them down almost from the start, even on the steamboats that brought them to Independence and St. Joseph. One steamboat, laden with sick and dying passengers, trying to land at Jefferson City, Missouri, for help, was driven off at cannon mouth by a group of frenzied persons, although the majority of the citizens later came to the assistance of the travelers.

Records at Independence, St. Joseph, and Kane's Crossing (Council Bluffs) indicate that twenty-seven thousand stampeders crossed the Missouri River on the ferries at these points in 1849. Bancroft, historian of the trail, estimated that one in five died of cholera alone.

Certainly far more were on the trail that year than those who ferried the Missouri at the points named. There were thousands of settlers already west of the river who added their proportion to the California rush. In addition, other thousands headed for California by way of Santa Fe and the southern route. Bancroft's estimate of one in five being struck fatally seems high. If it is justified, then the death toll must have been considerably above the estimated 5000.

Wagons trains that started early and crossed the Platte by June 1 escaped the cholera or were touched by it only lightly. But by mid-summer entire companies were being wiped out. This brought out the usual accounts of man's humanity to man, and his inhumanities. Sick and dying stampeders were being abandoned by comrades who rushed ahead, gold-mad, refusing to tarry for even a day. More numerous were the stories of others who risked their lives, delaying their journeys to help the sufferers.

Those who reached the mountains were safe. Little or no cholera was recorded among the stampeders beyond the Platte bridge, west of Fort Laramie. Cholera raged in the eastern states all year, taking thousands of lives. Later it was to invade California and turn Sacramento into a pesthouse and almost a deserted city, but west of the crossing of the North Platte, which is near the present-day city of Casper, Wyoming, the forty-niners no longer had that chill hand on their shoulders.

But there were other icy hands to replace it. There were the Indians. Always the Indians. The toll of lives they took in 1849 was comparatively light, although from the time the stampeders approached Fort Kearney it was not exactly good policy to wander out of sight of one's companions. The accounts of men who never returned from trailing missing livestock or from pursuing buffalo are detailed in many chronicles of the trail.

Many of these lost their way on the Plains, for they were from the green and forested east, not accustomed to turning to find that their back trail might have come from among any of those low, beetling bluffs and hills that all looked alike, and to discover that the driving wind of the Plains had already covered their tracks with blowing sand.

Of course those bluffs there to the southeast were the ones they had passed in the long pursuit of those three buffalo. Or were they? And did they really lie southeast? The overcast that had moved in confused a man as to directions. And so they kept going, never finding the trail again. Others were captured by Indians, tortured and slain.

Then there were fights among themselves. Gunfights, knife fights. These were young, virile men, thrown into situations that tried their souls, brought out the urge for violence, shortened tempers. Human life became less important than the miles—the endless miles that taunted a man. "Damn you, Bill, make them cattle move faster. Use the lash on 'em, I say, or I'll do it myself. I aim to git to the mines afore snow flies, even if'n you don't."

"Jest you try to whup my critters an' you'll be the sorriest man alive."

Or: "You there, prod them mules into thet ford or clear out o' the way. If you ain't got the spunk to cross thet stream, give others a chanct."

And so fists would fly or guns would explode. Organized companies had rules to take care of such cases, but the majority of the stampeders were individuals and acted accordingly. Many of the organized companies fell apart along the way as contending factions formed, each seeking authority. Former comrades became enemies. Such was the effect of the impersonal Plains on human nature. It had a way of finding the weaknesses in human make-up—and the strengths.

Geiger, the diarist, had his own day of real violence long after he reached California when he fatally knifed a man in a dispute over the Civil War. It is believed he fled to South America to escape the consequences. Geiger had seen death and near death on the trail. He had seen men drown at the Platte, had seen a young man die in the Carson Sink of a gunshot wound that was accidental, had seen another shot by his own gun in a similar accident at Fort Laramie.

There were many accidental shootings. The nerve-strung stampeders seemed to have a habit of dragging cocked and loaded weapons muzzle-first out of wagons and shooting themselves or innocent bystanders. It was just another of the hazards of the trail.

Also dangerous were the wagons and the livestock. Children fell out of wagons and were crushed beneath the wheels. So were grown men and women. Stampedes were a real hazard, not only from the buffalo but from the travelers' own livestock. Many companies numbered more than a hundred wagons, and such a caravan would carry upward of a thousand head of animals in its rope corrals or on graze at night. In addition, there would often be other caravans camped nearby. At places like the Platte ford or the North Platte bridge, scores of companies might be in the vicinity, awaiting a turn at the crossings. When a stampede started, far more than the original thousand head were likely to become involved. Such runs left many crushed bodies in the Plains grass.

Irene Paden, in her authoritative work *Wake of the Prairie Schooner,* decided that such stampedes grew more numerous as the companies neared the forks of the Platte, the livestock apparently becoming subject to a mass frenzy.

No doubt, the animals as well as many of their owners "had seen the elephant" by that time. This was an all-inclusive phrase, but usually meant that one had had it and was of a mind to turn back. The animals were still strong enough to rebel and take advantage of any chance to escape from the dust, the gall of the yoke, the crack of the bullwhip. Farther west, such frenzy seems to have died among the beasts. Reason: all spirit gone, no strength left to protest or run.

The livestock took the real brunt of the gold rush. Oxen, horses, mules. Even milk cows were put into harness. A person could have walked all the way across the dreadful Carson Sink on the carcasses of dead animals, say those who were there. On the trail as far back as Fort Hall they were failing, and one never had any doubt as to the route to follow. It was marked by carcasses. Both eye and nose were sufficient.

As for the fate of humans, a researcher in a letter to the House of Congress Commission on Roads in 1925 estimated that the California Trail took seventeen lives for each mile. This would place the total number of graves along the route at thirty-five thousand.

At first one is inclined to believe this figure also is too high. Still, when one considers the numbers who walked, or rode the two thousand miles from the Missouri border over mighty mountains, over the Plains, across the wastes of what is now Idaho, across the Nevada desert, the estimate is perhaps not too far off the mark.

Archer Hurlbert, in his book *Forty-Niners,* says that ten thousand persons had passed Fort Laramie by June 1, accompanied by fifty thousand head of stock. Hurlbert believed that, counting those coming up the Platte and those still leaving the border, and also others taking the southern routes, at least fifty thousand hit the trail to the mines in that first summer.

First summer is a term used loosely. The California rush was not a one-year phenomena. The volume was perhaps even greater in 1850, and that was when the graves began to multiply. By that time the trail was growing well beaten. In '49, because of ample rains, grass conditions were said to have been the best in years on the Plains. This kept livestock alive and averted disaster.

In 1850 conditions were different. What grass there was within reach of the trail in the spring was soon nibbled to the roots. The Indians became more hostile. The good rains that had helped in '49 did not arrive. Loss of livestock increased, and so did the privation and deaths of humans from exhaustion.

Outlaws appeared, massacring isolated parties, looting the wagons, and vanishing into the Plains. Often these wretches disguised themselves as Indians, thus increasing the enmity between the stampeders and the tribes.

Carson Sink became the graveyard of men's hopes and the literal grave of many. Food and help were sent out from Sacramento, San Francisco, Monterey, and other California communities when word of the horror in the sink became known. The year 1850 was a very bad year.

The worst of it was that by that time the bonanza was gone. The gold that could be taken in a dip pan on the streams had been found by the hordes that had arrived in '49. Millions in gold was still to be discovered, but the easy pickings were about finished. After '49 only the best of them, men with knowledge of geology and with fortitude and imagination, hit treasure. Some hit it very big. The others, by the thousands, subsisted on the crumbs from the table, and those were mighty scarce.

A few trading stores had sprung up along the trail in 1850. The Mormons were charging three dollars a wagon at their ferry on the North Platte. Men were still being drowned there, trying to raft wagons across the stream, which at that point was a swift mountain river, narrow and icy cold. Supplies at the trading store the Mormons had set up were scant. The gold rush had been considered a blessing by the Saints, but their stocks had been exhausted in '49, and the wagon trains they rushed in from the border still could not furnish supplies to meet the demand.

There was little real friendship between the Mormons, who remembered the savagery of their treatment at Nauvoo and other places, and the stampeders, who regarded Brigham Young's followers as immoral and heathenish. But there seems to have been little complaint about the prices that were charged, which evidently were not much out of line considering the circumstances. However, horse, ox, and mule shoes and nails became worth almost their weight in gold. Oxen were shod in leather from the hides of cattle that had died in yoke.

And still the great white sails kept rising over the horizon to the east and voyaging up the Platte Valley. Ezra Meeker, who made the trip twice, first in 1852, and again in 1906, the latter trip to publicize the marking of the old trail, in driving his oxen toward the crossing at Council Bluffs on his first journey, was puzzled by what appeared to be a great, dark shadow on the flats ahead. It was in the shape of an enormous flatiron, with the point concentrated on the two ferries that were floating wagons across the Missouri River.

The "flatiron" proved to be composed of hundreds of wagons and their camps. Thousands of stampeders were waiting with their equipment for their turn at the ferries. When a new arrival got in line, his wait was usually a week before his turn came.

This was in 1852, the fourth year of the rush. Hopes were still high of hitting it rich in California, although by that time it had become a state, San Francisco and Sacramento were booming cities, a railroad was being talked of, and folks in Hangtown were demanding that people forget that name and address them as citizens of Placerville.

Many today seem to have a picture of the Overland Trail as a faint pair of wheel ruts that were easily erased by weather so that a traveler often found himself lost in a maze of bluffs, ravines, and brush or on a trackless desert. Along with that is a belief that travel was a continuous battle against blizzard, sandstorms, floods, and hordes of fierce Indians.

A lot of stampeders did fight Indians. Plenty were hit by sandstorms and other blows from nature. Plains weather was as violent then as it is today and that's saying that the wagon people endured gully-washing cloudbursts, head-pounding hail, blinding dusters, cyclones, lightning in several varieties, including chain and technicolored, and several other brands of cussedness from the sky. These events usually took place in summer. If caught by winter on the Plains—brother!

But the trail, especially after the spring of '49, was a swath beaten so plainly that getting lost from it took some doing. Few of the boomers starved until they got far west. Their supplies, and what buffalo, antelope, and elk they downed, carried the bulk of them beyond Fort Hall on the big Snake.

If a company had underestimated its eating capacity it usually could get along, picking up items that had been abandoned by overloaded outfits. This held true along the Platte to beyond Fort Kearney as far as the fords. Sugar, especially, was plentiful, lying in boxes, kegs, and barrels along the way, for men had decided it was better to keep the oxen or horses alive than to cater to their own hankering for sweets. Indians developed a taste for sugar until some wretch added crystals of acid to a case of sweets, which wiped out the Sioux who had partaken.

As another commentary on human nature, some forty-niners, in abandoning articles, left notes welcoming the items to any who could use them. Others mixed sand with abandoned sugar, burned other articles, or smashed them to render them useless. Some burned wagons when forced to abandon them, thereby making sure they would leave nothing that might be of help to others.

Many friendships broke on the hard reality of the trail. More than one case is recorded of men, in ending association with each other, sawing their wagons in half, each going his way with improvised two-wheeled carts, drawn by the divided teams, or even by the men themselves. In the case of two particularly stubborn former partners, it is said neither would agree to the severing of the wagon crosswise for fear of winding up with the least desirable half. The impasse was solved by sawing the vehicle lengthwise, rendering it useless for either and for everyone.

All in all, the picture of small isolated outfits losing themselves on vanishing wagon traces is far from the truth. The trail out of Omaha in 1863 is described as being four hundred to five hundred feet wide, beaten iron-hard by the tires of wagons and blown free of dust by the winds.

The traffic that had accomplished this was fantastic in volume, considering the time and place, and the endless miles. Also considering that the Civil War was raging at this time. Except for a few lulls, travel remained consistently heavy after the first two tidal waves of the gold rush. Ezra Meeker said that in 1852 some sixteen hundred wagons passed his camp when he halted to help nurse a member of his party who had been taken ill. He also remarked that about half of his company continued ahead, leaving him and others to take care of the sufferer in spite of the pact they had made at the start to stick together through thick and thin.

Gold fever had been replaced by land fever on the Great Medicine Road. The Oregon branch of the trail quickened to new life. Thousands who continued to follow the forty-niner route toward California down through the City of Rocks to the Humboldt and on toward the Sierra Nevada, now clung to plows and harrows and bags of seed corn and wheat, rather than depending on miners' picks and shovels for a livelihood when they reached their destination.

Then came the gold strike in the Rockies. Denver City was born. The trail up the South Platte was crowded once again with stampeders, eyes aflame, goading their livestock to the point of exhaustion. Faster! Faster!

Along with that came the big silver strike at Virginia City, Nevada. This was the Comstock Lode that was to keep Washington financially sound during the Civil War. It changed San Francisco from a bawdy seaport into a prosperous city and a financial center. It once again quickened the blood of the nation's vital artery, the California Trail, with traffic now going both ways.

The Comstock Lode created millionaires who financed the Central Pacific, which, with the Union Pacific, gave the continent ocean-to-ocean transportation.

The trail was not the only artery which pulsed with life. Wagon traffic between Virginia City and the California settlements became unbelievable during the boom. It was said that teamsters who were forced to pull their vehicles out of line for repairs or other reasons, often had to wait hours before being able to find an opening to wheel back into the chain of traffic on the narrow trail.

Early in the sixties, the Overland Trail began to sink into trouble until it was more than hub-deep. The Indian war brought travel almost to a standstill at times. Militia from the border states came into the Platte Valley to escort wagon trains and stages. Companies combined into mass caravans that were hours in passing a point—a method of defense that was highly unsatisfactory because of its unwieldiness.

Even so, when traffic moved, it was enormous. The average number of vehicles passing Fort McPherson each day, bound both east and west, was placed at nine hundred. These were nearly all slow-moving ox wagons. The dust of their passing was a constant banner in the sky from horizon to horizon. A thousand tons of supplies a day was being delivered at Denver alone during the summer seasons. One Mormon caravan, bound for Salt Lake City, was more than five miles long, with the wagons loaded to their canvas hoods, and twelve yoke of oxen to each vehicle.

With this train were pushcarts powered by men and women. They were mainly foreign immigrants, and some observers have described them as coarse-looking and ignorant. The majority of them were uneducated, no doubt, but a man or a woman who had pushed a handcart nine hundred miles from the Missouri River, and still faced the continental divide and the miles to the promised land, was not likely to appear neatly garbed or jovial. Not only the Mormons had that lean and hungry aspect by the time they reached the Platte ford, everyone bore that characteristic stamp of the trail.

Billy Dixon described a Mormon caravan that he met between Julesburg and Plum Creek when he was swamping with a government supply train. He was only about fourteen at the time.

Dixon said there was not a man in the Mormon train. Women handled the oxen and wagons. They were Danes, wearing wooden shoes, and could not speak English. Some of the men in Dixon's train wanted to visit this all-female camp after dark, but were restrained by the wagonmaster with threats of being left behind if they were not back by camp-break at dawn.

Mark Twain in his *Roughing It* also described one of these Mormon wagon trains, indicating the tremendous volume of travel to Salt Lake City that went on through the years as new adherents arrived from Europe to join Brigham Young's growing empire. Twain remarked on the coarse-clad, sad-looking men, women, and children who had taken eight weeks to walk the same distance his stagecoach had covered in eight days.

1. A small band of buffalo in Wyoming in pioneer days.
(*Union Pacific Railroad Photo*)

2. Renowned plainsman Billy Dixon in his later years. (*Kansas State Historical Society*)

3. Mrs. Olive Dixon, Billy's wife. (*Kansas State Historical Society*)

4. Susan Magoffin,
believed to have been the
first white woman to have
traveled down the
Santa Fe Trail.
(*Kansas State Historical Society*)

5. Samuel Magoffin
famed Santa Fe-Chihuahua
trader, and husband of
Susan Magoffin.
(*Kansas State
Historical Society*)

6. A buffalo hunter's home near Sheridan. (*Nebraska State Historical Society*)

7. Buffalo hides awaiting shipment at Dodge City in 1874.
(*Kansas State Historical Society*)

8. Passengers sketched piling off a Union Pacific train to shoot buffalo when a big herd halts bell-stacked locomotive.
(*Union Pacific Railroad Photo*)

9. Great hunting parties came from Europe to join in the sport of killing buffalo. This shows the Grand Duke Alexis of Russia (seated center on sofa) with his entourage and American dignitaries. (*Kansas State Historical Society*)

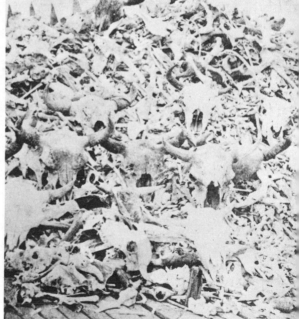

10. Buffalo bones waiting shipment by rail at Wichita, Kansas, in the 1870s. (*Kansas State Historical Society*)

11. Spotted Tail, famed Sioux war chief, who, along with some of his warriors, danced for entertainment of Grand Duke of Russia, while Custer's 7th stood guard. (*Union Pacific Railroad Photo*)

12. Sitting Bull, medicine man and chief of the Uncpapa Sioux.
*(Cody Ranch Photo)*

13. Shoshone Indians staring at the shine and splendor of the Iron Horse.
(*Southern Pacific Railroad Photo*)

14. Wagon train making its way through Echo Canyon in Utah Territory. But faster transport is already on its way. Note right-of-way for the Union Pacific which has been graded at right of picture. (*Union Pacific Railroad Photo*)

15. Sodbusters! Wheat being hauled to market at Minnesota prairie town in 1876, some of it by ox power. (*Northern Pacific Railroad Photo*)

16. General George Armstrong Custer, in his fringed hunting shirt, with Indian scouts and civilian scout when 7th Cavalry was guarding surveyors for construction of the Northern Pacific Railroad. Two of his greyhounds await call to begin the chase. Kneeling Indian is Bloody Knife, who died with Custer and his command on the Little Bighorn. (*Northern Pacific Railroad Photo*)

17. Still handsome and glamorously costumed, Buffalo Bill was sixty-nine years old when this photo was taken. (*Los Angeles Public Library Collection*)

18. General Eugene A. Carr, who was commanding the 5th U. S. Cavalry,
with Buffalo Bill as scout at the battle of Summit Springs
in Colorado on May 30, 1869.
(*Nebraska State Historical Society*)

19. Annie Oakley, "Little Sure-Shot," famous sharpshooter
with the Cody circus.
(*Cody Ranch Photo*)

20. Buffalo Bill in the ring simulating a buffalo hunt. (*Cody Ranch Photo*)

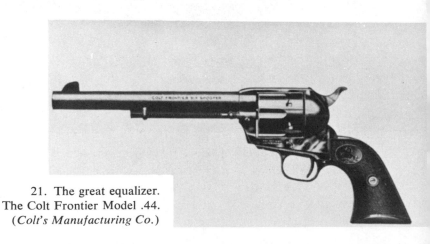

21. The great equalizer.
The Colt Frontier Model .44.
(*Colt's Manufacturing Co.*)

After the Civil War, travel over the trail continued to be heavy despite fierce Indian opposition. The path grew wider, deeper. Minor detours were made to avoid bogholes or other obstacles that had cropped up. A few bridges and roadwork here and there offered short cuts. Mainly the trail followed its original path. In wet weather, wagons bogged, and sometimes sixteen yokes were needed to pull them out. In dry weather, they rolled along, the wind blowing away the dust.

In places, the trail began to sink into the Plains. The blown dust formed high banks on either side so that in some stretches the wagons traveled almost hidden below the surface. So deeply cut was the path that, after more than a century, it is visible in many places. It can be traced, especially over South Pass, where it parallels part of the present-day highway that crosses that long sweep of sagebrush. Antelope hop away toward the hills beyond, badgers and gophers have made their home where the prairie schooners rolled, but the marks of their passage are still on the land. Out in the glare of the Carson Sink the tires and hubs of wagons abandoned more than a century ago sometimes can still be found when water conditions are right. It is not wise for inexperienced souvenir hunters to venture into portions of that seemingly smooth, hard surface. It is only a sun-baked crust beneath which lies a treacherous lake of saline-impregnated mud.

On the Oregon Trail beyond Raft River traces of the stampeders still are visible. A deep slash remains across a field owned by a rancher friend near Twin Falls, Idaho, where he grows beans and hay. This depression is always swampy, for surface water drains into it. This was where the white-sailed wagons cruised on their way along the Snake River toward the Columbia, their tires churning up dust to be blown by the wind.

The wagons continued sailing up the Platte and over the divide, year after year, until a new sound came from the east. It was the mechanical blast from a metal throat—the voice of the steam locomotive. The Union Pacific was on its way, laying steel across the Plains. The dust of the Great Medicine Road began to fade.

Also on his way into Plains history was a controversial figure —George Armstrong Custer.

## CHAPTER 5

## GEORGE ARMSTRONG CUSTER: HERO OR CUR?

The Custer story has been done to a crisp, reroasted and rebaked until it is in such a state it probably belongs with the fossils. The list of works on Custer already stretches from here to there on library shelves. The world, no doubt, is fed up with profound and solemn essays concerning the amazing doings of George Armstrong Custer. And the end is not in sight. More weighty words about Custer continue to emerge from the printing presses. So, one more drop of ink in the flood will hardly do damage.

In fact, if one starts writing about the western frontier, one collides head on with General Custer at about every fork in the trail. Custer rode here, Custer rode there. He slept here, he deserted his men there. He led his troopers to victory here. He retreated there. And so on. He had his great moments of glory. He was campaigning on the Plains when he was plunged into the depths of degradation, only to emerge again.

To many persons few other names are as synonymous with that errant word glamor as that of George Custer. To many the very sound of it arouses visions of battle smoke and war cries, of a dashing, long-haired vibrant personality, sword raised, leading a charge into battle while the trumpets blare and the band plays "Garry Owen":

> *We'll beat the bailiffs out of fun,*
> *We'll make the mayor and sheriffs run;*
> *We are the boys no man dares dun,*
> *If he regards his whole skin.*

No barroom was completely equipped unless it had a reproduction in vivid color of one of the paintings of "Custer's Last Stand" on its walls. The battle of the Little Bighorn has been done and redone in fiction and film.

On the other hand, no other figure on the American frontier scene has been quartered and hung by as many researchers. And praised and defended by others. Hundreds of thousands of scathing words have been said about Benedict Arnold, Aaron Burr, and such. John C. Frémont came in for his share. But it is on Custer's head that the real avalanche from pen and typewriter has descended.

For instance, Richard Wormser, in his fine history of the cavalry *The Yellowlegs,* says that "the best-known horse soldier the United States ever turned out was probably as useless as any man who ever wore stars." Wormser added that Custer was conceited, impulsive, disobedient, and incapable of learning.

A dissenting opinion: General Phil Sheridan, in a dispatch to General U. S. Grant, after the great Union breakthrough at Cedar Creek in the Civil War, which finally tolled the knell for the South, said, "General, I want . . . Getty and the brave boys, Merritt and Custer, promoted to brevet."

General George W. Getty commanded infantry in this battle in which Sheridan made his famous ride from Winchester to turn the tide. General Wesley Merritt commanded a division of Sheridan's cavalry as did Custer.

The dispatch added that Custer fiercely attacked the enemy and secured the artillery train.

Now listen to Frederic F. Van de Water in his *Glory Hunter,* an exhaustive, book-length account of Custer's career. Van de Water says the general loved fame with an insatiable ardor . . . all his life he rode for glory. The author also says some people believed Custer was insane.

The truth about Custer seems to lie between the varying views. Some of his critics seem to see nothing but vanity, incompetence, and a flock of other shortcomings in about everything Custer did. They belong to the school of debunkers.

On the opposite tack, his defenders glamorize him, but are forced to admit his faults. And Custer's faults were glaring, his vanity monumental. His greatest offense in the opinion of many of his critics was when he went to his death with 207 of his troopers at the Little Bighorn. It is the one for which he is the most bitterly assailed. He is accused of gross recklessness and of sacrificing his command in an attempt to grasp personal fame.

The question of why he did it, why he led his men over the brow of that barren hill into the hands of overwhelming numbers is still moot. Neither Custer nor any of his command were ever able to speak. They all died there.

Other military men, some contemporaries of Custer, made equal and sometimes greater errors, both in fighting Indians and in the Civil War. Some of those blunders, while not as publicized as the Little Bighorn, were more costly to the nation, but their perpetrators are forgotten.

Nothing Custer did seems to have been overlooked by researchers. In fact, Custer made it easy for them. He loved publicity, loved the limelight. Few men have been fated to be involved in as many colorful and dramatic events as George Armstrong Custer.

Born in 1839, he graduated from West Point in 1861, rated as a troublesome cadet who chafed under discipline and had narrowly escaped dismissal.

He fought through the Civil War and was involved in many bloody engagements from Bull Run to Appomattox. He soon wore the stars of a general, the youngest to hold that rank up to that time. It is charged that Custer did staffwork chiefly and that his career was marked by the many leaves of absence he was granted. If so, he saw a remarkable amount of action in between.

Sheridan, who believed in leading his men rather than ordering them into battle, made the cavalry a factor that was probably decisive in the final defeat of Lee. It had been an infantry war as far as the Union side was concerned during its earlier stages.

Custer apparently was a cavalryman of Sheridan's liking. Sheridan was Grant's strong right arm in the savage, long-drawn Wilderness struggle and the march on Richmond. Custer was often the point of Sheridan's sword.

Custer, with his uncanny way of being involved in events of great historical importance, fought at Gettysburg. He is credited with probably saving the Union side from disaster by disobeying an order—one of many offenses of this nature he is charged with. In this case, his division was ordered to move from the left flank of the Union line to the right. But Custer could see Jeb Stuart's

cavalry forming to sweep around the Union flank. He stayed
where he was and balked Stuart's plan.

Nearly a year later in the battle of Yellow Tavern during the
terrible Wilderness drive upon Richmond, Custer routed Stuart's
cavalry and Stuart himself was fatally wounded, costing the
South one of its great cavalry leaders.

Custer figured in the final thrust that brought Lee to the peace
table at Appomattox. A Sheridan dispatch to Grant on April 8,
1865, says in part: "Custer then pushed toward Appomattox
Courthouse, driving the enemy, who kept up a heavy artillery fire,
charging them repeatedly . . ."

He was wounded only once, slightly. Custer's luck, they
called it. During the course of the war he was reprimanded for
hanging some of Mosby's guerrillas. Mosby retaliated by string-
ing up Union prisoners, and Custer was blamed for this. His
defenders say that Sherman and Grant had issued a general order
to hang guerrillas. In fact, hanging was the customary fate of
such irregulars.

Custer is said to have been offered the first Confederate surrender at Appomattox. One researcher says that Custer brashly
dashed into the Confederate lines during the truce and demanded
the surrender of General James Longstreet, but was snubbed.
Another writer says this incident was related in Longstreet's
book, which was published thirty years later. Eyewitnesses on the
scene have attested that the white flag was actually offered to
Custer, and that he referred the bearer to Sheridan or Grant.

Custer is credited with coming into possession of the table on
which Lee signed the surrender. Phil Sheridan presented it to
Custer on the scene as a gift for Custer's wife, Elizabeth. Custer is
said to have ridden away from Appomattox Courthouse, steadying
the table on his head. Such a present from the dour, peppery
Sheridan would hardly have gone to an officer he did not believe
deserved it.

After the war, Custer, always colorful, always broke, and
reduced in rank, considered joining the army of Juárez in the
Maximilian affair in Mexico. Instead, he accepted an offer to
serve as bodyguard for President Andrew Johnson on a speaking
tour, an assignment of which Johnson, no doubt, knew the value,
for the presence of the dashing cavalryman certainly did nothing
to decrease attendance at the President's speaking engagements,

although it is probable the increase came mainly from the feminine ranks. Women could not vote in those days, or perhaps Custer might have run for President himself. It is believed he might even have entertained such ambitions at times.

The new 7th United States Cavalry was organized in the spring of 1867, and Custer was made its commander. This was the outfit that drank, marched, fought, and wenched its way over a greater part of the frontier west.

Custer's career as an Indian fighter is where he is attacked relentlessly. He was out of his element on the Plains. Born in green, lush Ohio, it was his nature to detest the vast distances and somber grandeur of prairie and plain. Instead of conforming to this environment, he tried to bend it to his own will. He detested the rude towns, Hays, Omaha, Leavenworth, and the like. He detested the dreary Army outposts, Fort Hays, Fort Harker and Fort Kearney. He loved dress parades and spit and polish, with military bands playing, steeds prancing, and ladies applauding in the reviewing stands. When it came to battle he preferred to charge and settle the issue at once—but with the band playing. War, to Custer, was romance, glamor, a heady wine. He never could understand men who did not see it that way.

He was a hard taskmaster, demanding rigid discipline and endless drilling in an attempt to make soldiers of poor material. He drove them as he drove himself. Troopers were not Custers. He seemed to have a physique of steel. Many of the troopers had enlisted, expecting an easy life. Some were buffalo hunters in need of food and shelter. Others were former guerrillas or deserters who had changed sides during the war, along with changing names. Some were wanted by the law back east. Others were callow tenderfeet who had come west in search of adventure and had joined up. A great many were European immigrants who could not speak English. Recruiting officers were lax in those days.

Custer, all his life, was out to win whatever game he played. If weaklings could not keep the pace, he had no patience with them. He was operating in a land where torture was the price of being captured. The weakness of a few could endanger all.

He placed men under arrest for minor infractions and inflicted harsh punishments. He tried to prepare them for soldiering in the furnacelike summers of the Plains and the bitter winters.

Never a man of patience, always on the search for fame and promotion, he suffered defeat, frustration, and even indecision on the Plains—a characteristic that had previously been foreign to him. He found himself opposed by a foe whose ways of life and methods of warfare were beyond his understanding. He was unable to match the Indian's method of ambush, indirection, and hit-and-run. He scorned and underrated a foe that never presented a solid front upon which he could charge, brandishing his sword. His camps would be raided unexpectedly after scouts had assured him there were no hostiles within miles. His supply trains would be hit and burned, and the Cheyennes, or 'Rapahoes, or Ki'ways, as the case might be, would vanish into the Plains before he could lead his men against them. When he sent subordinate officers out with details on scouting missions, they would be ambushed.

A wagon train with which his wife was traveling to Fort Wallace on the Republican River to join her husband was attacked by Sioux and besieged until a relief column arrived from the post. Libbie Custer was uninjured, but when Custer learned about it later he became aware that it had been a narrow squeak. Army officers had orders to shoot any white women under their care if their capture by Indians seemed certain.

All these things ground on the nerves of a man of Custer's temperament, because he could not come to grips with them. Some of his biographers view him as growing more erratic and reckless because he felt he was losing face, losing his life-long passionate race for more and more renown, more and more glory.

The biggest trouble he was to get into, except for the fatal day nearly ten years later, came in 1867. His company had been trying to pin down elusive hostiles on a long hard march, and as a climax he ordered a sixty-five-mile ride from the Republican River to the Platte.

The column lagged, men and animals suffered. Custer finally left his plodding command and rode ahead to the river with his orderly, the doctor, and a lieutenant, where they were camped when the company straggled in hours later.

The next day twelve men deserted. Custer, in a rage, ordered Captain Joel E. Elliott and Captain W. W. Cook to pursue them and "bring in none alive."

Those words brought to Custer his greatest disgrace—court-martial and a year's disbarment from the Army. He came within an ace of being charged with murder.

Of the dozen deserters, some of whom were mounted, nine escaped. Three were shot down by Elliott and Cook, and one died later of his wounds. Custer is accused of ordering the company doctor not to treat the wounded men, but this verbal command evidently was intended for the benefit of the ranks where the deserting spirit still raged, for he privately told the surgeon to treat the injured shortly after they were brought into the camp.

Meanwhile, Custer received orders by telegraph from Fort Sedgwick toward which he was heading, to return to Fort Wallace for supplies. A detail under Lieutenant Kidder of the 2nd Cavalry had been sent out from the fort with the same message in case Custer did not get in touch with a telegraph office. Kidder was unable to deliver the message. He and his men were ambushed by Sioux. Custer found their mutilated bodies.

Arriving at Wallace, Custer learned that his wife was at Fort Riley, and it was said cholera was raging there. Theirs was a love affair that was not broken by death. Until the end of her long life on April 6, 1933, in New York City, Libbie Custer defended her husband valiantly by word and pen. The books she wrote sang praise of the general and attested her devotion. She is said to have been the only officer's wife who followed her husband to every frontier post, no matter how primitive they might be, during the five, lonely years of campaigning on the lower Plains. She eventually followed the flag to the mosquito-plagued Fort Lincoln and was there the day the 7th marched away under Custer for the last time.

But that was almost ten years in the future. Alarmed by the cholera story, Custer again left his command and started the long ride to Fort Riley to join his bride of less than three years. He set out with nearly eighty troopers including his brother, Tom Custer. Nearly all the men dropped back on the journey. Two of these were cut off and killed by Indians. Custer arrived at Fort Harker late at night with only his brother and three other men.

The commander at Harker, Colonel A. J. Smith, awakened late at night, confusedly gave permission to Custer to proceed to Riley. The colonel realized his mistake in the morning and ordered Custer's arrest.

Arriving at Fort Riley, Custer found that reports of cholera were untrue. He was court-martialed, charged with leaving his command without permission, of ordering deserters shot without a trial, and other infractions. He was found guilty and suspended from rank, command, and proper pay for a year—a light sentence considering the charges.

Libbie Custer, in a letter to a friend, said proper pay amounted to ninety-five dollars a month, which they lost, but they had enough on which to live.

Custer was not the only military figure who had been beset by the headache of desertions in the ranks. It had been a major problem with the Army at frontier posts. Desertions often weakened commands in campaigns against the Indians to such an extent the remaining troopers were endangered as their ranks were thinned in the face of the enemy.

The problem extends through all military history. Theodore Roosevelt mentions it in his historical work as sealing the doom of General Arthur St. Clair's army of fourteen hundred men that was overwhelmed by picked warriors of the Delawares, Shawnees, Wyandots, and Miamis in the pre-Revolutionary fighting in the Ohio country. Deserters had quit St. Clair in such numbers before the fight his command was far outnumbered.

General Bisbee, in his book *Through Four American Wars,* tells of the difficulty of controlling rough troopers, especially when the men got their hands on whisky, which was as often as any could be found within miles. Bisbee, on one occasion, driven to fury by drunken, defiant soldiers, seized a rifle, cocked it, nearly becoming a killer before he controlled his rage. He related that on another occasion a lieutenant shot at a disobedient soldier and the bullet killed an innocent man.

Eugene Ware tells of an incident where a very unpopular second lieutenant was killed at Fort McPherson when a gun went off in the hands of a man in the ranks. Ware was appointed to inquire into the affair. Finding no evidence it was *not* an accident, nothing was done.

Custer's life was threatened more than once by his own men, but no bullet struck him in the back, although some researchers say the shot that killed Captain Louis Hamilton during the battle of the Washita was meant for Custer and that it came from the carbine of a 7th cavalryman. Such things are a grim occupational hazard for combat leaders who order men into dangerous situations.

Custer was not the only officer to lose his cool because of desertions and lack of fighting spirit in the ranks. General George S. Patton, the American Army's most capable tank commander in World War II, got himself into hot water by entering a military hospital and trying forcibly to boot men out of their cots and back into the battle line in the belief that were feigning injuries in order to shirk their duty. Patton drew a reprimand from General Eisenhower. The demands for his removal were very loud, for many war correspondents saw to it the American public was made aware of what was actually an unimportant incident. Fortunately, Patton remained in command. A cavalryman at heart, he did much to save the day during the battle of the Bulge by engineering a mass movement of tanks, men, and equipment to reinforce the battle lines at a critical time.

Libbie Custer and her husband, in all their writings, ignored the bitter setback the suspension gave to the general's ambitions. Sheridan, always Custer's staunch friend, came to their aid. The Custers occupied Sheridan's quarters at Leavenworth for a time, and then spent the summer in exile at the home Libbie Custer had inherited at Monroe, Michigan.

Sheridan had been placed in command of the war on the Plains, and things were going from bad to worse. His commanders in the field seemed to be either timid or unable to cope with the hard-fighting tribes. Indian raids increased. The last straw came for Sheridan when the 7th Cavalry, under Brigadier General Alfred Sully, was forced to retreat to Ford Dodge, unable to handle the situation.

Sheridan turned to Custer as he had so many times during the Civil War. He sent an appeal to General Sherman, who was his superior, saying that Custer's rashness was probably a necessary virtue in a cavalry commander and asked that he be reinstated although his year of exile was not up. He added, unnecessarily, that Custer was brave. Few of Custer's many critics ever differed with that estimate. In fact, it was sometimes pointed out as a fault.

Sheridan's request was reluctantly granted by Ulysses Grant, who never saw eye to eye with him in the matter of Custer. And so Custer emerged from exile, cocky, peppery, and wearing a uniform of his own design, carefully tailored. He found the 7th much deteriorated, and once again became the hard-nosed disciplinarian in an effort to make Indian fighters out of indifferent material.

He marched in November on a winter campaign. On a freezing dawn on the Washita River east of the Texas Panhandle, he surrounded the sleeping camp of Black Kettle, the same Cheyenne who had escaped alive on Sand Creek when the Chivington massacre took place.

On that bitter morning Custer ordered music. War, fighting, was still his romance. The band struck up. The musicians played until their instruments froze. By that time the music had been drowned out by the roar of Spencers and Colts.

Black Kettle is rated by many historians as having been a peaceful Indian. They assert that Custer mounted the attack only to enhance his reputation and make the public forget the year of ostracism. Black Kettle and his villages were not the first neutrals to be crushed by the juggernaut of war. Nor the last. That is, if they were really neutrals. It was related that men of the 7th found the bodies of two young white captives, murdered, in Black Kettle's village.

However, Black Kettle died there at least, along with many of his people. Custer placed the number of slain Indians at 103. One researcher declares that plainsmen and hunters scoffed at that figure. A squaw man was quoted as estimating that only about a dozen warriors were killed. This seems to clash with all other accounts.

Major Joel Elliott, one of those who had shot the deserters in the episode that brought about Custer's court-martial, lost his life on the Washita under circumstances that are still debated.

During the battle, Elliott shouted, "Here goes for a brevet or a coffin," and led nineteen troopers off into the brush in pursuit of fleeing Cheyennes. Elliott did not win his brevet. Neither he nor the nineteen men who had followed him were seen alive again. It was the old story of ambush. Firing was heard for a long time down the brushy stream, but the majority of the researchers say Custer made no move to send help.

For that, they have added a very black mark to Custer's record. Furthermore, some say he retreated from a victorious battlefield with his command still nearly intact, instead of advancing. The implication is that Custer lost his nerve. That, of course, contradicts everything in Custer's previous career. But they still add the black mark.

E. I. Stewart, in an intensive examination of Custer's career, says that Lieutenant Edward S. Godfrey, who had been sent by his commander to round up Indian ponies, had sighted many villages downstream whose presence had not been suspected. Custer often seemed to lack adequate scouting. Godfrey reported that warriors were swarming from the lodges, heading toward the scene of the fighting.

The men of the 7th had left their overcoats and rations cached when they had moved in to the attack at dawn. These had fallen into the hands of Indians. There were a dozen wounded men to care for, also the body of Lieutenant Hamilton, who had been killed. They had fifty squaws and Indian children as prisoners. No male Indian had been taken alive. In addition, they had captured seven hundred Indian ponies.

Another freezing night was coming on. More Indians were appearing on the bluffs. Custer evidently had no way of knowing how stiff the opposition might be. His failure to have such situations adequately scouted is blamed by some for his doom at the Little Bighorn later on.

He decided to retreat. The soldiers have a term for it. Let's get the hell out of here. For this, he has been roundly lambasted. It had been an easy victory up to this point, with the quarry unable to offer much resistance. Some critics seem to believe he should have driven ahead and killed more Indians.

There were many factors to consider. One was that although he had worked for weeks training his men before taking the field, they were not the battle-hardened troops he had led during the Civil War. Far from it.

Custer ordered the seven hundred captured Indian ponies slaughtered, a gruesome duty that was carried out. The lodges were set afire. His next order was characteristic. He again commanded the band to play. Even under those circumstances, with weary, battle-stained men in the midst of hostiles on a trampled, bloodstained battlefield, he ordered music.

Evidently the band's horns had thawed. The musicians struck up, and Custer and the 7th advanced upon the Indians on the bluffs. Whether it was the boldness of it, or there were not enough warriors to contest the march, no opposition came. The 7th rode away from the Washita where the lodges burned crimson in the twilight and the squaws were beginning their weird mourning of the dead.

The 7th joined their main supply train late the next afternoon, and men filled their famished bellies and replenished ammunition pouches. They continued the march—or retreat—to Camp Supply on the Canadian River. With the Custer love of flourish, they paraded into the post, the band playing, banners flying, to be reviewed by Sheridan, and cheered by the ladies.

Custer claimed victory on the Washita. His critics depict it as an example of his incompetence, and a failure. On the contrary, it apparently accomplished its purpose. Rarely again were the Indians on the southern Plains a real threat. More men would die in raids, more Indians would be shot down by the cavalry in retaliation, but these were rumbles of the fading storm. After the Washita, the handwriting was in the sunset for all the chiefs along the Arkansas to see.

The main battleground moved into the Southwest, and north, beyond the Platte. In those areas the war lingered for twenty years or more, dying down at times, often flaring savagely into new life. Custer's fate in 1876 was the last straw. But for the restraint of public opinion the Army would have fulfilled its threat to wipe out the Indians altogether.

Stewart, who wrote a foreword to an edition of Custer's own *My Life on the Plains,* expressed the belief that the general's decision to retreat from the Washita might have averted a disaster as great as the one years later at the Little Bighorn. Captain Benteen is said to have declared that Custer's book should have been titled Lie on the Plains.

It would seem that if Custer had decided to carry the fight to other Indian villages, as some of his critics say he should have done, and had escaped disaster, it would have entailed unnecessary shedding of more blood. Custer's attack on that freezing morning is credited with breaking the power of the hostiles on the southern Plains, so that settlers lived in less fear of losing their scalps.

Benteen, of F Troop, was one of Custer's bitterest critics. After the Washita campaign an unsigned letter was printed in a newspaper that was the basis of accusations that Custer had callously refused to send help to Elliott and the trapped nineteen. Custer forced Benteen to admit that he had written the letter, and threatened to use a whip on him, but failed to pursue the matter.

Jealousy and animosity raged among the officers of the 7th. There were Custer and anti-Custer factions. Benteen had been passed over in rank in Custer's favor during the Civil War. These feuds continued to the Little Bighorn.

A few weeks after the Washita battle, Custer and the 7th returned to the scene, accompanied by Sheridan. Custer's book offers a description. The frozen bodies of many Indians still lay on the field, although those of Black Kettle and Chief Little Rock had been removed. Also remaining were the carcasses of the seven hundred Indian ponies. The villages down the stream had been abandoned.

Custer said the mutilated bodies of Elliott and a majority of the nineteen troopers were found two miles away. It was evident they had made a desperate stand after being surrounded. Elliott's body was taken to Fort Arbuckle for burial.

So ended the battle of the Washita. At least on the Washita. It has been refought repeatedly with pen and typewriter by researchers since that day.

In his account, Custer said that during the afternoon, after the fighting had died down, a squaw brought a young Indian girl to him and placed her hand in his. Custer said his interpreter, with a knowing grin, told him the squaw was marrying the girl to him. Custer said he hastily declined the honor, remarking that he already had a wife.

Some researchers, including the late Mari Sandoz, say that, on the contrary, the commander kept the girl, Monahsetah, with him, and that a son named Yellow Swallow was born. Miss Sandoz, who was author of several works dealing with western Americana, also declared that other young Indian girls were taken into the tents of officers of the 7th.

For the next half a dozen years or so, Custer's career was relatively uneventful. That is, if you would look on such matters as being responsible for a gold rush, and a joust with the President of the United States as commonplace matters.

The gold rush was typical of Custer's flair for involvement in colorful, historical events. By the treaty of 1851, the great expanse of Plains north of the Platte River had been set aside as belonging to the Indians as their hunting grounds. The treaty specifically ordained that the buffalo land from the east slopes of the Bighorn Mountains to the sacred Black Hills be forbidden to white men. *Any* white men. Actually the entire "American Desert" west of the Missouri River was regarded as worthless and therefore "treaty country."

However, for years there had been rumors there was gold in the Black Hills, which were particularly revered by the Sioux and Cheyennes. Phil Sheridan had been wanting to set up a fort in the hills after his appointment as head of the Department of the West following the Civil War. This was ostensibly to control the tribes, but its real purpose would have been to explore the region.

On July 2, 1874, under Sheridan's orders, Custer set out from Fort Lincoln near the Missouri River settlement of Bismarck, North Dakota, in command of a "reconnaisance" force of a thousand men. Custer's command moved in an impressive march of three columns, the baggage train in the middle for protection.

This "scouting party" crushed the buffalo grass across the land to the Black Hills. There, experienced civilian miners with the military party confirmed the existence of gold in the hills. The famed scout, Charley Reynolds, arrived at Laramie in early August, after a dangerous ride, and filed Custer's historic message over Western Union. Gold in the Black Hills!

That broke the dam. Prospectors flooded into treaty country. The great Indian wars of the seventies followed. Custer and many men of the 7th, along with Charley Reynolds, became its most publicized victims as a result of the Little Bighorn disaster.

For a time, Custer followed prosaic garrison duties; then in the fateful spring of 1876 he testified in Washington at an inquiry into corruption and exploitation of the Indians by crooked traders with the connivance of federal officials. Orvil Grant, brother of the President, was involved.

Custer testified against the trading clique. That, of course, did nothing to elevate him in the President's esteem, and he had been far from being one of Grant's favorites in the past. After testifying, he left Washington without asking the permission of the War Department. He was ordered arrested, but Sheridan and General Alfred Terry intervened, and he was permitted to go into the field with the 7th.

He returned to Fort Lincoln and, with the band playing, set out on May 7, 1876, at the head of the regiment, to subdue the Sioux. According to the strategy, General Crook was to swing north from the Platte country toward Wyoming, General Gibbon was to march south from Fort Ellis, Montana, and Custer was to move in from the east in a pincer operation that would crush the tribes.

Elizabeth Custer went into camp with her husband on the 7th's first night under canvas outside of Fort Lincoln and traveled a dozen miles westward the next morning before he ordered her to return to the safety of the fort. It is said a pall of foreboding lay over the wives of the officers of the 7th when they marched away.

Toward midnight of July 5, the steamboat *Far West* returned to Bismarck, bringing news that had been mysteriously rumored at the fort for several days, from what source none knew, perhaps by the Indians' means of communication.

Soon after sunup, officers, ashen-lipped, went to the house where Libbie Custer lived. She is said to have taken the news as a soldier's wife is supposed to do. Bravely, resignedly. And despairingly. She had stood by him through victory and defeat, through disgrace and triumph. He had been the sun around which she had revolved. Now he lay dead at a place she had never heard of, the Little Bighorn River. With him lay the bodies of his command.

Since that time the controversy has continued. Custer was not the first commander to lead his men to their deaths. Nor the last. There were Braddock and St. Clair, whose incapacity cost the lives of hundreds of troops in the Indian wars before the Revolution. There was the charge at Balaklava when "into the valley of death rode the six hundred." Cries for the removal of "Butcher" Grant became loud during the terrible days of the Wilderness when Union soldiers were dying by the hundreds in Virginia swamps.

During World War II similar demands were made for the removal of General Mark Clark, who was in command of the bloody battle at the Rapido River in Italy. All those outcries died down. But every move Custer made has been examined with microscopic care. Every error and flaw—and there were plenty to find—have been pounced on and pawed over.

One wonders if it is not about time to let his bones rest in peace in Arlington along with those of others who died in the service of their country. There were many who made some of the same mistakes he made, and worse.

CHAPTER 6

## BUFFALO BILL CODY:
## REAL OR FALSE?

If the career of George Armstrong Custer is taken by some as only to be dangled at a distance while holding one's nose, and that only the worst of the subject's character be worth describing, how about one William Frederick Cody? His name and career are set down in Plains lore perhaps even more luridly than that of the general.

Buffalo Bill Cody was a contemporary of Custer. In fact, they were companions in some colorful events. Evidently they understood each other, for in their reminiscences neither has expressed anything but admiration for the other. This is unusual, for both were extreme extroverts who usually resented sharing the spotlight with anyone. Both Custer and Cody loved the limelight. By dress and manner they sought to attract attention. The fringed jacket Custer often wore in leading the 7th was an affectation aimed at setting himself apart from his fellow officers in their baggy, shapeless Army uniforms.

The fringe on Buffalo Bill's hunting shirts and jackets became even more famous. It fluttered in the streets of hundreds of cities, both in America and Europe. It became seasoned by cookfire smoke and skillet grease in Army bivouacs and camps of buffalo hunters. In his circus days, the fringe, white and expensive, brushed the sleeves of kings and dukes. Almost as much as his long hair was the buckskin jacket an emblem of his *nom de théâtre*—the King of Scouts. He loved that title, and also the one the Indians gave him—Pa-has-ka, or Long Yellow Hair.

Many reviewers dismiss William Frederick Cody with a sniff of disdain and the back of the hand to him. They take the position that he was a stuffed shirt whom Ned Buntline had invented out of hot air and had palmed off on a gullible public.

Mari Sandoz, in one of her books, dismisses Cody and also Wild Bill Hickok as merely a pair of stock tenders at stage stations. Cody and Hickok, no doubt, tended a lot of stock in their day, but they figured in several other things too.

Of course, it is difficult to separate the Buffalo Bill, circus performer, actor in dreadful stage melodramas, and hero of a series of ghost-written dime novels, from the Bill Cody, plainsman, buffalo hunter, and Indian fighter. He was the most colorful figure to emerge from the dust of the frontier.

Being colorful is sometimes an unforgivable trait in the eyes of some viewers. They could not believe that the handsome rider who led parades of his Wild West Show down the Main Streets of America was the same man who had scouted for Custer, hunted buffalo with the Grand Duke of Russia, figured in the legendary "duel" with Yellow Hand, had ridden for the Pony Express, had known Sitting Bull, Dull Knife, and other fighting chiefs.

Here, leading real cowboys and real Indians, some of whom remembered the Little Bighorn, was the person who had driven stagecoaches on the Plains when the Sioux were painted for war, had slain hundreds of buffalo for meat as the Kansas Pacific Railroad was pushed across the Kansas prairie. Here was the man who had performed before queens and kings and had permitted kings to take minor parts in his circus.

Here was a man who had been a close friend of Bill Hickok, and had even induced that maverick human to display himself on the eastern stage in one of the lurid plays in which Cody starred between stints of scouting for the Army.

Cody's name was used in an endless flood of cheap weekly novels that poured onto the newsstands before and after the turn of the century, along with such other classics as Diamond Dick, the Liberty Boys of '76, Nick Carter Detective, and many others.

In those offerings, Cody was presented as the first Superman. Slaying thirty or forty Indians, singlehanded, was weekly routine, along with other feats to match. Some of those yarns, especially the earlier ones by Ned Buntline, got mixed up with events in the life of the real Bill Cody. Being a showman, fully aware of the commercial value of publicity, he did not attempt to deprecate these legends, but by winks and smiles let them grow and expand.

He was born February 26, 1846, in Scott County, Iowa, but his real start to fame came when he is reputed to have been the youngest Pony Express rider to be hired. He had five sisters and a brother. Tragedy and violence came early in his life. When he was seven, Cody saw his fourteen-year-old brother killed when a horse fell. His father was wounded by pro-slavers in the bitter border strife of Civil War days and eventually died of his injuries. Helen Cody Wetmore and Julia Cody Goodman, his sisters, have left accounts of his life. Zane Grey is credited, along with Mrs. Wetmore, as author of one of these narratives, which seems to accept some of the legendary stories of Cody's doings as fact.

Cody traveled up the Platte at the age of eleven or twelve as a messenger with one of the bull trains operated by Russell, Majors & Waddell, the firm that was later to become famous in Overland Stage history. This trip carried him to Fort Kearney, outpost of the Indian country. There were always many lodges of "peaceful" Cheyennes and Sioux camped nearby, but, as a matter of fact, a scalp was not safe much beyond sight of Kearney's walls.

One story that always haunted Cody, and which was accepted as true by Mrs. Wetmore, is that he slew his first Indian on this journey. This, no doubt, was one of the fanciful items that grew out of the fiction works.

However, on his second freighting trip he had a real taste of violence. His outfit, of which a plainsman named Lew Simpson was wagonmaster, was captured by Utah militia under Captain Lot Smith. The wagons were burned, their owners being charged with illegal invasion of Mormon Territory. Cody and the others of the crew were allowed to make their way to Fort Bridger, warned never to enter Mormon country again.

There he met the already famous Jim Bridger. Also Kit Carson, another to be viewed with awe by a teen-ager. Young Cody was so impressed by the quiet, blue-eyed mountain man that, years later, he named his son Kit Carson Cody.

After his return to the border, he next took part in the Pikes Peak rush, but found no gold. He and his companions tried to save shoe leather by building a raft and floating down the South Platte, but the raft was wrecked near Jules Benti's trading post in the summer of 1859 and they lost all their belongings.

The Pony Express was being organized by Russell, Majors & Waddell. Cody was given a letter by Alexander Majors, introducing him to the notorious Joseph Slade, stagecoach division boss at Julesburg. Slade balked at hiring a boy so young, but finally assigned him to the stretch from Red Buttes to Three Crossings, west of Fort Laramie, believing it was about the "safest" assignment in his division, which was one of the most hazardous on the entire Pony route.

Cody was a rider for only three months, then returned to Iowa, having heard that his mother was ill. It was an active three months, if the stories are to be believed. For one thing, he is credited with making one of the longest rides in the history of the Pony, which was also a short history. He is said to have stayed in the saddle for more than 380 miles, when relay riders had been slain by Indians, in order to keep the mail moving.

Arthur Chapman, who wrote a history of the Pony, doubted that Cody ever rode for the organization. He based his view on the rule that no Pony rider under the age of twenty would be accepted. Apparently the rule was found to be impractical. Advertisements have been reproduced from San Francisco newspapers of that era which seek "young, skinny, wiry fellows not over 18 who are willing to risk death daily to ride for the Pony at $25 per week. Orphans preferred."

Hair-raising tales of escapes from Indians during Cody's Pony career have been told, the majority of them palpably generated by the novels, but there seems no question but that he had some bad moments and that the hair that was to become famous was very loose on his head at times.

Cody's next stint was to join William Hickok in a freighting venture from Rolla, Missouri. This interlude in the lives of both men seems to have been notable for the fact that nothing happened to interrupt the monotony of the journey. A rare lull for both.

The Civil War broke out, and Cody served as a dispatch rider between Forts Larned and Leavenworth in Kansas. Involved in this is a tale of again meeting Hickok, who was serving as a Union spy. Cody later was in the battle of Pilot Knob on the border. Except for another story of saving Hickok from being hung by mistake by the Union forces, the novels seem to have neglected to garnish his career as a soldier with heroic deeds.

A year after his regiment was mustered out at the end of the war, he married Louisa Frederici, whom he had met in St. Louis. He drove stage for the Overland from Fort Kearney to Plum Creek, which was not a particularly hazardous chore. However, he is credited with driving for Joseph Slade later on the division west of Julesburg, particularly the twelve-mile stretch beyond Independence Rock from Split Rock to Three Crossings. Cody well remembered this route from his Pony career, but it is said he came much closer to losing his scalp as a stage driver in an Indian ambush than when riding with the Pony.

He had grown into a stalwart young man. His stint as a stage driver, or "silk popper" as they were sometimes called, came in handy in later days when he was tooling six-horse coach teams around the narrow track in his wild West show arena with kings and future kings as his passengers.

He first met Custer in the spring of 1867 while scouting for the cavalry out of Fort Ellsworth in Kansas. The Kansas Pacific Railroad was pushing its way toward Fort Hays, reaching there in 1867. Cody, who had turned to buffalo hunting, became the official provider of meat for the tables of the construction crews. It was here that he picked up his title of Buffalo Bill. He was not unchallenged. There were several other frontier characters who desired to be known by that handle. Their deeds, or misdeeds, have helped confuse research into the doings of the real Cody. The same holds true for Hickok. There were any number of self-styled Wild Bills drifting around the frontier, and here and there, some, no doubt, posed as the real Hickok—after making sure that gentleman was far, far away.

Cody, according to records, brought down 4,280 buffalo in the 18 months he worked as a pot hunter for the K.P. As buffalo killing went, it was a commonplace achievement. Many hide-takers ran up scores far higher. Cody was not a hide hunter. He had no liking for the grime and grease of the skinning camps. Always fastidious of dress, he was beginning to be able to afford the colorful attire that was to become his trademark. He hired others for the skinning.

However, the words of officers and sportsmen who saw him in

action leave no doubt that he was an expert in the art of dropping the shaggy animals. Meat hunting, particularly, required "savvy." A bungler could stampede the source of supply so far from the consumer, in this case the terriers of the K.P. construction crews, that long hauls became necessary, with the ensuing problems of expense as well as spoilage. Cody was said to have an uncanny knack for bringing down his quarry within reasonable distance of the end of steel.

He officially clinched his right to the title in a hunting contest with one William Comstock, who claimed he was the one who should stand up as the real Buffalo Bill. Cody's detractors say this was another fabrication and that no such contest was ever staged. They ignore the fact that advertisements appeared in Kansas newspapers, paid for by the K.P., proclaiming the contest and offering excursion rates to the site, which was near Sheridan, Kansas.

Comstock claimed he could outshoot, outcuss, and outdrink any upstart buffalo hunter like Cody any day in the week and twice on Sunday. He was wrong on all three counts. The shoot was presented in three stages, or runs. Cody killed thirty-eight buffalo in the stated time on the first run, Comstock twenty-three.

He ran up proportionate advantages on the final two runs, and his challenger was thereafter fated to go through life as plain Billy Comstock. The heads of the slain buffalo were mounted by the K.P. and distributed through the East to lure hunters, and, preferably, settlers, to Kansas. Some of those heads, no doubt, are still in existence.

Cody's fame was now spreading. It became a feather in the cap of tourists to say they had seen Buffalo Bill in person, and an even greater feat if they managed to shake hands with that colorful scout. That was not difficult. Cody, a polite, gregarious man, was always easy to approach. He liked to plant a boot on the foot rail of a bar and spend a convivial evening.

Some viewers of the frontier take the attitude that Cody spent all his time in barrooms, and that the nearest he ever got to an Indian was the wooden kind in front of cigar stores. They point to his flamboyance as proof that he was not genuine.

Cody was flamboyant, right enough. He stood out from the run-of-the-mill with Roman candle brilliance. He was not the hell-for-leather, come-on-men type of warrior that was Custer, nor was he the steely gunman and pistol artist that was Hickok. He did possess that elusive quality—color—and he won his spurs on the Plains.

He was chief of scouts in several Army campaigns against the Indians, and was praised often for his skill by those who rode with him. He is officially listed as engaging in eight actions against Indians during one campaign alone, and was awarded the Medal of Honor, a distinction that was rescinded by act of Congress, because he was a civilian.

W. E. Webb of Topeka, Kansas, was a member of the party of naturalists and fossil hunters who hired Cody as a guide at Fort Hays in 1872. Webb wrote a book titled *Buffalo Land,* which was published in 1874, in which he speaks of Cody as a spare and wiry figure, and the best guide he ever saw. Webb said, in the flowery language of the day, that the mysterious Plains were an open book to the scout, and that he led his party over it through the black, starless nights, never losing his way. However, Webb pointed out that the fact Cody could slaughter buffalo was not remarkable since this animal was dangerous only to amateur hunters.

General Bisbee, then a captain, hunted with Cody when the latter was scouting for the 3rd Cavalry during an expedition against hostile Arapahoes in the Bighorn Mountains. He voiced great respect for Cody's ability at locating game, but took satisfaction in recording how the scout had a rare case of buck fever and missed an easy shot at an elk.

One of the most dramatic Indian fights in which Cody was involved was the battle of Summit Springs, south of Julesburg, on May 30, 1869.

Tall Bull's Cheyennes had attacked and wiped out all but two white women of a wagon train, and had fled south with the women as captives. Cody scouted for General Eugene A. Carr's 5th Cavalry on a long, hard pursuit that started from Fort McPherson, more than a hundred miles east of Julesburg.

The detachment, five hundred strong, overtook the Cheyennes at Summit Springs and staged a surprise attack on the village. The harsh tally was fifty-two Cheyennes dead and seventeen women and children captured. One trooper was slightly wounded.

One of the captives, Mrs. G. Weichel, was rescued alive, but the other, Mrs. Thomas Alderdice, was brained with an ax by a squaw when the attack began.

Cody was credited with having slain Tall Bull during the Summit Springs attack, but this, like so many battle episodes, has many versions, with various troopers in the outfit claiming it was his bullet that downed the chief.

General Carr, who had no ax to grind, wrote some years later: "Mrs. Tall Bull, the chief's wife, says it was Cody who shot her husband." Cody was praised by Carr in his official report of the affair, and the adjutant general was ordered to pay him a special hundred-dollar bonus for his skill in trailing down the attackers of the wagon train.

Mrs. Weichel's rescue was to be re-enacted over and over, matinee and night performances, in Cody's wild West show and sometimes three times on holidays. For many seasons it was the high point of the program, with the agonized captive about to die at the hands of the Indians, and the last-minute arrival of the cavalry, trumpets blaring, guidons flying, guns gushing flame and smoke from blank cartridges. The role of the Cheyennes was usually taken by real tribesmen who traveled with the circus, and the truth is that some of them might have been involved in the actual massacre of the wagon train years before.

Cody never laid claim to saving Mrs. Weichel personally. Some unidentified trooper in the 5th had that honor. But the demands of circus business made Cody the rescuer during show time, amid the hail of wads from blanks.

And plenty of blanks were used at each performance of the "Bill show." For that reason it was one of the first "topless" entertainments. Topless tent, that is. Otherwise the spectators might have been overwhelmed by powder smoke before the program ended.

All the approaches to Cody's adventures have been colored through the years by the boom of circus drums and the blare of pitchmen. "Step up, folks! Step this way and I will tell you about the world-famous scout and Indian fighter, the Honorable Colonel William Frederick Cody, the man who killed the famous chief Tall Bull in the battle of Summit Springs, who slew Cheyenne Chief Yellow Hand, in mortal hand-to-hand combat, the man who was chief of scouts for the Army in many campaigns, the greatest plainsman, the greatest rifle shot of all time who has been prevailed upon to demonstrate his skill for the benefit of the public."

The pitchmen laid it on very thick. They implied that he was a real gun-swift who had taken care of badmen by the dozen, in addition to scores of Indians. There is no record of Cody ever drawing a weapon in anger against a white man, and his Indian fights took place with combatants on both sides shooting to kill.

As a marksman, he was not in the same class with Wild Bill Hickok, but he was far from being a novice. One of his turns in the circus was to break glass balls tossed by a beautiful Indian maiden as he rode at a gallop on his famous horse Charlie.

Some critics point derisive fingers, saying he used rifle shells loaded with bird shot, which scattered, and with which any novice could have found the targets. Agnes Wright Spring, in a history of Cheyenne and Black Hills stagecoaching, relates that he broke twenty-three out of twenty-five glass balls at Cheyenne in a rifle match, using a weapon without sights.

There is little doubt that he used bird shot. He performed in circus arenas, surrounded by onlookers, or on streets with people gazing from doors and windows. Solid shot would have endangered lives.

However, any pitchman's claims as to Cody's pre-eminence as the top marksman with the show would not hold water. At various times there were phenomenal trigger-experts in the arena. One was his first partner, Dr. W. F. Carver, who was a dentist and a champion crack shot. Carver could never understand why Cody received all the plaudits, while he, Carver, who could outshoot the colorful scout in target contests, was virtually ignored. Their partnership ended, and Carver became one of Cody's most bitter critics.

There were other gun experts with the show at times, including the famous Annie Oakley, who was one of the premier attractions. Some of them had known days when their targets were shooting back at them in their real-life careers on the frontier, either as lawmen or the opposite. Annie, of course, was not in that category.

One eyewitness, who was on the Plains and can be taken as an expert in matters of gunmanship, is Luther North, brother of

Frank North, organizer of the famous company of Pawnee scouts that were so valuable to the Army during the war against the Cheyennes and Sioux.

Luther North, who was a captain in one of the Pawnee units, rode with Cody many times. Luther was proud of his own skill as a marksman, and mentioned several moments when he had outshot Custer during hunting trips, to the general's chagrin. He also said he could outshoot Cody in target matches. It was a different matter when mounted and hunting game. He relates in his book about his career that he personally saw Cody kill sixteen buffalo with sixteen shots while riding at full gallop on a horse not accustomed to such antics. Luther added that Cody was the best shot from a running horse he had ever seen.

The publicity Cody gained from the Summit Springs matter paled into insignificance in contrast to that he received from the Yellow Hand "duel." Disputes over that one still seethe in a cauldron of ink about as fiercely as the storms over Custer's doings. But, before that came up, many things happened to Buffalo Bill. To mention one item, he became at one point in his career, heaven forbid, an actor. On one occasion he was to return to the Plains from the footlights as dramatically as in any of the lurid stage roles he attempted to portray.

Ned Buntline was the person who influenced the scout into attempting an acting role. This ultimately led Cody to become head of a circus. Buntline, whose name is more famous to this day for the "Buntline Special" Colt than for his dime novels, dangled attractive bait before Cody in winning his assent. The bait, of course, was money. Cody could always use money. And spend it with equal facility. He was usually in need of funds.

The Buntline Special was a six-shooter with a barrel twelve inches long that its originator had made especially as gifts for famous western persons such as Wyatt Earp, Bat Masterson, and other peace officers around Dodge City. Plastic imitations have been sold by the thousands in modern times on toy counters.

Several recipients of the genuine Special had the barrels sawed to standard size, but Earp is said to have carried the complete model, finding the muzzle length effective in "buffaloing" obstreperous persons.

Buntline was a pen name, his real name being Judson. In addition to being a producer of dime novels and a promoter, he was a very hard case in his own right, having used a six-shooter a time or two to settle disputes in his favor.

Cody apparently became acquainted with Buntline while acting as an Army scout. From then on, his career became an intermingling of fact and fiction. In winters, he was an actor, taking applause—and sometimes the howls of derision—of ticket buyers in the eastern cities, as well as frightful roastings at the hands of newspaper critics. In summer, he was often on the Plains, scouting for the Army, or acting as a hunting guide, usually with celebrities such as the Grand Duke of Russia.

The Grand Duke was only nineteen when he visited the Plains, along with a retinue of companions. The ostensible object was to hunt wild game, principally buffalo, the real purpose was to make merry.

Cody was introduced to high life on the royal hunt, such as champagne before breakfast. He was young and always in festive spirit, too. So was Custer, who was among those present. They viewed the world through rose-colored wineglasses. They all wore fancy, fringed buckskins, even the Duke. It made quite a flutter. It was certainly quite a party. The pens of correspondents must have smoked as they described the pomp and glitter of it as the dashing, romantic Duke, the golden-haired Custer, and the equally ebullient Cody galloped off, side by side, to hunt down the buffalo in his native lair—well protected, of course, by the 7th Cavalry, and attended, hand and foot, by servants.

Many a buffalo was slain, many a feminine heart at Fort Hays and Fort Harker trembled at the thought of being rescued from distress by any one of this trio. Many a bottle was left empty and deserted, with gaping mouths, on the prairie.

Some of the hunters, including Cody, are said to have been packed home across a mule after a day of shooting and champagne. Cody was not used to bubbling wine served in beer mugs. Spotted Tail and his Sioux gave a war dance for the entertainment of the visitors. Sheridan, Custer, and Cody watched with some apprehension, and Custer had his cavalrymen braced for trouble. They knew Old Spot very well and were set on a hair trigger in case he decided to try for a royal scalp. But the chief and his warriors merely danced.

It was soon after this that Cody began his stage career. Buntline induced him to appear in a melodrama titled *The Scout of the Plains.* Wild Bill Hickok and Texas Jack Omohundro were lured into joining the cast. Omohundro was a former scout, and had been a trooper under Jeb Stuart in the Confederate cavalry.

Cody and Omohundro were instant hams. Hickok, always intractable, was never in his element, and was finally let out of his contract by Cody. Hickok, for one thing, persisted in firing blank cartridges close to the legs of Indians who were part of the company. The unscheduled dancing that resulted on the stage was often a feature of the performance.

At the end of the first season Cody went back to the Plains, then returned to the footlights in eastern cities with Omohundro, spending the winter treading the boards, deaf to the hoots of onlookers and the barbs of critics.

He continued to follow this bizarre way of life. Then came the year of 1876. A fateful year in the lives of many men, as Buntline might have written it. Custer went under at the Little Bighorn, along with Tom Custer, the famous scout Charley Reynolds, and many other men of the 7th who had been Cody's friends. In the spring of that same year, Kit Carson Cody, aged six, passed away. Wild Bill Hickok was murdered.

His son's death was the first real shadow on Cody's life, which, from then on, was to become a succession of bright heights and somber depths. He was at the bedside when the lad, to whom he was deeply attached, died at the Cody eastern residence at Rochester, New York.

He returned to the stage to complete the season's engagement when a second interruption came. A message arrived notifying him that his old friend, General Carr, of the 5th Cavalry, wanted him to rejoin the outfit as a scout. The 5th was at Fort Laramie, preparing to take the field against the Sioux, who were at the zenith of their fierce war on the whites.

Cody could not refrain from seizing the chance to dash upon the stage at a dramatic moment, read the message, then charge off into the wings as though about to mount his horse and ride all the way to the buffalo country to the rescue of the cavalry, although his location at that moment was Philadelphia.

As a matter of fact, although he did not know it, of course, he was on his way to the Yellow Hand affair, which has aroused the warmest disputes concerning his career.

Adhering to his love of the dramatic, Cody reported to Carr at

Cheyenne clad in gaudy Mexican-style breeches and sash, bolero jacket, and picturesque *vaquero* hat. It was the costume he had been wearing the night the message had reached him as he was about to enact his role in a lurid Plains melodrama. History does not record whether he wore the costume all the way from Philadelphia to Cheyenne, nor have Carr's comments upon viewing this spectacle been handed down to posterity. Being acquainted with Cody's love of the spectacular, and being also his good friend, it is likely Carr only chuckled. He needed Cody, no matter how bizarre his apparel.

Cody's arrival is said to have lifted the spirits of the men in the ranks. The fortunes of the Army in its attempt to subdue the Indians had not flourished, to say the least. There had been too many ambushes and tragedies such as the Fetterman massacre, the costly Beecher Island fight, the disaster at the Platte River Bridge. There had been too many forced, hard marches under inefficient leaders, too many stragglers picked off and tortured by hostiles. Morale was low.

At this time, Custer was marching from Fort Lincoln with six hundred men of the 7th, which raged with its internal jealousies and distrust of its officers. General George Crook was moving north from the Platte with a thousand men. General John Gibbon was pushing south from the Yellowstone with an equally strong command. It was a pincer move, aimed at crushing Crazy Horse and all of the rebellious tribes.

Everything went wrong. Crazy Horse hit Crook with a thousand warriors on June 17, 1876, and Crook's men narrowly escaped the disaster that soon befell Custer. Crook fell back—and waited. Custer divided his command into three units—a fatal error. Gibbon was late reaching the agreed rendezvous. Crook preferred charges of incompetency against his subordinate, General J. J. Reynolds and two lesser officers. The trap that had been planned for the Sioux had turned into a shocking reversal for the Army.

The news came to the 5th Cavalry on July 5 that Custer had been annihilated by the same Indian strategists the 5th was expected to face. Therefore the 5th was in a very dubious mood when it moved out of Fort Laramie. Its mission was to prevent Red Cloud's reservation Sioux from joining Crazy Horse. Carr was replaced by General Wesley Merritt, who had been consid-

ered a top cavalry officer in the Union Army. He was a witness to
the "Yellow Hand" affair.

This event has been the most severely debated of any of Cody's
activities. In this one, a minor chief named Yellow Hand, or Yellow Hair, was killed. It is often referred to as the Cody-Yellow
Hand Duel. There was no duel as such things are pictured in the
public's mind. However, it seems to have been one of those rare
items—a shoot-out between two men.

As pictured in the dime novels, battle-hardened files of cavalry
and a great party of Cheyenne warriors are drawn up, face-to-
face. The fierce chief, Yellow Hand, is represented as riding between the opposing lines, brandishing his scalping knife, and point-
ing out Cody. "I know you, Pa-has-ka," he shouts. "I will fight
you, and one of us will die. No other will die. We will settle this
between us."

And, of course, Cody, the knight in buckskin, fights the duel
and emerges victorious. He scalps his foe, brandishes the trophy,
and shouts, "First scalp for Custer!"

It didn't happen that way. The encounter took place on July 17,
1876, on Warbonnet or Hat Creek, in northwestern Nebraska.
Cody and Merritt, leading the main body of cavalrymen, were on
high ground. The regiment's supply train was approaching, following a draw below, when several warriors were spotted splitting
from the main body of Indians in the distance, with the intention
of cutting off two troopers who were riding in advance of the
train.

Cody, seeing a chance to trap those Indians, was given permission by Merritt to lead half a dozen troopers and two scouts
into the draw below. As usual, from then on, the accounts vary.
Again we must relate it from the majority view. Cody was seen to
ride ahead of his group, not knowing a lone Sioux was approaching around a bend in the draw. On the bluff, a trooper named
Wilkinson asked permission to shoot at the Indian. Wilkinson fired,
the Indian ducked back of the neck of his pony and sent a return
bullet which almost bagged Merritt.

A Signal Corps man claims to be the only one who saw the
finish of the fight. He is quoted as saying that Cody and the Sioux
met unexpectedly, that Cody fired and wounded his foe, the same
bullet downing the Indian pony. Cody's horse stumbled, the scout

jumped clear, knelt and killed the wounded Indian with a second shot. Then Cody took the scalp.

The slain warrior proved to be a minor chief, Yellow Hand, or Yellow Hair, depending on tribal interpretation of his name. The part about waving the scalp and war bonnet and shouting that this was the first scalp for Custer, is controversial. However, it was typical of Cody's love of the spectacular. In addition, Indian sources are said to have confirmed that Yellow Hand was carrying a war bonnet, which he donned, then removed before meeting Cody. Apparently it was still on his pony when he went down. This might give substance to the many lurid paintings of Cody brandishing the scalp and bonnet, with one foot planted on the body of the fallen chief.

Afterward, all manner of dispute arose. Several men claimed to have been shooting at Yellow Hand, and each was sure it had been his bullet that had killed the chief. Some went so far as to declare that Cody was not even present at the time. That seems to discount any version they might have given.

The Red Cloud Indians decided not to test the 5th and returned to the reservation. The 5th replenished supplies and marched up the Bozeman Trail, joining Crook's command. Cody was named chief of scouts in the campaign, which was officially titled the Bighorn-Yellowstone Expedition. He had under him several noted scouts, including Frank Grouard and Baptiste Pourier, better known as Little Bat.

The campaign covered a lot of ground without much result, and Cody finally asked for his discharge. A fight took place later at Slim Buttes, which Cody missed—by design, his critics say, although his career does not indicate that he went out of his way to avoid danger. His friend and shadow, Buffalo Chips White, was killed in the Slim Buttes fight.

With one exception, that ended Cody's connection with the Indian wars, although he was to spend much time and to lose a fortune in investments on the Plains and to die there.

The Summit Springs and Yellow Hand affairs were only the highlights of his career as a scout. He is praised by many in their recollections of frontier events, particularly by Army officers for whom he carried dispatches many times through dangerous Indian country.

But only one career was ending. He was entering a new way of

life that was to be as filled with greater triumphs, greater down-
falls than the one he was leaving.

First came the formation of the wild West show. This was
named the Honorable W. F. Cody and Dr. W. F. Carver Wild
West. It opened at Omaha, May 17, 1883. It met the bad luck in
its first season that seems to follow circuses the world over.
A steamboat carrying the show and its meager equipment sank in
the Mississippi River. What little was saved went to creditors.

However, the show managed to raise enough capital to stagger
along, but it was a hand-to-mouth existence. Then came the turn.
A well-known couple in the circus world, Mr. and Mrs. Frank
Butler, left a rival outfit and joined the Cody show. By this time
Doc Carver had parted company with Cody and the circus.

Frank Butler was a crack shot, but was overshadowed by his
wife in the ring. She was the famous Annie Oakley, better known
as Little Sure Shot, whose feats with pistol and rifle were legendary.
To this day complimentary tickets to entertainment affairs are
often called "Oakleys" after Annie because one of her tricks was
punching holes in playing cards held in her husband's hands. Free
tickets are usually punched when given out.

From then on the show began to make money. Taking a gamble, Cody eventually rented Madison Square Garden in New York
City, an outrageous affront to protocol.

What few attempts had been made in the past to present the
wild West type of entertainment in the sophisticated city had been
met only with boredom. Back in the 1840s P. T. Barnum had put
on some such a show, but it had been staged across the river in the
Jersey mosquito flats. Barnum had made money out of it, but the
profits came mainly from boat fares, Barnum having cannily leased
all the ferryboats for the day. He had come into possession of a
herd of young buffalo that had been brought east by some promoter
who had gone broke, and had staged a buffalo hunt. But all in all,
it was a makeshift affair.

Now, in the face of the scoffers, the real wild West and Buffalo
Bill came to Manhattan. Genuine cowboys, some of whom had
not been exactly model citizens in the past, were with the troupe,
using "stage names" in case a Texas sheriff showed up with a
warrant. But they could ride. And how! And shoot!

There were real Indians. Live Sioux who gazed at patrons with
flat, Stone Age stares, and seemed to be measuring their topknots

for size. And why not? Some *had* taken scalps. Some had fought Custer on the Greasy Grass.

Sitting Bull himself traveled with the Bill show. He was paid fifty dollars a week and was entitled to extras. One of the extras was the right to keep all the revenues from selling his pictures to patrons.

The old Sioux chief is sometimes pictured as a cowardly medicine man who carefully kept himself out of harm's way in the Custer fight and other battles. Gall, the Uncpapa Sioux, was the war chief who led the Custer annihilation. However, Sitting Bull is credited by Flora Warren Seymour in her *The Story of the Red Man* with rallying the more rebellious factions of the Sioux nation and other red people as far east as the Chippewas into joining the war against the Army.

There is some kind of a sermon, no doubt, in the thought of the bronze, square-jawed, squatty chief, he who had smoked the pipe with the likes of Crazy Horse, Dull Knife, and Spotted Tail, raking in small coins from the nervous hands of city slickers and country bumpkins whose only previous encounter of this kind had been with painted effigies of the Bull in shooting galleries or in front of cigar stores.

During the circus's tour in the States the chief met with animosity, for Custer's memory was still vivid in the mind of the public. He was taunted with having fled to Canada ahead of avenging United States troops to save his own scalp. However, when he toured Canada and Europe with the show it was a different story. Sitting Bull was regarded with awe and great respect.

Sitting Bull was not the only famous Indian leader who was unable to resist the lure of circus life. Geronimo, the great Apache chief, took part in a wild West show that was staged in Oklahoma by the Miller Bros. 101 Ranch, which later became a road circus.

Cody's show flamed brightly in the entertainment world, and continued to prosper. It survived the vicissitudes that seem to beset all circuses—train wrecks, fire, wind, mud, rain, great heat. It made money for Cody, who spent it as fast as it poured in.

The show reached greater heights when he shipped it to Europe. And so did he. He learned to handle himself at dinner tables set with linen and crystal. He was entertained by the Prince of Wales, later to take the throne as Edward VII. He met Prime Minister William Gladstone and other high-ranking men in London. Queen

Victoria attended the circus and was so charmed she ordered a command performance at which her guests included many of the crowned heads of Europe.

Four kings rode around the arena as passengers in a genuine Deadwood coach, with Cody handling the six horses in wild, wheel-skidding turns around the track. The Prince of Wales sat at Cody's side on the box, waving his top hat.

The Grand Duke of Russia rode Cody's famous show horse, Charlie, in the chase after buffalo, which was a daily part of the program. The Yellow Hand "duel" was fought over and over, following the Ned Buntline version, to the music of the band. Cody rode through the smoke of blank cartridges to rescue Mrs. Weichel at Summit Springs from the painted Sioux, who were real warriors at fifteen dollars a week.

Rosa Bonheur, famed French painter of horses, did Cody's portrait, complete with steed. Annie Oakley shot a cigarette from the mouth of the German Crown Prince, the future Kaiser who was dethroned in World War I. Royalty developed a very strong flair for ham acting and was ready to try to perform in the circus arena at the nod of a ringmaster's head.

After a long tour the show returned to America. Charlie died during the voyage and was buried with honors at sea. Cody was at the zenith of his fame, and of his financial status. The world was his apple. His champagne bottle, perhaps.

However, business in the States did not prove to be as lush as he had anticipated. The Cody name seemed to have lost some of its magic, perhaps from overexposure. The fact was that the American public was indulging in one of its most outstanding whims. It had accepted its idol without question at first, but now was searching for the flaws with which to destroy that same image. Debunking was becoming the order of the day, particularly among writers in need of fresh approaches to sell their wares.

One of Cody's two daughters passed away. The dark clouds were gathering. He took the show back to Europe for a long tour, and the skies seemed to lighten.

He had bought a ranch near North Platte, Nebraska, in partnership with Frank North, but had not really been a part of the Plains since 1876. However, while he was in Europe, the false wind sprang up that fanned the deadened spirit of the Indian nations into new life—the Messiah craze.

Cody had left the show temporarily to return to Washington with some of his Indian supers to refute charges the red men were being mistreated by the circus in Europe. General Nelson A. Miles, in command of the Department of the Platte, knowing the Indians held Cody in great respect, and that he was trusted by Sitting Bull, believed the former chief of scouts might calm the rising tide of superstition that was growing with the ghost dancing.

The Indians seemed to be rallying around Sitting Bull, who had long since left the circus and had returned to the Plains. A request was sent to Cody asking him to see the chief and talk him into agreeing to be taken into custody.

This, of course, was meat and drink to showman Cody, very good medicine for the ego of a man who was seeing the tarnish of time setting in on his glories.

He traveled by train to Bismarck, North Dakota, then by wagon to Fort Yates. Wrapped in a borrowed overcoat and robes of buffalo fur he set out alone in a wagon on a bitterly cold day in December 1890, to find Sitting Bull's village. However, James McLaughlin, the Indian agent, interfered and had Cody intercepted, placed under guard, and sent back to Fort Yates.

Cody's defenders say the act was prompted by jealousy on the part of Indian Department officials. His detractors say the affair was none of Cody's business and he was there only for publicity purposes.

But, whatever the human motives, there is no doubt it figured in sealing the doom of Sitting Bull. Indian police were sent out to accomplish what Cody might have achieved without bloodshed. A parley was held at which it became evident Sitting Bull was ready to submit to custody. He was old and had seen so many of his people die at the hands of the white men. He had traveled with the whites, knew their numbers, their strength.

He was taunted as a coward by his firebrand son. Intertribal feuds erupted. Shooting started. Sitting Bull was killed. That ended the ghost dancing. Sitting Bull, *Tantaka Inyotake,* was no more. All that remained of the Indian wars was the slaughter at Wounded Knee two weeks later.

That was Cody's last joust with danger, glamor, fame, self-glorification—whichever term researchers into his life choose to use. He knew when he returned to the show that the old life on the Plains was a thing of the past. It was ended there, and it was ended for himself.

Hard times set in for the circus. His investments, such as his ranch in Nebraska, which he had named Scout's Rest, his pioneering projects in Wyoming, especially his promotions at Cody, Wyoming, plunged him deep into debt. The last performance of his wild West show under canvas was staged—where, but Julesburg, the place from which he had started up the trail to fame as a boy rider for the Pony Express. The show was attached for debt a few days later in Denver.

He traveled for a few seasons in the decline of his years with circuses that used his name. Sells-Floto & Buffalo Bill Wild West, Pawnee Bill & Buffalo Bill Wild West. But as an employee.

His last public appearance was in 1913. He came to such a financial state he wrote a letter to the government, inquiring about the ten-dollar monthly pension that went with the Medal of Honor that had been awarded him years before. His letter said the money would be a godsend. His request was denied, because he had been a civilian scout and the money and medal only went to enlisted men and commissioned officers. In his heyday, he had been paid 150 dollars a month, along with remounts, food, ammunition, and the companionship of high officers when he had scouted for the Army.

Some residents of the Plains, who remember him from those sad days, refer to him scathingly as "that drunk." There are few or none alive who knew him when he rode with such as Custer and Crook and with Hickok.

He died January 10, 1917. His tomb is on Lookout Mountain in Colorado, which commands a mighty sweep of the Plains where he rode in the great days. Visitors come by the thousands each year to gaze at the vista and marvel at the career of the man.

One writer of the West brushes off William Frederick Cody as just another Indian scout, who "never shed much human blood in anger in his life."

Let that be his epitaph.

The same cannot be the epitaph of his friend, James Butler Hickok, the gunman.

CHAPTER 7

## PISTOL POPPERS

The American public, which fondly rates itself as very hard-nosed and objective, on the contrary is a sucker for press agentry, ballyhoo, and balderdash. It is driven in mass formation in this direction or that by publicity experts who are fully aware of the sheeplike instinct of humans to ride with the majority in fear of being the only ones who are wrong.

The public often picks its idols or its villains on sudden, lightning-flash whimseys that have little to do with fact or sound judgment. The herd instinct of avoiding independent thinking is not confined to the general public. It is very much present among the so-called experts who attempt to predict or evaluate events of interest.

Historians and researchers are no more immune to this mass huddling than other stratas of so-called experts. They shrink from swimming against the tide. Many of them have another common trait. Once an idol is built high in the public's mind, often by their own writings, it becomes fashionable to dig for clay feet in order to tear down what they had created. Debunking is the word for it. Once one of them sights the quarry, the hue and cry arise and the chase begins. Powerful personalities whose ways of life do not agree with the critic's ideas are singled out to be dissected and exposed as frauds. To be flamboyant and colorful, as were men like Frémont, Custer, Cody, and Wild Bill Hickok, has made them particular objects of the chase.

On the other hand, criminals like Jesse James, who was bold only when he had a gun in his hand and was dealing with peaceful, unarmed citizens, and the psychopathic killer Billy the Kid, as well as other murderous brutes, are too often glorified and treated with tender consideration.

Jesse James is represented many times as a sort of Robin Hood who was persecuted by the mean, old Pinkertons. In reality, of course, he was a thug who learned the art of murder as a youth, preferred crime to earning an honest living, and preyed on society all his life.

In the same category were outlaws like Sam Bass. Folk songs have been written about this one. Sam Bass was such a kind and loving person that whole communities in Texas tolerated and protected him and his gang of cutthroats, not out of admiration, but because of fear of terrible reprisal if they sought help from the law.

Billy the Kid is said to have slain twenty-one persons, one for each year of his life, until he was exterminated by Sheriff Pat Garrett in New Mexico. His principal feat was to shoot down two deputies in cold blood after he had got his hands on a gun while a prisoner in the Lincoln jail.

This unlovely person has been glamorized in writings and drama, until he is now seen in the mind of the public as a sort of good-humored cowboy who just got into shooting scrapes by accident with tough hombres who deserved being killed anyway. It became necessary to place a strong fence around his grave at Fort Sumner, New Mexico, because souvenir hunters were chipping away the tombstone. So vandals backed up a derrick on a truck and made away with the entire stone.

Another strong conviction that seems to have been planted in the public's mind by dramatists and fiction writers is that almost everyone in the West who walked on two laigs had to depend on the speed (blinding) with which he could whip out a weapon (six-gun, hawg-laig, old cedar, lead-squirter, etc.) and the accuracy (awesome) with which he could (1) shoot a pistol out of his opponent's hand without damaging said opponent's fingers; (2) shoot (drill) his foe through the shoulder in case that individual's presence was needed farther along in the plot; (3) kill (rub out) any number, from two to five in as many shots without being scratched himself by the hail of return fire.

Along with the fastest-gun-in-the-West belief that has been built up there is its companion legend, the gun-for-hire thing. One would be led to assume that the livelihood of the major part of the male population of frontier towns was gained from being paid to kill someone. If these sources are to be believed, the only effort one had to put out to find a gunman was to walk out of a saloon and beckon to the first male in sight, who would come running, his pistol loaded and ready.

Of course, no other situation in fiction, stagecraft, or real life grips the imagination as does the man-to-man "shoot-out." Hand in hand with this is the legendary image of the professional bounty hunter and killer that has been built up beyond all bounds of truth.

Zane Grey is given credit for starting it with his Lassiter character in *Riders of the Purple Sage*. But Grey's Lassiter is worlds apart from glorifying the brutes of the frontier.

Also carried to incredible extremes in the name of entertainment are those long-drawn fist fights in which men knock each other all over the barroom floors for minutes, using fists, chairs, clubs, or whatever is handy, then dust themselves off and go on their way, carrying neither bruise nor contusion. This is a long way from reality, of course.

That is not to say there were no such things as violence or gunmen in the old West. There was and there were. Plenty of violence, and quite a few individuals who qualified as genuine gunmen. The latter killed many people, particularly each other, which was a point in their favor. A lot of law-abiding citizens killed some of them, helping rid the West of one of the flaws in its make-up.

Some of the gunmen were even fast on the draw, but it was mostly a stunt for exhibition purposes. The sad fact is that practically all of our frontier badmen, gunmen, gunnies, trigger-sharps, or by whatever brand they might be called, did not depend on how rapidly they could yank a six-shooter, hawg-laig, old cedar, etc., from its holster, leather, tie-down, etc., when they were out to perforate, salivate, puncture, or plug an opponent.

Nor did they wait for the other man to reach, grab, snatch, or draw first. The truth was that when men were out to shoot to kill they sought each other, pistols already in hand and cocked. They did not usually advance openly down the middle of a dusty street with nothing but thin air at their backs. It might not have been the gallant way, but they generally crept between buildings, preferring to catch their quarry with back turned, playing cards, drinking beer at a bar, shoeing a horse, or even sleeping, so that they could draw a bead undisturbed by any opposition from their prey.

Of course there have been meetings, face-to-face, in which opponents actually blazed it out. This usually proved fatal to both sides. Therefore, it was not a very popular method of settling accounts.

The most famous of these encounters, naturally, is the Earp-Clanton battle in the O K Corral at Tombstone, Arizona, on Oct. 26, 1881. In that case, three of the Earps and Doc Holliday marched side by side down the street in Tombstone, guns in their hands, wheeled and strode into the corral where five of the Clanton gang waited, also armed and ready.

The shooting lasted about thirty seconds. It was not a quick-draw affair. Everybody was set and ready beforehand. Three of the Clanton group were killed. At least three of the Earp contingent suffered wounds, two of them slight, a remarkably light toll in a gunfight at such close quarters.

It is notable that after the echoes died the Clantons had seventeen empty shells in their pistols, but only three bullets had wounded their opponents. The Earps are said to have emptied an equal number of cartridges and scored eleven hits, six of which tore into young Billy Clanton after he was down and dying. So much for accuracy at close range when the other fellow is also shooting. Nearly all of the men involved came about as close to fitting the description "cold-nerved gunmen" as you'll ever come across in western lore, fact, or fiction.

Whether the bad guys or the good guys won this fight is still hotly disputed in Tombstone. But, sorry to say, it has been remarked that the good guys generally finish last. In fiction and on the screen, the hero usually wins. Not so in real life.

Dueling, in which the antagonists paced it off and fired, was commonplace until public opinion had this practice stopped. The rakehells and firebrands of the days before the Civil War were always popping at each other over matters of cards, wenches, and such. One of the old-time favorite dueling grounds is still a tourist attraction on the outskirts of New Orleans. Some of the duelists, especially from the gambling fraternity, were regular visitors on this field and usually left under their own power. Aware the likelihood of being called out was a hazard of their occupation, they were well skilled in perforating their opponents by dint of much practice with dueling pistols, which are awkwardly balanced weapons. A bullet in the belly usually puts an opponent out of business quickly and generally permanently.

Two of the most famous duels in America saw the bad guys walk away unscathed while the nation lost talented men. Aaron Burr killed Alexander Hamilton. In California an opportunist politician, David S. Terry, slew famed California senator David Broderick in 1859.

Cody's "duel" with Yellow Hand has already been detailed. Then there was Kit Carson's meeting with a huge French-Canadian in a trappers' rendezvous back in the beaver days. Like the majority of such events, accounts vary. It seems evident that each man had friends and foes who saw the affair from biased viewpoints. Many of these stories apparently have been colored by researchers who became equally biased. Carson, who was the most noted mountain man of them all, and who has escaped the debunking process, at least thus far, no doubt had his critics and deprecators in his own time. Such is human nature. Carson was also human.

According to Stanley Vestal's biography of the man, the duel was over a pretty Arapahoe girl who favored Kit, and whom his rival had tried to violate in spite of her chastity belt. Other researchers indicate it might have been just friction between men of opposite temperaments. The French-Canadian's name is variously given as Shinan, Shunan, and Shunar. His differences with Carson came to such a pass one day that the mountain man ran to his tent to get his rifle. One historian remarks that any sane man who knew Kit would have got the blazes out of there, for when Mr. Carson seized up a weapon in anger someone usually got ventilated. In this case it was Shunar.

Carson's first bullet tore into Shunar's arm. All accounts seem to agree on this. Vestal indicates that Carson must have found a second weapon with which he slew his quarry, then scalped him. Does all this sound something like Cody's "duel" with Yellow Hand?

As far back as researchers delve, there were duels and killings by whatever weapons were at hand. The invention of gunpowder permitted smaller men to meet brawny opponents on equal terms.

A peasant with a blunderbuss was a better man than a plumed knight with only a sword.

In the old West, Mr. Colt was the great equalizer. One of Mr. Colt's most noted disciples was James Butler Hickok, better known to posterity as Wild Bill Hickok.

Hickok, probably more than any other man who ever lived on the frontier, qualified for the title gunman. He figured in many sanguinary events where gunsmoke so obscured the truth that various versions of all those affairs have been handed down. Like his contemporaries, Cody and Custer, many researchers refer to him with acid-tipped pens. They dismiss him as a vicious killer, and those who attempt to sort out the facts of his career are sometimes denounced as "apologists."

There is no doubt that he killed many men. His first role as an aide to the Grim Reaper came at an early age while he was employed at a stagecoach station at Rock Creek, Kansas. He had been assigned to that post by the stage company while he was recovering from injuries sustained in an encounter with a bear in Raton Pass while working as a freighter.

Bad blood between Hickok and David McCanles, the proprietor, resulted in a grim fray in which McCanles and two of his friends were killed. Some accounts say a woman finished off one of these with a hoe as he lay wounded, and that a stage driver did the same for a third victim who had crawled into the brush. The fight was said to have been over the favors of a woman—an item that was to bring Hickok's guns into play more than once later on. The law made little effort to detain him.

That was the first of many Hickok six-shooter episodes. He became a buffalo hunter and Army scout, then was made sheriff of Ellis County, Kansas, in 1869. Hays City and Fort Hays were within his jurisdiction, and that was a job tough enough for any man—even Hickok.

The buffalo hunters were there. And the soldiers. And the Kansas Pacific construction crews. Not to mention the Texas trail drivers who declared a blood feud against the gun sheriff. Gunmen such as John Wesley Hardin and Ben Thompson, almost as famous as Hickok, were there, jealous of their reputations.

However, there was a difference between Hickok and men like Hardin and Thompson. Hickok often carried his gun as a law officer, and many of his powder-smoke episodes were related to that task, coming either while he was wearing the badge or resulting from grudges that carried over after his tenure was finished. Men of the Hardin, Thompson stripe were gamblers who cold-bloodedly preyed on weaker men.

Many attempts were made on Hickok's life at Hays, and he killed at least two men there. Some of these affairs had their roots in an earlier short career when he brought law and order to Fort Riley, wearing the badge of a deputy U.S. marshal. It was at Riley that he met Custer.

Also, previous to his service at Hays, he had figured in a killing at Springfield, Missouri, on July 21, 1865, when a man named Dave Tutt went to Boot Hill.

Hickok's tenure as sheriff ended at Hays, and he returned briefly to hunting and scouting. He made the mistake of going back to Hays to visit old friends. Or perhaps to revive old feuds. And one that had smoldered flamed into violent life. He had handled some of Custer's 7th cavalry roughly during his term as an officer and they remembered.

What was probably Hickok's most dramatic gunfight erupted in a Hays barroom. When the gunsmoke cleared two troopers lay dead and another seriously wounded. Few of Hickok's slugs had missed. The soldiers had scored no hits. Hickok left Hays for the last time. One researcher says the brush was beaten for days by troopers who meant to shoot on sight. They did not come upon their quarry, perhaps luckily for them, if they did conduct such a hunt. It is possible they were careful to look only in the wrong places.

Hickok was appointed marshal of Abilene, Kansas, on April 15, 1871, a task that made the Hays job seem like child's play. There have been many other rough, tough towns in the history of the frontier. Cheyenne had buried "its man for breakfast" during the U.P. boom. Ogallala was uncurried and wild during the trail days. Dodge City, after the Santa Fe terriers arrived in force, was no model of deportment. But Abilene, when Wild Bill became marshal, probably had more fur on it than the others.

Ben Thompson ran a saloon there, dealt crooked cards, and killed victims who objected. Hardin was present also, along with a swarm of lesser lights in the gun world. The buffalo hunters were still around. Above all, there were the Texans. The cattle drives were coming in big.

There is a story that Ben Thompson made Hickok eat crow one day in the Bullhead saloon at Abilene, the marshal refusing an invitation to go for his gun. That might be true. Wyatt Earp is also said to have "gone up a tree" in Dodge when Clay Allison, the curly wolf of the Washita, came to town to die or win fame by killing the famed peace officer. That might be true also.

Both Hickok and Earp lived to fight another day, and fight they did. There is no question but what they played the odds, tried to make sure the situation was in their favor before wading in. They liked to have a solid wall at their backs, a pistol in their hands, facing their opponent. But to indicate that either man was yellow is amusing.

In fact, Hickok had already chastened Thompson by forcing him to tone down a coarse painting that appeared over the door of his Bullhead saloon. He added to his edge over Thompson by killing Thompson's partner, Phil Coe, before the summer was over, without retaliation by Thompson.

The killing of Coe took place October 5, 1871. It was the climax of the smoldering feud with Thompson, and there seems little doubt the basic cause was a dispute over brothel and saloon graft.

Hickok is charged by his critics with shooting Coe from a sneak. On the contrary, it would appear that the marshal expected to face odds, for he had warned Mike Williams, who was a special policeman and Hickok's friend, to stay back of him. Williams, when the guns began roaring, rushed into the scene from another direction, and Hickok's bullets struck him down like a lightning bolt, the marshal believing he was another enemy.

The accidental killing of Williams evidently shook Hickok. Joseph G. Rosa, in his biography of the gunman, says he ran wild that night, cleaning out dives and brothels in a rampage of fury.

But that seems to be the end of his career as a gunman. He was let go as Abilene marshal a short time later. The city council evidently had enough, not only of Hickok and all gunmen but even of that source of revenue, the Texas trail driver. The Farmers Protective Association sent a formal request to the cattlemen of Texas stating that their "evil" trade was no longer wanted. After that the cowboys decided to roll their spurs in other towns.

Many things have been said about Hickok by researchers, little of it flattering. The killing of Dave Tutt at Springfield was one of the many cases where he is accused of murder. However, this seems to have been one of those rare events when two men hunted each other in the streets of the town with guns in their hands. The guns roared in Springfield's public square and Tutt lay dead on the sidewalk.

The charges flew that Hickok had fired from a window or a doorway before Tutt was aware of his presence. This is similar to some accounts of the McCanles affair earlier which assert that Hickok shot down at least two men, without warning, from the cover of the stage station.

Mari Sandoz, in her history of buffalo hunting, says flatly that Hickok helped murder the Indian chief Whistler, who a few years earlier had saved Hickok's life in an Indian ambush. Rosa's account of Hickok's life says that a mix-up in names might have occurred, and that a buffalo hunter named Wild Bill Kress probably was the guilty man.

In the spring of 1876—again that fateful year—Hickok married a dashing circus woman named Agnes Lake, a tightrope walker and bareback rider whom he had met five years earlier. There are stories that he later married Calamity Jane at Deadwood, but these are pure hokum.

He was murdered at Deadwood in the Dakota Black Hills on August 2, 1876, while playing poker. A drunken man thereby wrote his name in the annals of the West. The name was Jack McCall. Killing Hickok was his only way of attracting attention to a worthless life.

A Deadwood jury that consisted of characters similar to McCall freed the man on the grounds of self-defense. Even Hickok's most caustic critics have gagged on that one. Hickok's friends saw to it, however, that McCall was brought before a neutral jury later on. The man was convicted of murder and hung at Yankton, South Dakota, March 1, 1877.

Since then the disputes continue about events in Hickok's life. Hickok was a cold-blooded murderer. Hickok was a brave lawman. Hickok was a coward. Hickok was a man of steel. Hickok was effeminate.

That last one is really far out, for those same persons go on to show that some of his gun troubles were over women. One reason Bill Cody let Hickok out of his contract as a ham actor was Hickok's habit of becoming too realistic in romantic scenes with female members of the cast on the stage. Hickok was usually in his cups during his stage career. When it came to being an actor, the charge of lack of courage held true against him. He could only force himself to face an audience by recourse to brave-making stimulants.

There are many accounts of his skill as a marksman, some in the realm of fantasy. Stuart Lake's story of Wyatt Earp's career quotes Earp as saying he witnessed some amazing feats of marksmanship by Hickok, who was a close friend. These stunts are said to have included such things as splitting a bullet on a dime, and driving a cork into a bottle at twenty paces. It is the consensus that Earp must have been telling it tall and scary when he related such things to Mr. Lake.

However, there is little question as to Hickok's actual skill with a pistol. For instance, Custer, who prided himself on his marksmanship, told of seeing Hickok put half a dozen bullets into a knot on a tree past which they were riding at a gallop.

There is no record that Hickok was the "fastest gun in the West." Apparently, when the occasion demanded, he drew his weapons, fired, and that was it. Other men have taken far more lives than Wild Bill. Ben Thompson, John Wesley Hardin, Billy the Kid, to name some. These gunmen never wore a law badge and were therefore never exposed to the same pressures and grudges that such jobs entailed.

Such men actually deserved the brand of killer, for they seemed to relish the taking of human life. Billy the Kid boasted that he had not counted Mexicans in listing his murders. Victims of the Thompson, Hardin variety of killers were often men befuddled by drink who objected to being fleeced at gambling tables, or were half-baked young hoodlums trying to make a name for themselves by facing up to a noted gunman. They had little chance against their opponents.

Probably no other man of his era had a target on his back, as the saying went, as did Hickok. There are stories that owners of Texas herds posted important money for any of their cowboys who "got" the two-gun marshal. After Hickok had worn the badge in a frontier town that place was no longer rated as really tough. He was a town-tamer. He walked the "line" each night, nattily dressed, sometimes in evening clothes complete with top hat and cape lined with scarlet silk.

But, beneath the coat the two .44s were always strapped. He walked arrogant and scornful among the Texans and cavalrymen whom he hazed and buffaloed with the barrels of his guns when they got out of line. For the uninitiated, "buffaloed" means bringing the barrel of a Colt six-shooter very forcefully down upon the skull. The feud between Hickok and the trail men had its roots in the Civil War. It was nourished by Hickok. It carried over to other trail towns and other marshals. It was especially to plague Wyatt Earp at Dodge later on.

Hickok never hesitated to shoot to kill and there was no doubt that he had the advantage the majority of the times. But often his opponents were out to kill him. He consorted with the roughest elements, prostitutes and gamblers. No doubt, as marshal, he received pay-offs from these sources. He liked to gamble, but was an easy mark for men with sharper card savvy. He drank, and sometimes went on rampages, leaning on the fear that men had for him and his reputation.

From the time as a young man when he was frightfully mauled by a bear, he seemed to have walked with Death only a stride back of him, and to have had to walk ever faster to stay ahead. Only a man accustomed to the Presence would have pinned on the badge at Abilene after having emerged alive from the cauldron at Hays City.

After Hays City and Abilene he would never sit with his back to a window or door. With one exception. That exception was the warm, quiet afternoon at Deadwood when he waived the rule and took a vacant chair with his back to a door, rather than trouble a friend to change places. Then the Presence overtook him.

Wyatt Earp is the other most-famed gun marshal of frontier towns. Stuart Lake rated Earp above Hickok in both cold nerve and gun speed, in fact rated him as the greatest peace officer in the history of the West.

Earp, like nearly all whose names arose above the others, either through publicity or ability, has his debunkers. Lake, in his biography, painted Earp in too-shining armor, but there can be no question that his subject rated eye to eye with Hickok as a town-tamer. It is charged by some to this day that the Earp-Clanton shoot-out in Tombstone was murder on the part of the Earps and Doc Holliday, and that the Clantons were misunderstood cowboys. Some contend the Clantons were not even armed.

The debate as to who was the fastest gunman on the draw continues to this day. It is mainly mere rhetoric to pad out lines in the book or article. There are modern claimants. Contests are held. Occasionally, aspirants shoot themselves in the legs while practicing. Small boys are given plastic pistols and holsters as Christmas presents with which to practice the quick draw and imagine themselves blasting down opponents.

Tom Rynning, who was captain of Arizona Rangers, says one of his men, Jeff Kidder, was the fastest he had ever seen. Rynning, you can believe, was an expert in such matters.

In Rynning's life story, written by Al Cohn and Joe Chisholm, the Ranger leader tells how Kidder handled himself in a gunfight in a Naco cantina. He had been trapped there by rurales with whom a feud had erupted because of the wounding of one of the rurales' *comaradas* a time earlier. Kidder, caught between four opponents entering from front and rear, shooting as they came in, drew and opened up. Three rurales fell dead. Kidder, two live shells in his gun, wounded another, then missed with his last shot and was slain before he could crawl across the U.S. boundary a few blocks away. This sounds something like Hickok's fight with soldiers at Fort Hays almost half a century earlier.

There were many other law officers who knew very well which end of a Colt the bullets came from, such as Pat Garrett; Billy Tilghman, one of the most respected of the frontier lawmen; Bat Masterson of Dodge City renown; Charlie Siringo, the nemesis of cattle rustlers. Then there were the members of the non-badge set who merely toted guns—and used them, such as the Thompsons, Hardins, etc. The majority of them left little impression in the annals of the communities they infested.

However, there was one part-time gentleman, part-time rascal, part-time gentle husband, and part-time ruffian, who did cut a considerable furrow across the face of The Mighty Land. His name was Joseph Slade.

CHAPTER 8

# HUMAN EARS FOR WATCH FOBS
# AND OTHER DROLL STORIES

Joseph Slade, who was stage station boss at Julesburg
when the Sioux and the Cheyennes—and the road agents—were
riding, is ranked as one of the roughest, toughest characters to in-
fest the frontier. He was generally known as Jack Slade.

His reputation as a bad man spread so far he was almost as
much a landmark on the Overland Trail as such places as Independence Rock and South Pass. No trip by ox wagon, saddleback, or stagecoach was considered complete unless the traveler
bellied up to a bar in Julesburg and asked—in a back-of-the-hand
whisper, of course—that the notorious killer Slade be pointed out
to him.

The tourist might discover, to his horror, that the gentlemanly,
quiet-spoken person to whom the question was addressed was
none other than Mr. Slade himself. When sober, Slade was said to
be as well mannered and likable as the next man. When traveling
with John Barleycorn, it was a different story. A Jekyll and Hyde
affair.

Captain Slade. That was the way he wanted to be addressed.
Other handles have been given him. Apparently Mr. Slade was
known as Jack, Alf, William, and Joseph. In addition, such labels
as the Terror of the Plains and the Bad Man from Bitter Creek
have been attached to his list of brands.

Slade's career is a bar sinister on Julesburg's escutcheon. If
only he had refrained from using the ears of the founder of the
town as a watch fob, much might be forgiven. Such goings on
give a community a dim reputation.

The gentleman who lost his ears was Jules Benti, who had several variations in his surname in the various accounts of his activities, but all agreed that his front handle was Jules. Perhaps, if a vote had been taken at the time of the founding, what citizens there were around might have put thumbs down on naming the place after Jules. He was not the type of person after which up-and-coming communities are usually christened.

Jules founded a ranch and trading store where Lodgepole Creek joins the South Platte, and presided there in some prosperity, if not entirely in peace. He is believed to have been a French-Canadian, a big man, and very tough. He had cut his eyeteeth in the fur business, and was not what could be pointed to as a pillar of rectitude. He is credited with having killed his share of men in eye-gouging, knife-wielding, knee-fighting brawls in trappers' rendezvous and Indian camps. Researchers might disagree about the temperaments of such frontier people as Custer, Cody, and Hickok, but they are unanimous in the opinion that Jules was what is called in the Southwest a *mucho malo hombre*. A very, very bad guy. The toughest in town.

That was until Jack Slade came along and took those laurels from him. Jules, because he was first on the ground, had been appointed stage station master at the upper crossing of the river by the Central Overland, California & Pikes Peak Express, which was the long-handled name for the Overland Mail.

The Julesburg section of the line, officially known as the Fort Kearney-Cheyenne Division, had been plagued by road agents, some of whom garbed themselves as Indians, but who usually did not bother with any disguise. The situation became so troublesome that Jules's primary task was to get rid of the outlaws.

Jules was eminently qualified for the task, but his appointment as agent, no doubt, was made only after a great deal of soul-searching by the front office in Omaha, particularly by Alexander Majors of Russell, Majors & Waddell, overlords of the Overland, who were to be succeeded by Ben Holladay within a year or so. Majors opposed indulgence in stimulants, a practice that was very prevalent in the West. He was against the use of tobacco and profanity. When the Pony Express was formed, all riders were required by Majors to sign a paper promising to abstain from such vices.

These requirements may have been adhered to among the Pony

riders, who were often too young to be admitted to saloons and such, but there is no evidence that Majors' creed attracted a very wide following on the frontier as a whole.

Certainly Jules was not one of these. Some accounts total the number of men he had killed as a baker's dozen, but this seems an exaggeration. Nevertheless, it was not long before the stage company had reason to regret its choice. Jules not only failed to improve conditions on the line but apparently helped in their deterioration. The only item he seemed to have improved was his own prosperity. One method of accomplishing this was to steal company horses and buy them back with company funds. He was also believed to have connived in holdups of the stages he was supposed to protect, having surrounded himself with a number of kindred spirits.

One of Jules's peccadillos was a flair for making "whisky flour" when he was in his cups. He would roll a barrel of flour into the dusty street, dilute it with whisky, and stir the batch with a hoe, evidently enjoying the fumes. Contemporary accounts fail to let us know the aftermath. Whether he baked bread from his batch, or merely passed the dough around in a spirit of conviviality is not clear. Observers unanimously lamented Jules's idiosyncrasy as a waste of good whisky. The waste of flour does not seem to have been equally deplored.

Eventually, Jack Slade arrived on the scene, sent out by the front office to replace Jules and restore order along the stage division. Slade, a native of Illinois, had fought in the war with Mexico and styled himself as Captain Slade, if you please, a title that nobody seems to know was real or assumed. Like several other men who were noted for taking human lives, he was a paradox. Many accounts describe him as courteous and easy to get along with.

Nevertheless, his life could not have been quiet in the past, for he is said to have been carrying in his anatomy several assorted pistol or shotgun slugs. This collection was soon to have additions.

Jules was hurt, of course, when Slade displaced him. Jules hung around the vicinity, pouting, and making it plain that he was not taking his dismissal lying down. It came to a head when Slade seized several horses belonging to the Overland that Jules was using for his personal benefit.

Jules fortified himself with a few slugs of whisky that had escaped being made into bread, lay in ambush, and filled Slade with more lead. In his book *Vigilante Days and Ways* N. P. Langford quotes a supposed eyewitness to this affair who said Jules first emptied a pistol of five shells, then used a shotgun on his quarry. Slade was carried into the stage station with thirteen new items of metal in his frame.

Jules suggested that the easiest way to dispose of Slade, once he had ceased breathing, was to dump his corpse into an empty packing case and bury him. Slade, hearing this, arose from what everyone believed was his deathbed to state, with emphasis no doubt, that he would live to wear Jules's ears as a watch fob.

At about this time, unfortunately for Jules, Ben Ficklin, route superintendent for the Overland, arrived by stage. He was palpably a man of instant decision, for he forthwith had Jules strung up by the neck. This accomplished, Ficklin, who was a busy man, departed on his way, secure in the knowledge that Jules had been adequately punished. However, like Slade, Jules was tough. When cut down he was still alive. He was one of the few who have walked away from their own hanging. He repaired to the mountains with some of his cronies and began a new career of horse-stealing and preying on the stages.

Slade was taken to Chicago for medical attention, and returned to Julesburg, all the punctures in his body vulcanized. He had not forgotten his vow involving Jules's ears. Eventually, some of his men captured Jules and brought him to the station as a prisoner.

Again accounts differ. Langford's source says Slade wounded Jules, then gave Jules a chance to write his will before finishing him off. Other versions have it that Jules was tied to a corral post and used as a target while Slade polished up his marksmanship. This is said to have continued for hours with fingers, etc., being shot off to demonstrate Slade's skill. Finally the finishing shot. And then the ears.

All versions agree that Slade was ten devils riding a cyclone when he was under the influence of John Barleycorn. And most versions agree on the target-shooting method. All agree on the ears.

Slade used the ears as a watch fob, as he had promised. He carried them everywhere he went. Occasionally he had other use for them. Bartenders from Fort Kearney to Cheyenne, from Julesburg to Denver, were shocked by having Jules's ears slapped down on the bar in payment for booze. "Make change for that, my friend!" Slade would bellow.

At any rate, Jules was done in. Slade cleaned up the division. He did it the same way he had taken care of Jules. He hung men without trial, without benefit of doubt. He ran others out of the country so fast and hard they never found their way back.

His notoriety spread. When sober, he was still described as quiet and polite. When drunk he was a demon. He shot up stage stations. He wrecked saloons and brothels. In Denver the storm warnings went up when he hit town. When he was in his moods, even men who considered themselves his friends were not safe. It appears that he was one, above all, who should have signed Alexander Majors' pledge of abstinence and abided by it.

However, like nearly all frontier personages, Slade suffered from the telling and retelling of incidents. One account numbers his kills at twenty-six, obviously far fetched. It also relates how he shot a man in the back, then slew the man's wife and her child and three or four witnesses. Added is the statement that it was men like Slade who gave Holladay's stagecoach line a "bad reputation."

On the credit side, Slade cleaned up conditions as far as outlawry and holdups went until Overland passengers had only Indians to fear. That peril, of course, was sufficient for years as the great Indian wars burst over the Plains.

One person who stepped from a stage at Julesburg—with some trepidation—to meet Slade was Mark Twain. He describes the moment in his book *Roughing It*. He said Slade was so friendly and gentle he could not help warming to the man.

Slade's outbreaks became more frequent, more violent. He had married a beautiful girl. Maria Virginia Slade's comeliness was almost as renowned along hundreds of miles of trail as Slade's reputation for cussedness.

When Ben Holladay swung the stage route farther south, by way of Denver, in order to avoid the increasing Indian trouble on the South Pass route, Slade changed his headquarters to a beautiful spot west of Denver and named it Virginia Dale. Travelers looked forward to arrival there and to meeting the woman for whom it was named. They were not disappointed in either respect.

The Army and the stage company had put up with Slade to the point where he could no longer be tolerated. He passed that point when he wrecked the sutler's store at an Army post. The

Army had enough. It cracked the whip on Ben Holladay, and Holladay listened. Slade was fired. To the surprise of everyone, he gave up his post meekly to his successor and even aided the new boss in inventorying equipment.

He and his wife left for Fort Bridger, but joined the gold rush to Montana. He arrived there at an unfortunate time for him. Bannack, Alder Gulch, and Virginia City had sprung up after the rich Alder Creek gold strike. Gold seekers swarmed to the diggings. Also more than the usual quota of gamblers, prostitutes, outlaws, thieves, pickpockets, footpads, and run-of-the-mill crooks. Murders, robberies, crimes of all kind, became daily fare.

Henry Plummer, sheriff of the county, not only made no effort to perform his duty but was on the side of the roughs and opposed to the honest citizens. No person was safe in his home or on the street. Scarcely a stagecoach on the run between the Montana diggings and Cheyenne escaped at least one stop by holdup men. There were cases where the same stage was held up more than once, but, of course, the robbers who got there first, profited the most. They grew so bold they did not bother wearing masks.

However, Montana's gold had attracted a strata of citizens who were not only honest but could be as hard and violent as the roughs themselves. Harder, in fact. And more ruthless. Among them was the redoubtable John X. Beidler. "X" as he was known and dreaded. "X" became the mark of death, the brand of the hang rope. He was the firebrand of the organization that was formed. The Vigilantes!

Vigilante Committees came into being in many crime-ridden frontier towns, always with results. A massive Vigilante movement rid San Francisco of a lawless element that had practically taken over the city in its early days. The group's method of action was a classic example of a citizenry being forced to take the law into its own hands when enforcement bodies became helpless or corrupt.

Next to the San Francisco group, the Vigilantes in Montana were the most effective. Bloodthirstiness has been charged to both committees, particularly to the Montana group. "X" has been accused of bringing about the hanging of suspects with merciless speed and without benefit of a hearing or defense.

Both organizations probably went too far, and suffered from the same disease all such uprisings seem to generate—lust for more and more power until the citizen is in danger of being destroyed by the thing he created. However, few voices have been raised to say that "X" and the Montana Vigilantes made many mistakes. And no one at all claims that their efforts failed to bring law and order.

As soon as the bodies began appearing, swinging by the neck from corral gates and trees, a great exodus started from the Alder Creek communities. Plummer, however, refused to believe he was not strong enough to win. He paid for that arrogance with his life. On a wintry Sabbath afternoon he had callers at his home.

He attempted to draw a pistol, but was thwarted. Along with accomplices Ned Ray and Buck Stinson, he was marched to a gallows that he had erected, and where he had officiated at the hanging of a murderer by due process of law the previous summer. True to the tradition of outlaws who are brave only when the advantage is their, he begged for his life. He pleaded with the Vigilantes to cut off his ears, his tongue, leave him naked in the freezing night. Anything to spare his life. He pleaded on his knees, tears streaming. He called on the Vigilantes to witness that he was too wicked to die, too wicked to face his Maker.

Ned Ray, defiant, asking no mercy, was swung to his death, cursing the Vigilantes. Stinson, who offered to confess too late, followed Ray. Plummer was given a moment to pray. Then he was lifted into the eternity he dreaded. He was twenty-seven years old.

The Vigilantes were relentless. One by one, they overtook and captured five more ruffians whose names were on the list with the black "X" marked against them. An Army howitzer was used in one instance to blast a suspect in a cabin where he was besieged. The others were caught and hung.

Six more names appeared on the list of doom. Virginia City was surrounded by Vigilantes, and the search began. One of the wanted men managed to escape by crawling along a weed-grown ditch past the cordon. The other five, headed by Boone Helm, who had made a sorry reputation for himself in Nevada's Virginia City before shifting to the Montana counterpart, were taken and hung, side by side, from the same beam in an unfinished building whose sides were open so that all could see and heed.

The graves of Boone Helm and his companions are on a ridge overlooking Virginia City. Wooden markers have been restored, the names repainted, for the town, once a ghost, is now a tourist attraction. The graves, along with the building in which they were executed, are among principal points of interest.

Jack Slade was not involved in the Plummer gang's operations. He was not an outlaw and there is no record that he ever drew a gun on anyone in Virginia City. But he made the mistake of making a nuisance of himself at a time when the hang rope was hungry and patience with violence was at an end.

He engaged in various business ventures, and made money by taking the risk of hauling cargo hundreds of miles through dangerous Indian country from steamboats that were stranded on the Missouri River by unusually low water.

But his drinking increased despite the efforts of Maria Virginia, who remained faithful to him. He resumed his habit of wrecking saloons and stores. He finally went too far by terrorizing a judge before whom he was being arraigned after one of his sprees.

The Vigilantes had been busy with murderers. Slade was not on the list, but his reputation had followed him. Except for property damage and a habit of bullying peaceful citizens, he had committed no felony in the territory. Nevertheless, the Vigilantes met. Such was the temper of the times that merely a hint they were meeting and that a name was before them was usually enough.

Someone warned Slade, who was in town and drinking, telling him the bell was about to toll for him and that he had better get himself aboard a horse and begin making fast tracks. Right now!

Slade headed for his horse, then decided he'd have just one more drink before leaving. While he was indulging in this libation six hundred Vigilantes gathered. When he emerged from the saloon he became instantly sober. According to Langford, he had been a Vigilante also, but there is no record of his having taken part in its deadly proceedings. He knew what this meant, knew that his drink had been indeed one for the road. His last.

He pleaded with them. Someone sent for his wife, who was at their ranch ten miles from town. He was given time to pray, then was stood on a dry-goods box in the entrance to a corral, a noose placed around his neck, and the rope slung over the log arch. Then he was pushed to his death.

His body was cut down and carried to a hotel. His wife arrived on a lathered horse—too late. She upbraided the Vigilantes, few of whom had loitered to face her wrath. So bitter was she against Montana and its executioners she refused to permit her husband's body to be buried in its soil. She bought a lead coffin and had his remains preserved in alcohol. Some observers are said to have callously remarked that this hardly seemed necessary in view of the quantity of this stimulant that Slade had imbibed during his lifetime. After months of legal proceedings, she had the casket taken to Salt Lake City, where Slade found his final resting place.

Jack Slade, Joe Slade, Alf Slade, Captain Slade, was executed without trial for crimes he had not yet committed. A precaution, no doubt, on the part of the Vigilantes, to save the lives of possible victims of Slade's erratic whims.

The moving hand of the Vigilante Committee had written and passed on in its harsh task. Its tenure was nearly ended when Slade was executed. Perhaps the summary manner in which Slade was treated sobered the community, warning citizens that the thing they had created was getting out of hand. Only a few more were to know the terror of the knock on the door at night, and to hear the words, "We want you."

The hang-noose knot with its traditional thirteen loops is, bleakly, almost as much an emblem of the old West as the Colt six-shooter. It has been immortalized in fiction and film until it is commonplace in even the play of children. By weight of repetition, the importance of the rope and the gun has been ballooned out of all proportion to their true place in the winning of the West.

They did have their place, nevertheless. The Colt six-shooter holds the premier position as a bringer of law and order as well as settling matters outside the law. But the hang rope was no minor item. Placerville was not originally known as Hangtown on a mere whim. If the Colt was the great equalizer, the rope was the final judge. Too often, its verdicts, though fatal, were not just.

Every settlement, every mining camp, every railroad and trail town, had not only its share of gunfights and its man for breakfast but it also had its lynchings, right or wrong.

The name of Isaac Parker, the "hanging judge" who presided over the federal court at Fort Smith, Arkansas, is, of course, always in the front rank when the subject of the noose comes up. Parker's jurisdiction was the western district of Arkansas, which extended as far as the Colorado line. That included all of what is now Oklahoma, which meant that his district was infested with probably the toughest collection of outlaws, fugitives, and all-around ornery citizens in the nation.

Parker enforced the law to the letter. During his term he condemned one hundred and sixty-eight men and four women to death. Of these, eighty-eight men went to the scaffold. Commutations and reversals by higher authority spared the others. All four women escaped execution.

The eighty-eight went to their doom on the scaffold in the courtyard at Fort Smith, which has been restored as a historical relic. It was built to accommodate as many as twelve condemned men at a time, but the high record for a single day's swinging was six. This exceeded by one soul the mass executions of Boone Helm and his pals by the Montana Vigilantes.

There have been many other multiple hangings in the West, the majority the work of Vigilantes or lynch mobs. One of the first summary executions by enraged citizens took place at New Albany, Indiana, when masked men burst into the jail and swung to their deaths four members of the infamous gang of Reno brothers, who, among murders and other crimes, were credited with having staged the first holdup of a train in America. Three of the executed men were Reno brothers.

Three other brothers named Weaver, who had been neighborhood bullies and small-time thieves, finally wore out the patience of citizens in Harper County, Kansas, and were strung up in a schoolhouse in 1886.

Four brothers and their father were executed at ropes' ends in Modoc County, California, as late as 1906 by men who were never identified, but were said to have been cattlemen who have vowed to end rustling in their range.

Even later, in 1920, three men were taken from jail by a mob at Santa Rosa, California, in the peaceful vineyard country, and their necks stretched to telephone poles. Lynchings were not confined to the West, of course. They have taken place in nearly every state.

However, mob lynchings seem to be going the way of other quaint customs, such as the pillory, the ducking stool, the branding stake, and the whip. Even legal executions have been ruled out by the courts, although voters in some of the states are restoring the death penalty for some crimes.

## CHAPTER 9

## SKY ABOVE, GRASS BELOW

Wheat and corn are members of the grass family, the long-grass family, of course. To say that these items live up to their names on the former buffalo range in Kansas, Iowa, and Nebraska, is a first-class understatement.

Travel through Kansas along in midsummer and you'll see grass in the form of wheat until you almost begin to rebel at the sight of a loaf of bread. North of that is the habitat of the taller variety—corn. On one occasion, heading west in late July, this writer beheld a large proclamation painted on the side of a barn in Illinois not far from the Mississippi River. It stated: You Are Now Entering the Great American Corn Belt.

Whether intended as a warning or a boast, it told the exact truth. Across Iowa and Nebraska, what one viewed from the highway was corn. Corn, corn, corn. The blue sky overhead, and the tall corn on either side. This green tunnel continued until a higher elevation was reached on the Plains in western Nebraska.

The prairie was the long-grass country. Bluestem sod predominated along the eastern areas where rainfall was more plentiful, fading into needle and slender grass as moisture dwindled westward.

Beyond, on the still more arid Plains, lay short-stem country, which was where the buffalo foraged on the famed grazing buffalo grass. This, along with grama, was the low-growing native of the Plains. It cured on the stem and was very nourishing even when pawed from beneath frozen snow.

Ogallala is about in the middle of the short-grass country. Both in the narrow way and the long way. The short-grass belt does not extend far east and west, but it starts in the Texas Panhandle and stretches all the way into Canada.

Long grass, in favorable places, grew as high as a buffalo's eye before the granger and his plow came along. The short grass rarely would cover more than the fetlocks of an Indian pony—or a Texas bronco.

Buffalo ranged in both belts. The early Longhorns from Texas kept more to the long grass in the beginning. Grazing was rarely a problem on the virgin prairie, although finding water at the right time and place was another matter.

When Kansas passed laws to quarantine cattle against Texas tick fever, and barbed wire began to fence off the trails, the drives took to the drier upper Plains in western Kansas and eastern Colorado. The buffalo and grama grasses were there and the herds did not suffer from any lack of graze, although water became a greater problem than before.

That was the era when the northern ranges in Montana and Dakota Territory were being stocked. That was when the trail towns lived throught their hectic chapters, with cowboys jingling spur chains on the plank walks and whooping it up in the music halls, blowing in three months' pay in a night on the fancy girls or at the poker tables.

The heat of summer lay often on the Plains, a scourge to man and beast. In winter, the blizzards raged. As they do to this day. A man who fans himself in his office on a July day in Kearney, and turns the air conditioner higher when the temperature in the street is 100 degrees or better, huddles beside a heating stove six months later with the thermometer hitting 30 or 40 below, and a gale moaning across the Plains.

They talk about the weather on the Plains, not because nobody does anything about it, but because they have so much of it. They have thunderstorms. A mild term for some of these displays. Cowpunchers on trail drives used to leave their horses, throw away their spurs, six-shooters, knives, and any other articles containing steel or iron. They didn't want to attract the personal attention of any of the bolts of lightning that were streaking around them.

There was lightning in carload lots when one of those hell-benders broke, generally to finish off a torrid, humid afternoon, although some violent ones seemed to occur after midnight. Some meteorologists believe the Ohio River Valley is the home of the most violent thunderstorms on the continent. The Ozark Mountains, too, can cook up some ear-benders. But the ripsnorters that visit the Plains will do until better ones come along.

Trail men have told of Longhorn herds moaning in almost human terror beneath the fury of these storms. Countless stampedes were caused, often taking the *remudas* with them, leaving crews afoot for days.

On one occasion at the Red River ford, a herd of three thousand head began running during a storm and nearly a dozen more drives, waiting in the vicinity to wade the river, joined in. Some thirty thousand cattle in many brands united in one giant stampede. Cowboys worked for many days rounding up and sorting out the brands.

The late G. H. Mohle, of Lockhart, Texas, tells of the trials of cowboys in the book, *The Trail Drivers of Texas,* which was edited by the late J. Marvin Hunter. In 1869, Mohle was with a drive of three thousand Longhorns that had great difficulty with high water at the Canadian and Arkansas rivers. That was only the start. The herd was sold to a California buyer at Abilene, Kansas, who hired Mohle and the crew to drive it to the West Coast.

A cyclone struck their camp on the Republican, overturning the chuck wagon and blowing tents away. Reaching the Platte, they had to search for twenty-five miles before finding a ford safe from quicksand. Indians ran off all but five of their *remuda* of sixty-three horses.

These things delayed them until winter struck. Beyond Julesburg, they were immobilized by blizzards for days at a time. There were poison springs that took toll of the herd. They stuck it out until they reached Utah, then gave it up and took a Union Pacific train east on the first leg of the trip back to Texas. Such was the life of a trail driver. Weather was his biggest opponent.

Another trail man, S. H. Woods, in the same collection, tells of a terrible thunderstorm at night while en route to the crossing of the Platte near Julesburg. "Fox fire" stood on the ears of their mounts, the odor of sulphur being strong in the night. The storm caused a stampede in which several other herds were involved, requiring a week's riding by the crews before order was restored.

Fox fire, as this cowboy called it, St. Elmo's fire as it was termed by others, was a weird side show of some of the violent storms. Many cowboys have told of seeing the tips of all the horns of the cattle bearing tiny candlelike cold flames when the great storms were brewing.

Then there were days of summer heat when a saddle horn became blistering to the touch. The same sun that makes the wheat and corn grow, beat down on the buffalo and the cowhand, sometimes running the temperature up to 105 in the shade.

Shade? That was something a cowboy, trailing a herd across the Plains, found only when the sun went down. A man might ride all day without seeing a shrub more than knee-high and might not see a tree for a week at a time. The only hope for respite from the sun was to find a rock or a dry wash big enough to offer a shadow. As for houses, they were even more rare than trees. The wide-brimmed hats that became the fashion with cattlemen had many uses, but one of its main features was that it offered a semblance of shade for its wearer.

Then there were the hailstorms. Sometimes the hail came down as big as hen eggs. Such a storm did considerable damage at Cheyenne in August 1876, and cut a swath northward toward Deadwood. Riders caught in such bombardments often abandoned their horses and crouched with saddles balanced over their heads as shields against the rain of ice balls.

Blowing sand was another hazard. The cavalry, especially, suffered from this source during the Indian wars in the Platte Valley area. Goggles were often a part of the issue to troops. Many forty-niners carried green goggles as protection from blowing sand as well as sun glare. The eyes of oxen often became so inflamed the animals were blind.

But, above all, there was the dust. The insufferable, eternal dust, the pitiless dust. It was the great affliction of the trails, the evil that, more than any other cause, broke the strength and the spirit of travelers. It often hung over the caravans for days, a choking pall that seemed to increase instead of alleviate the burning heat of summer sun. It coated humans, wagons, livestock, sifted into blankets and into food. Men, women, children, breathed it, slogged through it ankle-deep, fought it futilely, and sometimes sank down, sobbing, huddling, covering heads, not wanting to continue the battle against it.

William Henry Jackson, famed picture maker of the trail, described the dust, when his outfit halted to rest at Fort Kearney on June 26, 1866, as so thick at times one could not see a rod ahead. In addition, the great Indian war was raging and the military would not permit trains numbering less than thirty wagons to proceed westward beyond the fort. It was required that every man in all caravans be adequately armed, with supplies of ammunition.

But there were the good days when the wind or the rains of the previous night had conquered the dust for a time, when the clouds floated white and fleecy overhead, the wind ran soft and light-footed across the undulating sea of grass, and cowboys sang songs, forgot their homesickness, and dreamed great dreams. There is no beauty like that of the Plains when it smiles, and it smiles often. It is a smile that makes men forget the interludes of heat, the sandstorms, the quicksand in the rivers, the lightning bolts from the sky, even the dust.

To the list of very real hazards in the pioneer days was that dreaded element—fire. Prairie fires have figured in fiction and legend to such an extent that the average opinion is that the danger from this source was, to say the least, exaggerated, and that lurid stories of the enormous holocausts stemmed from the imaginations of men like Ned Buntline.

However, prairie fires were a real danger to hunters and wagon trains and even to considerable bodies of troops at times. The major habitat of these blazes, of course, was in the long-grass country. Here, in years, when the spring growth had been lush, followed by hot, dry weather, a prairie fire could be a fearful thing indeed.

The majority were touched off by lightning. Carelessness of hide hunters who let campfires get out of hand started many blazes and sometimes the hunters paid the price of their own folly by being trapped. Indians set grass fires to handicap the cavalry by wiping out grazing for the troopers' mounts. This tactic was especially used by the Sioux after the Custer fight. They burned off grass along Wind River and the Rosebud ahead of Crook's column to such an extent that his livestock began to suffer. Cody and other scouts risked their lives seeking out draws and rises that had escaped the fire so that the horses might find sustenance.

This was a weapon that was used by both sides. The biggest

blaze of all, of course, was the one set by the Army in 1865 in an attempt to starve the Sioux and Cheyennes.

On another occasion, a hide hunter's camp where Billy Dixon was present narrowly escaped disaster when sparks from a camp-fire touched off tall grass. All that saved the wagons was that, by luck, the teams were still hooked to the vehicles and the hunters were able to career their equipment out of the path of the flames.

Witnesses have described the beauty of the fires—especially at night—a sinister beauty.

Not all of the blazes were destructive, especially in timbered country, common belief to the contrary. Before the coming of the white man the Indians habitually burned off the summer's growth of small brush and grass in order to give better sustenance to big timber and to hold down the growth of thickets that would only offer fuel for conflagrations and destroy the trees.

This method of conservation was not necessary on the treeless Plains, of course, but in the uplands, especially in the forests of the Northwest, it was practiced by the tribes. Old hunters who were in the Oregon timber country before a modern school of thought prevented the burning of undergrowth, have told of walk-ing as youths beneath the big trees, stalking deer, elk, and bear amid parklike beauty. Now one gazes at a maze of tangled brush. Each year fires, the majority of which are started by lightning, feed on this jungle and destroy mature trees.

Returning to the Plains and its weather, there were—and are—the winters to consider. Like the one in 1872 when buffalo, drift-ing with a terrible blizzard, stalled a Union Pacific train in Ne-braska, piling up against the cars for shelter from the wind and snow until the train was in danger of being derailed.

Plains lore is filled with stories of hardships that travelers en-dured in the great blizzards. They took lives then, they take lives to this day. Mrs. Henry Inman, wife of the historian of the trail, was snowbound near Salina for thirty-six hours aboard a Union Pacific train and shared with other passengers a collection of mince pies, believe it or not, that she had in her trunk and intended to deliver to relatives at an Army post who had not enjoyed that luxury in many a moon.

Seventy-one years later the situation was repeated, and under even worse conditions, when a train was stalled in North Dakota in minus 50-degree weather. It was not dug out until three days had passed, even with modern equipment.

In November 1871, a bull train loaded with wood was caught by a blizzard five miles from Fort Hays. All the cattle froze and nearly every man in the train lost a hand or a foot from frostbite.

A March blizzard raged for five days in Wyoming, in 1878, and Cheyenne hotel guests emerged from second-story windows onto snowdrifts that had piled against the buildings, blocking lower floors. Many buildings collapsed and many lives were lost on the stagecoach lines.

General Bisbee, bound for Julesburg from Fort Laramie, decided to leave his escort and cross the ice on the river on foot because he considered it too dangerous for the army ambulance in which his wife was riding. He had important information which he wanted to forward from Fort Sedgwick. He broke through the ice, with the temperature 20 below, ran two miles to the fort, and escaped without loss of fingers or toes.

But the year they still talk about with muted voices was '86. The winter of '86 and '87. The Year of the Big Die. The year that left the cattle industry prone and almost penniless. It was a long time recovering.

Although the cow industry retained the ruddy hue of prosperity, built up during past years, the fact was, as the winter of 1886–87 approached, an inner fever was already draining its strength.

Texas cattle had moved into Montana and the Dakotas, into Wyoming and Colorado, by the hundreds of thousands, stocking the range from which the buffalo had been eliminated. It was the era of the cattle boom. Beef was the magic word. Eastern capital was investing in cattle, vying for range rights in the upper Missouri country.

Six-shooters often decided title to grazing land. It was the day of the cattle baron, the hired gunman, the rustler. Wars with sheepmen began as the woollies moved in. British investors arrived. The Plains, which had seen grand dukes, monacled earls, and pompous counts ride to hounds and kill buffalo, now had to adjust its eyes to the sight of ranch owners posting on English saddles and calling a halt to work at midafternoon in order to sip tea at the chuck wagons.

There had been warnings, both from nature and from the beef markets at Kansas City and Chicago. The winters had turned

unusually cold, and ranchers had suffered losses up to ten percent
of their cattle the previous year, but this merely cut the surplus
and helped steady prices that were none too high and had a
tendency to plunge at the slightest excuse.

Theodore Roosevelt was ranching in the Badlands at the time
and was always to remember 1886–87. The summer of '86 had
been exceedingly hot and dry after a wet spring that promised a
bumper crop of grass, a promise that failed under withering heat.
Streams shrank, cattle thinned from having to rustle to find grazing. Hip bones jutted, ribs fluted.

The morning of November 15 dawned mild, but an ominous
pall gathered to the west. This deepened and moved eastward.
By daylight the next morning a gale was blowing. Then came
snow. The temperature plunged below zero.

The wind became so fierce riders took refuge wherever they
happened to be caught—in line camps or in gullies or the lee of
cutbanks. They figured to tough it out as they had toughed out
other Plains storms.

This one was different. It didn't quit. Wind, snow, more wind,
more snow. And the cold. All human life was forced to remain under cover. Lamps burned day and night in the ranch houses and
the towns, both for light for the inmates and to guide any travelers
seeking safety.

The winter of the Big Die had started. The death rate among
humans was light, but, by January, all ranches in the upper Missouri country knew they faced ruin. Cattle were freezing in their
tracks. Those that hung on, drifting with each succeeding storm,
were flanked by packs of wolves that had come down from Canada. Only the wolves and the buzzards fattened that winter.

Where drift fences had been built or homesteaders had stretched
wire to protect their fields, cattle massed in heaps and died, with
the wind burying them under drifts of snow. In one January storm
an outfit north of the Missouri lost half of a stock herd of three
thousand head it had trailed in from Oregon the previous summer.

Cowboys and owners, riding line during lulls when they could
venture from shelter, stared unbelievingly at grim sights. Frozen
cattle were lodged in trees above their heads. They had climbed
there on frozen snowdrifts to eat bark and branches, had died
there, and other storms had blown the ground clear below.

Carcasses choked gullies and ravines, sometimes forming bridges on which a horse and rider could cross.

The *average* minimum for two months after November 15 was 11 below zero. Lows of 44 below were recorded by the weather bureau. Cattle ate sagebrush to the roots. They began to invade the towns in search of food, or perhaps just to find humans in the hope the humans could help them. Five thousand head invaded Great Falls, Montana, gnawing at trees planted for shade on the streets, smashing rubbish cans in search of food.

The chinook finally came in March. Rivers flooded and draws became deadly torrents. The stench of rotting carcasses became unbearable on the range. Ranchers and their riders were as gaunt as the cattle that had survived. So were their bankrolls.

Granville Stuart, naturalist and cattleman, estimated that out of 1,000,000 cattle in Montana, 600,000 had perished with a loss of $20,000,000. The Niobrara Cattle Co., Texas-owned, lost 30,-000 head of its herd of 40,000. Some outfits reported ninety-five percent losses. The majority of the ranchers were bankrupt or heavily in debt. Theodore Roosevelt gave up ranching, returned East, and went into politics.

Ranching in the northern range was never the same. Smaller brands, fenced and better controlled, came into being. The wheat farmers moved in, and that was the final knell of the open range.

The loss was not confined to the upper Missouri range, although that region was hardest hit. The winter of 1886–87 is remembered in the Platte Valley and in Colorado, and even down on the wind-swept expanses of the Staked Plain.

But they still haven't done anything about the weather on the Plains. The storms still rage, the winds still howl, the blizzards moan. Avalanches still sweep down the slants of the Rockies, taking lives at times. Ranchers drop hay to livestock from planes when the animals are drifted in. Trains still get stalled. The snowplows on the U.P. and other railroads have polished blades during many of the winters.

Cattle and sheep still die, pile up against fences or in coulees, when riders, blinded by wind and snow, are unable to turn them as they drift. Ranching is still a gamble.

And so is farming on the prairie. Remember the Dust Bowl of the 1930s?

CHAPTER 10

MONEY OR YOUR LIFE!

From Funk & Wagnalls New Standard Dictionary, 1914
edition:

**bandit** (ban'dits or ban'di'ti). One of a band of highwaymen or
robbers, especially one infesting the mountain districts of Spain,
Italy, Turkey, etc.; a brigand; originally a proclaimed outlaw. **Banditt; bandito, banditty.** Syn.: see robber.

A common practice by cub reporters of a past era was to refer to a holdup man as a "lone bandit." The purists on the copy
desk were always waiting for that one, and greeted it with the
howls of derision that are reserved for the ignorant. It was in the
same class with that other classic cub reporter blunder: "the dead
man was seen walking up the railroad track."

Since then, somewhere along the line, copy desk purists and
Funk & Wagnalls to the contrary, the lone bandit is with us almost every day in the newspapers. Any thug who mugs a citizen
or rolls a drunk in an alley often rates the term. Essentially however as F.&W. decided, the bandit was a member of a band.
The Plains knew both varieties—lone and plural.

Even before the 1914 edition of the dictionary, the robber,
singly or in groups, could no longer be regarded as indigenous to
Italy, Turkey, etc. By that time America had long since earned its
right to be listed among the nations into which this unlovely form
of viciousness had been introduced.

The banditti of the West operated under rather commonplace
names. Good American names, such as James, Bass, Reno, Logan,
Younger, Dalton, Cassidy, and so on. They had such solid Christian
front handles as Jesse, Sam, Bill, Harvey, Cole, Emmett, and
Butch. Often brothers and cousins ganged up to engage in the fun.

There were the James boys, the Daltons, the Renos. Nearly all wound up at an early age in graves or in prison, or as fugitives in foreign countries.

The banditti, of course, were not the exclusive burden of the Plains. Probably the worst of the lot east of the Mississippi were the Harpe brothers, who operated along the Natchez Trace and the Ohio River. Their speciality was shooting down, without warning, travelers along the trace and luring flatboat crews ashore by false distress signals. They left few witnesses alive.

As population increased and spread beyond the Mississippi, as gold was found in California, the Rockies, the Dakotas, and in Arizona, the lure of quick profit attracted more and more thugs into the game. Stagecoaches were the main early target, being vulnerable to ambush because of the nature of the wild country over which they traveled.

"Hands up!" That became the watchword on the stage lines.

Lone travelers were equally victimized. "Your money or your life," was the customary greeting.

Much loot was taken by both methods. Treasure stages were held up and tens of thousands of dollars taken at a time. Shotgun guards gave their lives in defense, bandits were slain, drivers murdered. It was an era of wild adventure, grim drama, great heroism, and cold-blooded killing.

At times the banditti outnumbered the law by such wide margins that the badge-toters were helpless. Things came to such a pass in Panamint City, the wild silver camp in the mountains west of Death Valley, that mine owners smelted their cleanups into great cannonballs of silver which were chained to drays and carried down the grade on their way to refineries. Their eight-hundred-pound weights balked the banditti.

None of the outlaws who operated against the Overland and other stage routes have been rated as vicious as the savage Harpes, but they were, by no means, looked on as gentle and righteous citizens.

Black Bart, the California highwayman who wrote poetry, is about the only one who was regarded with any real respect by the sheriffs and Pinkertons. Black Bart, it is said, never injured a victim, nor even a lawman, in his sometimes humorous holdups, which is probably why he is pointed to in the memoirs of the sleuths as an example for others who aim to take up crime for a living. He was finally captured and turned out to be a mild-ap-

22. Front Street, Dodge City, in the '70s, with its famous sign prohibiting the carrying of firearms, an admonition that was not always heeded. (*Kansas State Historical Society*)

23. This photo might be that of a sedate, placid businessman or banker. In fact it is that of Wyatt Earp, of Dodge City and Tombstone gun fame. (*Kansas State Historical Society*)

24. Three who rode together. Wild Bill Hickok, left, Texas Jack Omohundro, center, and Buffalo Bill Cody. This picture was taken when the trio were actors in dreadful melodramas, touring the East to mixed applause and catcalls. Omohundro, a kindred spirit to the more famous pair, had been a Confederate cavalryman under Jeb Stuart before moving to the Plains. (*Cody Ranch Photo*)

25. Jack Slade, stage boss at Julesburg, who killed the founder of the settlement and wore his ears as watch fobs. (*Julesburg Historical Museum*)

26. Trouble, trouble! Chinese laborers dig out stalled Central Pacific train in the Nevadas.
(*Southern Pacific Railroad Photo*)

27. Power drive. A battery of eight (one out of picture) wood burners pushes a bucker plow through snowdrifts on the Central Pacific in the 1870s.
(*Southern Pacific Railroad Photo*)

WILLIAM A. PINKERTON.

28. William A. Pinkerton. (*State Historical Society of Missouri*)

29. This rare photo shows a very young Jesse James (*right*). His brother Frank is seated. With them is a companion, Fletcher Taylor.
(*State Historical Society of Missouri*)

30. The Dalton gang, ready for the undertaker (*from the left*) Bill Powers, Bob Dalton, Grat Dalton, and Dick Broadwell. (*National Archives*)

31. This is the road agent poet, Black Bart, who plagued Wells Fargo stagecoaches on the California trails until he was captured in San Francisco. He turned out to be an apparently sedate citizen named Charles E. Bolton, who was given a brief sentence. (*Wells Fargo Bank History Room*)

# $800.00 Reward!

# ARREST STAGE ROBBER!

1.

On the 3d of August, 1877, the stage from Fort Ross to Russian River was stopped by one man, who took from the Express box about $300, coin, and a check for $305.52, on Grangers' Bank of San Francisco, in favor of Fisk Bros. The Mail was also robbed. On one of the Way Bills left with the box the Robber wrote as follows:—

"I've labored long and hard for bread—
For honor and for riches—
But on my corns too long you've trod,
You fine haired sons of bitches.
                    BLACK BART, the P o 8.

Driver, give my respects to our friend, the other driver; but I really had a notion to hang my old disguise hat on his weather eye." (*fac simile.*)

*Respectfully B. B.*

It is believed that he went to the Town of Guerneville about daylight next morning.

2.

About one year after above robbery, July 25th, 1878, the Stage from Quincy to Oroville was stopped by one man, and W., F. & Co's box robbed of $379. coin, one Diamond Ring, (said to be worth $200) one Silver Watch, valued at $25. The Mail was also robbed. In the box, when found next day, was the following, (*fac simile*):—

*here I lay me down to sleep
to wait the coming morrow,
perhaps success perhaps defeat
And everlasting sorrow
I've labored long and hard for bred
for honor and for riches
But on my corns too long youve tred
You fine haired sons of bitches.
let come what will I'll try it on
My condition cant be worse
and if theres money in that Box
Tis munny in my purse
                    Black Bart
                    the Po 8*

32. This offer of reward and samples of Black Bart's poetry were sent to law officers by Wells Fargo throughout the territory where the mysterious masked road agent operated. (*Wells Fargo Bank History Room*)

33. Carry Nation of Medicine Lodge, Kansas, militant prohibitionist. (*Kansas State Historical Society*)

34. Interior of wrecked saloon at Enterprise, Kansas, after a visit by Carry Nation. (*Kansas State Historical Society*)

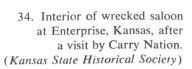

35. D. R. "Cannonball" Green, for whom Greensburg, Kansas, is named, who ousted Carry Nation from his stagecoach when she snatched an offending cigar from his lips. (*Kansas State Historical Society*)

36. Go! Frederic Remington drawing of Pony rider leaving relay station after swift change of horses. (*Wells Fargo Bank History Room*)

37. Pony Express saddle. (*Wells Fargo Bank History Room*)

38. Payload. Sketch of Overland Mail stagecoach, carrying capacity load of passengers at fast clip over the trail. Note the Chinese passengers riding on rear seat on top. (*Wells Fargo Bank History Room*)

39. Racing across Humboldt Desert, Central Pacific crew, the majority Chinese, speeds new track eastward.
(*Southern Pacific Railroad Photo*)

40. The Winner! Construction boss J. H. Strobridge, standing left on flatcar, and his crew celebrate at Victory Camp after laying more than ten miles of track in a day to win ten-thousand-dollar wager Charles Crocker of Central Pacific had made with Thomas Durant of the Union Pacific.

(*Southern Pacific Railroad Photo*)

41. Freighter's nightmare. Typical scene when supplies were being hauled to railroad construction camps in mountain country, as Central Pacific was being built.
(*Southern Pacific Railroad Photo*)

42. Laying track on the Kansas prairie near Fort Hays for Kansas Pacific Railroad, on October 19, 1867. Buffalo Bill Cody was supplying K.P. crews with fresh buffalo meat daily.

*(Union Pacific Railroad Photo)*

pearing citizen of San Francisco named Charles E. Bolton. He served a short prison term.

Bart was the exception to the rule. Butch Cassidy, of the Hole in the Wall gang, is adorned with plumes by some researchers. There is no evidence Cassidy murdered any holdup victim in cold blood. His companions did, and he was often a witness to such crimes.

Cassidy and his outfit belonged to the later era of banditti. Stagecoach robbery had its rewards, but there were literally hundreds of them every year, and of that number the vehicles carrying treasure were few and far apart. The haul usually consisted of cheap watches, wedding rings wrested from the fingers of fainting women, and worthless trinkets found in the cases of traveling salesmen.

However, as railroads built into the West, and settlements sprang up, it became profitable to open banks. Thereby, the banditti had new sources of profit, although the reaping was not quite as easy. Bank holdups and train robberies became the fashionable way to go for the gangs. Both methods generated the most bloody and noisy episodes in the crime history of the frontier.

Site of what is believed to have been the first train robbery in America was not the Plains, but an obscure country hamlet in the flatlands of southern Indiana, Seymour by name. In October 1866, the Reno brothers—Frank, John, Simeon, Clinton, and Bill—held up the express car of an Ohio & Mississippi train and got away with ten thousand dollars. This led to the mass lynchings of four of the outlaws previously mentioned in this narrative.

From then on, the Pinkertons were kept busy chasing train and bank robbers in singles and bands. Many of these were former guerrillas who had got their schooling with Quantrill or other looters during the Civil War by raiding unprotected border communities where the majority of the men were absent in the armies. They murdered old men and boys, raped women, and burned peaceful homes.

One graduate of the Quantrill school was:

> *Jesse James was a lad*
> *That killed many a man;*
> *He robbed the Danville train;*
> *But that dirty little coward*
> *That shot Mister Howard,*
> *He laid pore Jesse in the grave.*

Jesse James has been dramatized so many times in fiction and film that his name has become a legend. He is often portrayed as a sort of American Robin Hood. But in fact he was a leech on society.

He and his gang, of which his brother Frank was one, included many other desperadoes at times, such as the Younger brothers. They were such a scourge along the Kansas-Missouri border that decent settlers avoided the area, putting a damper on the early growth of those states.

The outstanding drama in the Jesse James story was the bitter feud between the outlaw and the Pinkertons. It became a personal matter between Jesse and Allan Pinkerton after Jesse's mother was maimed by a bomb set off by the Pinkertons at the James home. It was a blood grudge between a desperado and a relentless bloodhound. Many criminals died, many lawmen died, but the chief antagonists survived until Bob Ford's bullet ended the feud.

The James gang staged numerous bank holdups, but their first train robbery, according to the records of William A. Pinkerton, took place fifteen miles east of Council Bluffs on July 20, 1873, when they wrecked a train, murdered the engineer, wounded the fireman and several passengers, and escaped with considerable treasure.

Aided by the Younger brothers, they held up a train at Gadshill, Missouri, on January 31, 1874, got 10,000 dollars, and later killed two Pinkerton men and a Missouri sheriff in a gun fight in which John Younger died with his boots on. Jim Younger stopped a bullet in this fray, but recovered.

The James brothers robbed a Union Pacific train at Munsey, Kansas, in December 1875, getting 55,000 dollars. A Missouri Pacific express holdup at Otterville, Missouri, July 8, 1876, netted seventeen thousand dollars. One of Jesse's gang, named McDaniels, was killed by the Pinkertons when resisting arrest.

Disaster struck Jesse's outfit when the citizens of Northfield, Minnesota, rallied after the outlaws had killed J. L. Haywood, a cashier, in a robbery. Considerable powder was burned. When it cleared, outlaws Bill Chadwell, Clell Miller, and Charley Pitts lay dead. Jesse, along with Bob and Jim Younger, was wounded. Frank James got Jesse to a Missouri river boat to safety. Cole, Jim, and Bob Younger were caught a few days later and given long prison terms. Bob died in prison. Cole and Jim were pardoned after a quarter of a century. The men of Northfield accomplished in a few minutes what the Pinkertons had been unable to do in years of pursuit. They put an end to Jesse James as a desperado to be feared. The Northfield fight came on September 7, 1876.

Bob Ford, who was a member of the James group, murdered Jesse at St. Joseph, Missouri, on April 3, 1882, for the ten thousand dollar reward on his head. Bob and his brother Charles, who was present at the killing, were sentenced to death by a jury, but were pardoned by Missouri governor Crittenden and were paid the bounty. Frank James surrendered and was allowed to go straight.

Jesse had been shot in the back when he stepped on a davenport to straighten a picture on the wall. This scene became the climax to the drama *Jesse James, Outlaw* that was presented for years by many traveling stage troupes. This tear-jerker was alternated with such other presentations as *Over the Hills to the Poorhouse* and *Uncle Tom's Cabin*.

The action of the men of Northfield contradicts a shopworn theme, much used in fiction and drama, that entire towns in the West were terrorized into hysterics by the very thought of having a bad man or gunslinger appear in their midst. In some areas, outnumbered citizens did look the other way, knowing that criminals were walking their streets, but this was the exception and not the rule. Eventually, in nearly all cases, they ended such reigns of fear by ousting or killing their unwelcome guests.

Nearly every household in the West had guns hanging on antler racks or placed handy at bedside, and with men around who had learned how to use them at places like Shiloh, Chickamauga, and in the Wilderness. A lot of them had fought Indians, shot buffalo. They had only contempt for the likes of Jesse James and his ilk.

Among Jesse's ilk was Sam Bass.

> *Sam Bass was born in Indiana;*
> *It was his native home,*
> *And at the age of seventeen*
> *Sam Bass began to roam;*
> *He first came out to Texas,*
> *A cowboy for to be . . .*
> *A kinder-hearted fellow,*
> *You seldom ever see.*

The legend of Sam Bass is still nourished in folk song. Like Jesse James, his name has a ring to it, a name that should belong to a man of daring. It is also easy to rhyme in doggerel verse. He is popularly credited with leading the gang that made the biggest "score" in a Plains train holdup, when, as a matter of fact, it was planned and led by another man.

One fine fall evening in 1877, a Union Pacific express ground to halt at a water tank at a whistle-stop station, Big Springs, Nebraska, a few miles from Julesburg. It was promptly boarded by six masked men who proceeded to rob the express car.

The robbery was the brain child of Joel Collins, with whom Bass had traveled, committing minor crimes. Boxes in the express car yielded sixty thousand dollars in cash. Cool cash, for these were newly minted twenty-dollar gold pieces, bound from the San Francisco mint to a destination in the East.

Not satisfied with that spectacular haul, they robbed the passengers of jewelry and wallets that netted a few hundred dollars more. The loot was split up at a rendezvous under a lone tree along the South Platte, and then the gang cut out in various directions.

Of the six, only one, Tom Nixon, apparently escaped the hand of the law. The last heard of him, he was in Honduras some years later. Joel Collins and Frank Hulfish were killed by officers near Ellsworth, Kansas. Jim Berry met the same fate at Mexico, Missouri. Henry Underwood spent years in an Indiana prison.

Sam Bass, with his share of the loot, headed for Denton County, Texas, where he had worked previously as a cowboy. He bought drinks for the house in some of the bars, paying for it with Big Springs gold, thereby being acclaimed as a sort of golden-hearted desperado who robbed the rich to buy drinks for the poor. There is no record that he bought a second round nor that he distributed any of his Big Springs money among the needy.

Instead, he became a sort of old-man-of-the-sea on the back of Denton County and surrounding areas. He gathered about him a number of his own kind and these banditti began preying on their fellow men, staging small holdups and train robberies and letting their neighbors know exactly what would happen to them—or their wives and children—if anyone sold them to the law.

However, Sam was sold to the law, and not by the neighbors. He met the same fate as Jesse James, betrayal by one of his band, Jim Murphy. Murphy tried to tip off the law that the Bass gang was en route to rob a bank in Round Rock, Texas. After several mishaps and narrow squeaks from being caught by Bass, he succeeded. In a gun battle in Round Rock, two law officers were killed and Bass was fatally wounded, dying a day or two later. Jim Murphy died months later after swallowing poison, some say by mistake, others say it was slipped into his drink.

According to Pinkerton records, other members of the Bass outfit ended up thusly: James Pike and Joe Herndon, life in prison; Al Collins and Arkansas Johnson, killed resisting arrest; Seaborn Barnes, killed at Round Rock. Bass was twenty-seven when he died.

Big Springs, Nebraska, dozed for more than three quarters of a century after the visit by Bass and Joel Collins in 1877. Then, in 1965, Duane Earl Pope, a "lone bandit," held up the bank in that small community, which is still only a whistle-stop on the U.P. He murdered three bank officials, including a woman clerk, but was caught and sentenced to death.

Sentence, after three years of legal pondering, was vacated because of a ruling by the U. S. Supreme Court that this particular section of the law was illegal on the grounds it gave juries the exclusive power to order such executions. The slayer was remanded for sentencing. Pope is now serving a life term.

Among the banditti of the West were the Daltons, whose exploits of murder and robbery have also been depicted in the Hollywood studios, often with some of the leading stars taking the roles of Bob, Emmett, or Grat, according to which way the script pointed.

Their operations lasted less than two years, but they were exceedingly busy during that span. They favored no particular locality. They ranged from California, where they murdered a helpless locomotive fireman in Tulare County, to sticking up "Katy" trains in Oklahoma Territory. "Katy" was the popular term for the Missouri, Kansas, and Texas Railway.

What did the Daltons in was the desire for real fame. They weren't satisfied with train robberies where they had the advantage of surprise and superior numbers against unarmed victims. They became overconfident and decided on doing something Big. Not one bank at a time, but two. The James boys had never knocked over a brace of banks at one time, had they? Nor the

Youngers? Nobody had. It would be something to write home about, to brag and strut about.

So they rode into a small, peaceful farm and cattle town in southeastern Kansas on the morning of October 5, 1892. Five of them—Emmett, Bob, and Grat Dalton, Bill Powers, and Dick Broadwell. That was the day the name of Coffeyville was written into the history of the frontier, along with that of Northfield, Minnesota.

Within twenty minutes after they entered the outskirts of Coffeyville all of them were dead except Emmett, and he had so many slugs in his carcass they were still digging for them after he had been pardoned and released from prison in 1907.

Again John Citizen, law abiding and not looking for trouble, turned out to be far tougher than the banditti. First, the outlaws met more than their match in the person of an iron-nerved official in Coffeyville's First National Bank, Charles T. Carpenter. He delayed the Daltons, saying the time lock on the safe would not open for several minutes, thus giving the citizens of the town time to arm. Which the citizens did very promptly.

The citizens began to shoot. The outlaws, trapped, fought back. When the gunsmoke cleared away, four citizens were dead and three were seriously wounded. The Dalton gang, however, would never ride again. Bob and Grat Dalton, Dick Broadwell, and Bill Powers lay dead. Emmett paid with fourteen years in prison. He died in 1937 in Hollywood, California, where he became somewhat of a celebrity as an authority on guns and outlawry.

Only Bill Dalton, who had been unable to make it into Coffeyville that morning because of a disabled horse, remained of the old bunch. He continued the family tradition of living without working for nearly two years. On May 23, 1894, he and some pals stepped into the First National Bank at Longview, Texas. Bill handed a note to the president which read:

Home, May 23.

First National Bank, Longview:
This will introduce to you Charles
Sprecklemeyer, who wants some money
and is going to get it.
B&F

They got two thousand dollars, but paid a fearful price. Citizens killed Jim Wallace, one of the gang. Bill was killed two weeks later at Ardmore, Indian Territory, while resisting arrest.

Another example of the way John Public failed to tremble in the presence of thugs took place on May 1, 1884, at Medicine Lodge, Kansas, a small community in the southern part of the state. Four masked men rode into town that morning, intending to hold up the Medicine Valley Bank. They met resistance right from the start. They killed cashier George Geppert and mortally wounded bank president E. Wylie Payne, but they left their leader dead on the bank steps.

The other three rode away, but were pursued by a posse of angry citizens, reinforced by Texas cowboys, for Medicine Lodge was a trail town, with the drives passing through.

The quarry was surrounded in the Gypsum Hills southwest of town. The trio meekly surrendered. Unfortunately for them, bank president Payne succumbed to his wounds about sundown. The coroner's verdict the next day was that the three prisoners came "to their deaths by hanging at the hands of a mob of persons, identity unknown."

The outlaw who was killed on the bank steps turned out to be John Henry Brown, city marshal of Caldwell, also a trail town in Kansas. One of the trio who was hanged was his deputy, Ben Wheeler. The other two were cowboys, Billy Smith and John Wesley.

News that the Caldwell lawmen had turned to moonlighting by robbing banks in neighboring towns was a sensation. John Henry Brown had built up a good reputation in Caldwell, but was reputed to have been a former gunman with Billy the Kid in the Lincoln County war.

At least they have not been immortalized in folk songs. Nor were others, like the Burrows brothers, who robbed trains, women, children, and banks in the Southwest; the Sontag brothers, who were thorns in the sides of Wells Fargo and the Pinkertons in the upper Midwest in the 1890s; Bill Doolin and his cutthroats, who took over for a time where the Daltons left off and ended up in about the same place. Being unsung, their names are not household words like the others. Almost to a man, they ended up slain by officers or in prison.

Not the least of the outlaw bands was the Wild Bunch. In

fact, it probably was the toughest of them all. Its wide and varying membership could list the greatest number of crimes of any such gangs.

Some of the more prominent members had names easy to remember:

Robert or George Parker, alias Butch Cassidy, described as affable, gentlemanly, who took a victim's money with a smile at gunpoint. He is sometimes regarded as the Wild Bunch leader;

Harvey Logan, alias Kid Curry, who was actually the leader;

Big Nose George Curry;

Harry Longbaugh, alias the Sundance Kid;

Ben Kilpatrick, the Tall Texan;

Tom Ketchum, alias Black Jack.

And so on. They were ruffians who gloried in fancy names and worked hard to build reputations as very tough hombres. They held up stagecoaches. They robbed banks. They looted trains. They held up citizens, rolled drunks in alleys.

One of their most sensational feats, one that ranks with the sixty-thousand-dollar haul by Collins and Bass at Big Springs, took place near Malta, Montana, in July 1901. Kid Curry led the Bunch when a Northern Pacific express was stopped and more than forty thousand dollars taken from the express car.

However, there was a flaw. There usually seems to be one in the exploits of outlaws. The loot was not in readily spendable gold as had been the coins taken in the Big Springs job years earlier. These were bills. They looked like ready cash. They were crisply new. They were so new they hadn't been signed at the banks that had issued them. Efforts to forge the signatures of the bankers usually were clumsy and had a tendency to put the Pinkertons close on the trail of the guilty.

They never quite got over laughing at the Bunch for that one. Then there was the time they robbed a train at Tipton, Wyoming, blowing up an express car whose door a spunky messenger refused to open. Then they blew up the safe. They blew it so completely that the air was filled with greenbacks being swept away by the wind, with the outlaws scrambling through the brush in an effort to salvage something for their efforts.

Kid Curry and two pals robbed a train at Parachute, Colorado, in the spring of 1904. They were cornered by a posse. The Kid's pals escaped, but he committed suicide. News that Curry had taken his own life sent a shock through the outlaw world. Why, the Kid had been the best, the toughest. Hard as they come. He was the man who had fought a fist fight with rough, old Pike Landusky, a lawman for whom a town in Montana was named. The Kid got licked, of course, taking a terrible beating, but he sure squared up with Pike Landusky. He got himself a gun and killed Mr. Landusky, the latter being unarmed at the moment.

The cold-blooded murder had given the Kid premier standing in those circles that believed devoutly in the creed that good guys do not deserve any kind of a break, not even a chance. This is not to give the impression that Mr. Landusky was exactly a good guy. He is said to have slain an unsuspecting Indian and to have made a tobacco pouch of the red man's skin. The number of persons who have claimed to have tamped tobacco into their pipes from Pike Landusky's copperskin pouch is said to be amazing.

Butch Cassidy rode with the Bunch in bank robberies and train holdups, and spent his time hiding from the law in such places as Hole in the Wall, Robbers Roost, and Star Valley. He finally fled to South America, along with the Sundance Kid and a woman named Etta Place. There they took advantage of their training in the States by holding up mine paymasters and such until they met the inevitable end. This came in bleak Bolivia where they were trapped by *soldados*. The Sundance Kid died game. Cassidy took the Kid Curry route, killing himself.

As for some of the others: Black Jack Ketchum, hanged at Clayton, New Mexico, April 26, 1901; Big Nose George Curry, killed by a posse in Utah; Ben Kilpatrick, killed by an express messenger while attempting a Texas holdup; Lonny Logan, a lesser member, riddled by Pinkerton bullets at Dodson, Missouri, February 28, 1900.

And so it went with other criminals who attached themselves to the Bunch from time to time. The list of prison sentences, escapes, murders, pursuits by posses, gunfights with sheriffs and Pinkertons, would fill pages. Much loot was taken, little of it was in their pockets when they were run to earth. Write your own moral. Coin a phrase. Such as: Crime Does Not Pay.

The outlaw spirit did not die with the fading of the frontier, of course. The sad truth is that the lesson has not been learned. The holdups of those days seem to be small potatoes in comparison with modern events. Bank robberies have become so commonplace, especially in big cities, they rate scarcely more than a paragraph in the newspapers unless the loot is on a major scale or the circumstances out of the ordinary.

The one that topped them all was the seven-million-dollar train robbery that was staged in England in 1963. About a score of the participants have been arrested over the space of half a dozen years for that one. Jesse James, the Daltons, the Youngers, must turn over in their graves at the thought of how easy the pickings would be if only they hadn't been born too soon.

Then, again, it might occur to them that their path of crime led only to the grave and that the jails and prisons are overflowing with inmates.

Many persons eagerly accept incredible tales that some of these criminals did not meet the fate history has recorded. They believe stories that Jesse James did not fall dead with Bob Ford's bullet in his back, but lived to a ripe old age in peace and quiet —on the profits of his misdeeds, no doubt. Some stories have it that he turned up in California. Others have Texas as the scene of his resurrection. Their belief is that the grave in Missouri is occupied by the body of someone else.

According to those "in the know," Butch Cassidy did not kill himself in Bolivia. Wyoming old-timers are quoted as solemnly saying that Butch came back to his old stamping grounds, not as an outlaw, but as a peaceful cowboy who rode in off the range to drink and pass the time of day with his old friends at the bar, then rode off into the sunset again.

The same fantastic beliefs cling to Sam Bass, Billy the Kid, and almost every other lawless character who died by violence. Some persons just don't seem to want to let them die with their boots on.

CHAPTER 11

HERE'S HOW!

And then there was John Barleycorn.
The old West had many faces. It was a bold and daring West.
That, beyond a doubt. It was a peaceful West—although, ad-
mittedly, this could be only applied in some places after the
Vigilantes had acted. It was a reverent, God-fearing West. A
cowboy's complaint when he first viewed Ogallala, that there
were thirty saloons and "not one church steeple" in sight, did
not hold true in the majority of settlements.

However, it must also be admitted that in boom towns, such
as Denver, Cheyenne, and the like, the fandango parlors and
bordellos outnumbered the religious edifices by wide margins.
But, while there were the Wesley Hardins, the Mattie Silks, the
Ben Thompsons, the Sally Purples, there were also the Father
de Smets, the Marcus Whitmans, and other devoted men and
women who gave their lives to preaching the word in the wilderness.

The West had its benign face. Beggars fared well on frontier
streets. It had its harsh face. It hung men for offenses that draw
merely a slap on the wrist from the law in present-day courts. It
revered women and children and strung up horse thieves. It
rigidly observed the Sabbath, but on Saturday nights, it had fun
shooting at the feet of dudes and Indians.

And it drank its liquor straight. The West, let's face it, was
a drinking West. True, it was the home of prohibition. The
Kansas of wild Dodge and Abilene and Ellsworth and Hays
City, was the birthplace of Carry Nation, the saloon window-

smasher, and was one of the first western states to go dry. But it was also the home of the bootlegger and the speakeasy. Nobody who really wanted to imbibe had to look far to find means of quenching his thirst.

The West prided itself on being able to hold its liquor. It would seem that a sizable proportion of the male population had considerable training in this respect. Perhaps overtraining, at times. Some of the citizens of Leadville once decided to drink Oscar Wilde under the table, when that celebrity visited the mining camp on a lecture tour. They considered him an easy mark because of the ruffled sleeves, mincing manner, etc. You know the answer to that one. Mr. Wilde, his ruffles still unruffled, delivered his lecture on schedule that evening while his drinking partners remained sleeping peacefully on the barroom floor.

The West had no monopoly, on its knowledge of John Barleycorn, but the deeper one goes into its doings and undoings, the heavier the evidence grows, gallon by gallon, that the frontier moved westward on a wave of alcohol.

The journals of Geiger and Bryarly tell of taking on fifteen gallons of whisky at Fort Kearney in '49 and jettisoning tools and some food to make room for the jugs. Their company hit cold weather, with rain, and there was a great clamor for a few snorts on one particularly raw morning, but only those on stock guard were granted a brimming horn to drive the chill from their bones.

However, the investment was considered worth while when they reached the South Platte ford, and gazed with dismay at the expanse of surging water. The booze was dealt out generously. Fortified with this Dutch courage, the crossing was made successfully without loss of even those who had got a little high. In fact, there was singing and whooping instead of apprehension during the operation.

Fur traders in the beaver days packed along barrels of whisky or sometimes grain alcohol, which they diluted with whatever was handy. Some of their problems involved keeping such prize cargo out of the hands of semi-friendly Indians who insisted on moving in on them at times for social purposes. One outfit hastily buried the kegs when they discovered they were about to be visited by a large party of Sioux. They had to tough it out for days, because their guests lingered on. Eventually, they had their wish to be alone. Digging up the kegs, they proceeded on their way, reviving their spirits, no doubt, with libations.

Whisky, of course, was the leading stimulant, and it came in all flavors and makes. The cowboys of a trail outfit strung up an itinerant trader whose product they had bought at two bits a drink when he showed up with his wagon and barrel along the way. Someone happened to peek into the barrel and discovered quids of tobacco floating there to give the concoction tang and body. Also the head of a rattlesnake. Often such hootch was merely alcohol, diluted with water and flavored with paprika and brown sugar.

However, whisky was far from the exclusive beverage. Enough champagne was drunk on the Plains, and, if it had been dumped into the South Platte all at once it probably would have washed Julesburg to a new site down the river. The Grand Duke Alexis was by no means the first to bring that form of heady wine to the West. Memoirs of Army officers tell of special events being toasted in champagne at Fort Kearney.

Of course, men in the ranks preferred whisky for their normal libations and got away with it in considerable quantities. Whisky for troops in the field was drawn from supplies at Fort Kearney in amounts as high as seven barrels at a time. But, champagne was the status drink when citizens or officers were able to afford it. Champagne flowed heavily in the boom mining camps such as the two Virginia Citys, Leadville, and Tombstone.

Ships brought the vintage around the horn, unloading it on the *embarcaderos* at San Francisco and Sacramento by the thousands of cases, when those places were much more in need of other necessities. Champagne toasted the big strikes in the Mother Lode at Grass Valley, at Sonora, at Placerville, and at Whisky Flat, despite its name.

Bubbling glasses were lifted at Virginia City, Nevada, when the discovery of the Big Bonanza was confirmed in the *Territorial Enterprise* by Dan De Quille, the famed newspaper mining expert, who was an associate on the staff of that publication of Mark Twain. De Quille was asked to enter the Consolidated Virginia mine and measure the bonanza, which had been blocked out. He cut his original estimate in half for the sake of conservatism, placing the value of the find at approximately $116 million. His original figure proved to be nearer the truth. The

huge block of rich silver ore did not take up anything like the
space that cases of incoming champagne occupied in the ore-
wagons jerk-line freighters used to haul cargo over the Sierra
Nevada from the steamboat docks at Sacramento. Virginia City
swam in champagne—and other beverages—until the bonanza was
exhausted.

So did Virginia City, Montana, although there it was gold, not
silver, they toasted. To this day, souvenir hunters pick up frag-
ments of champagne bottles in the brush around the big boom
camps. Rhyolite, Nevada, in the pass above Death Valley, was
a champagne town. The big find around Rhyolite, the last time
this writer passed that way, was to come upon the neck, or even
the whole body of a champagne magnum. These had been pretty
well prospected, but the remains of the ordinary fifths were
plentiful in the sage and creosote.

Rhyolite flamed like a rocket when Shorty Harris made the
Bullfrog strike. Some of the greenish "jewelry" ore, streaked
with wire gold, was on display at the Bottle House, although the
Bullfrog had petered out years before. The Bottle House? It
was built of bottles, naturally. Bottles of all kinds, champagne,
whisky, gin, beer. Rhyolite was a champagne town in the beginning, then turned to whisky as the Bullfrog began producing
more *borrasca* (worthless rock) then bonanza. Presently it was
on a beer diet and when the citizens could not even afford that
it became a ghost town with the Bottle House standing as a
monument to the past.

There was another Bottle House. This was a half dugout,
down in the heart of Death Valley itself, near Stovepipe Wells.
It had been a barroom in its day, catering to forty-mule teamsters
and cross-country freighters who made the long haul from Owens
Valley. In winter, that is. Stovepipe Wells closed for the summer,
and closed early in the season. Who could keep beer cold in
those days at temperatures up to 130 in the shade?

The West did not overlook other forms of indulgence. Gin,
rum, and brandy were next on the list of popularity after whisky.
Buffalo Bill, when he was scouting for Carr's 5th Cavalry, was
sent back to Laramie to buy supplies which proved to consist of
five gallons of whisky, five gallons of brandy, and two cases
of Old Tomcat gin. Proving that the Army was not entirely
addicted to whisky as a stimulant.

There were times, of course, when the available supply of the usual forms of thirst-quenchers failed. In such cases it was often necessary to fall back on bitters to keep throats from parching until the next shipment of booze, probably delayed by Indian trouble, arrived. Hostetter's, Log Cabin, Plantation, and Tansy Bitters were among brands popular on the frontier.

Bitters were usually carried by many of the saloons as a reserve supply. That source failing, many druggists usually could produce a bottle, if needed, from their stock. The frontier doctors often carried a supply sufficient to tide over a patient in need. Bitters, or "tonic," under many brand names, was regularly prescribed by many physicians to female patients who complained of lethargy, fainting spells, lack of interest in housework, inability to appreciate husbands, etc. The "tonics," which were usually about eighty-proof alcohol, seemed to work miracles—temporarily, at least. When the effects wore off, the only remedy, of course, was more of the same.

Eugene Ware's adventures as an officer during the Indian wars include the sad tale of the bitter end to a stock of bitters. Artemus Ward, the humorist, stagecoaching west to learn how the persons who had followed Horace Greeley's advice were faring, alighted at Fort Kearney during a whisky draught.

When the great man, accompanied by Ware and other officers, approached the post bar to toast the occasion in the appropriate manner, the extent of the tragedy became plain. The only beverage in the place was Hostetter's Bitters.

Artemus Ward, questioning the bartender, learned that the supply consisted of eighteen bottles of Hostetter's. This, it developed, was exactly what Mr. Ward needed to assuage his thirst and that of his fellow passengers, who greeted him back aboard the coach with open arms, and at once began diminishing the contents of the eighteen bottles.

However, bitters, brandy, and Tomcat Gin to the contrary, it was whisky on which the West floated. While Kentucky products held a high place in sales appeal, imports from Tennessee, Georgia, and other states below the Mason-Dixon line were highly regarded also. In fact, Tennessee moonshine was much favored, as it was later during national prohibition when it went by many names, the most popular being white mule.

Some concoctions were stilled or stirred together in the West.

Forty-rod was the usual term for it. A libation the mountain men drank came to be known as Taos Lightning because of the way it got immediate results. Some of the Mormons who opened trading posts along the trail, and who did not drink because it was forbidden in their religion, sold an equally potent mixture referred to as Mountain Thunder. It was also placed under the generic term of panther juice, which included many varieties.

Rum was a favorite drink of many, and the truth is it probably averaged of much higher quality than whisky, for much of it came up the Missouri on steamboats, or up the Platte and down the Sante Fe trail in wagons, and was keel-aged, having been shipped out of New Orleans after arriving from the islands. Beer, of course, was the volume drink. Breweries sprang up almost as swiftly as did brothels in the boom camps.

However, there were teetotalers. Jack Crawford, the poet scout, who wrote verses concerning his activities, carried a quart of whisky on a dangerous ride with dispatches from Cheyenne to Crook's army during the Sioux campaign. The quart was a gift for Buffalo Bill Cody, who was scouting for Crook, from Colonel Jones, owner of the Jones House in Cheyenne. Cody remarked as he began sampling the contents that Jones used rare judgment because Crawford was the only man he knew who could have brought the bottle through unopened. Crawford was a teetotaler.

Another famed scout, California Joe, went to the opposite extreme. He imbibed too freely and nearly disrupted Custer's expedition against the Indians on the Washita by mistaking troops he was supposed to be guiding for hostiles and opening fire on them.

Saloons, of course, were where the conviviality reigned. They sprang up with mushroom speed wherever two or three home-steaders halted their wagons to discuss the possibility of staking claims and forming the nucleus of a settlement. They were on hand, sometimes in the form of a plank laid on two kegs, or a spigoted barrel in the tail of a wagon, when the stampeders came into Cherry Creek, Alder Gulch, Sun Mountain, or Bodie.

Some developed into glittering, gilded establishments with plate-glass mirrors and crystal chandeliers. Nothing was too opulent for the carbonate kings at Leadville and Denver. Virginia City, Nevada, had its Bucket of Blood for the bonanza barons.

Tombstone sported its Birdcage, which is still in existence as a tourist attraction as is the Bucket of Blood. There was the ornate Gold Room in Cheyenne, which Hickok is said to have wrecked during a spree. Many establishments all over the West claimed to have the longest bar or the biggest mirrors or the fanciest chandeliers. Some had silver dollars set in their bars or even in the floors.

Many examples of ornate bars are to be seen in the casinos of Las Vegas and Reno, where they offer new courage to the dice and blackjack and slot players. One excellent example of a massive bar, surprisingly, stands in a crossroad beer parlor in the remote, cotton-ginning town of Pahrump, not far from Death Valley.

Leadville, high in the Rockies, sported some very ornate places for whiling away the time, largest of which was the Great Saloon, which had a gambling hall, dance hall, and theater, and luxurious rooms on the floors above. It catered to the better element, allowing no vulgarity or rough stuff, so it is said. These rules limited its clientele, for Leadville, in the days of the big strikes, was as hairy as they come.

The Orient in Tombstone was a gathering place for people like the Earps, sometimes the Clantons, and others who packed guns and knew how to use them, but its principal purpose was to serve drinks, along with the use of a few gambling tables, whereas the Birdcage had a stage, girls, and private rooms.

Chalk Beeson's Long Branch in Dodge City is often represented as a gaudy dance hall, swarming with tinseled percentage girls. It was in fact a drab, narrow establishment with a small bar at the right and a shelf as a back bar over which hung a framed mirror.

Other saloons which had considerable reputations or notoriety as places of pleasure and conviviality were also ugly, cheerless, unwashed, unswept traps with rude bars, stained with tobacco juice, tarnished foot rails, and cuspidors that had needed attention for days. Their back bars were often made of the remains of packing boxes, with cracked mirrors, and sported sucker glassware, meaning beer mugs and shot glasses with thick walls and bottoms that held less than half of their apparent capacity.

Good whisky commanded prices of from two to four bits, according to the opulence of the town or camp. The carbonate and bonanza kings generally scorned such petty piking and usually ordered by the full bottle. There is little evidence they bought for the house, a custom that is popularly ascribed to them, but seems to have been wishful thinking rather than reality.

Then, of course, there were the ladies. The scarlet ladies, the ladies of the night, the lost souls, the girls of pleasure. In other words, the prostitutes, sometimes referred to as harlots or whores. They operated in places known as bordellos, brothels, chippie joints, houses of ill fame, and many other terms.

Julesburg had its line after its portable Hell on Wheels had moved on to Sidney, albeit a small one. It had such competition it never amounted to much. Ogallala, down the river, was a wild cowboy town where one did not have to look more than beyond one's nose to find any type of diversion, including pistol play. However, in winter, Ogallala died.

Not so Denver. Considerably farther from Julesburg, nevertheless it was a comfortable eight-hour ride on the U.P. local, with a smoking car, a bar, and a roaring stove, which the train crew kept well stocked, to sit by and maybe a little poker to while away the trip.

When one alighted at Denver he was in a big city. A metropolis. Hansom cabs in which to ride. A variety of hotels from which to choose. Glittering music halls, opulent saloons, which were open twenty-four hours a day, come blizzard, come storm. There was the magnificent Tabor Grand Opera House for awe-struck eyes. One might even get a glimpse of Senator H. A. W. Tabor himself, the carbonate king. Also of Baby Doe Tabor, whose romance with the senator rivaled anything that even the *Police Gazette* or *Frank Leslie's Weekly* printed.

And, of course, there was the line. It stretched along Holladay Street, and its leading lights carried such names as Mattie Silk, Molly B'damn, Velvetass Rose, Slanting Annie, and Red Stockings. Scores of prostitutes beckoned from doors and windows of the ugly, unpainted, false-fronted shacks they occupied.

Some of the more elaborate establishments had their own business cards, which were liberally distributed. Visitors might gaze upon a brass band being driven by on a circus wagon which advertised the "virtues" of a brothel.

Holladay Street had been named in honor of Ben Holladay, the stagecoach king. He may have basked in the renown, but after his death his heirs took a dim view of the honor and swung enough influence to compel the city council to change the name of the thoroughfare to the prosaic title Market Street.

Leaving the ladies to their various devices, the visitor had his choice of saloons, or cafés, as some preferred to be known. These ranged from grand to the dregs. The same went for the gambling halls. Faro bank was the popular game, reputed to carry better odds in favor of the player than other forms of chance. Other games that are offered to this day at gambling houses everywhere, were available—stud or draw, twenty-one (blackjack), keno, chuck-a-luck, dice, roulette, slots, wheels of fortune, policy drawings and many others.

After a few days in Denver, the recreation seeker could use his return ticket, if he'd been wise enough to buy a round trip, and head home, broke, but educated.

If one really wanted to see life in the raw, there was the hog ranch on the Sweetwater River. This was operated by Ella Watson, originally of Rawlins, who became better known by the adopted title of Cattle Kate. She was one of the few females in the West to die at the hands of lynchers.

She was a woman of considerable strength and ample proportions, who could handle a horse and shoot as well as the average man. The brothel she established in partnership with one Jim Averill was a one-woman affair usually, although at times other prostitutes held forth there.

The profits of the hog ranch proved to be far greater than what could normally be expected of such an enterprise so far from population centers. Only a man hunting trouble, or wanted by the law, would wander so many miles back into the coulees. Furthermore, the ranch was a stopping point for men traveling to and from Hole-in-the-Wall. These gentry did not favor the presence of strangers when they visited the ranch for entertainment and refreshments.

That was the heyday of the big cow outfits in Wyoming. The owners were being surrounded by homesteaders, patch-saddle ranchers, wolf hunters, and drifters, who always seemed to have meat in the pot when they sat down to a meal. It wasn't buffalo meat. They called it slow elk. But elk were about as scarce as buffalo. Cattle were very numerous. Other men's cattle.

Beef on the hoof was disappearing with increasing regularity.

Trails of cloven hoofs led frequently to the corrals at the hog ranch, then away in the direction of Cheyenne or Sidney, where disposal through shady dealers was not difficult.

Some owners even saw cattle wearing their brands in the hog ranch corrals. Kate and Averill had grown arrogant, believing they had the ranchers buffaloed. They began taunting the owners, challenging them to do anything about it. They had the backing and sympathy of the small ranchers, and Kate felt sure nobody would turn a hand against a woman, even though she was a rustler. Such a thing just wasn't done in the West.

She was wrong. The ranch had visitors one day. Twenty of them. They asked Kate and Averill to take a ride with them. Kate just knew they were bluffing. She continued to needle them. She kept it up until the noose was around her neck. Then she became a little worried.

"Aw, you men, stop tryin' to skeer me!" she said a trifle shakily. "You know you—"

The horse was quirted from beneath her, as was the mount on which Averill sat. They died slowly, clutching at the nooses that strangled them.

The lynching was the spark that touched off the Johnson County war. It was the greatest and the last land war between big and small ranchers. The big owners imported gunmen by the special trainload, who were surrounded and humiliated by the greater number of opponents. The country became more amenable to small settlers.

At the opposite end of the scale was another female—Carrie Nation. Even to this day, you'll find saloons that have gilded replicas of hatchets fixed to walls, or above back bars, bearing Carrie's name. She was a woman of sizable proportions also, with a firm jaw and a will to match, as well as a total disregard for jeers and catcalls. In all other respects, she differed from Cattle Kate, especially in the matter of morals. She was a pillar of rectitude. She was a reformer.

John Barleycorn has had his ups and downs through history. Attempt after attempt has been made to bury him in a drunkard's grave. The temperance movement started in the East long before the Civil War, with Maine adopting prohibition in 1846. Other eastern states followed suit, although some modified the regulations after a few years. The Eighteenth Amendment dried the entire nation—theoretically—in 1920, but was repealed after a little more than thirteen years when the citizens decided it was not enforceable, and was putting great wealth and power in the hands of hoodlums like the Al Capone mob. It certainly brought into full flower the speakeasy, bathtub gin, and home-brewed beer.

Many sections of the nation are still dry, legally. Sales of liquor are regulated in various ways from state to state, city to city, county to county, and even township to township. John Barleycorn is still on the defensive, but he has been in that category for centuries. John is very durable.

The state of Kansas went dry in 1881, the citizens being hopeful of putting an end to its reputation as a swinging state, this reputation having been built up energetically from the time the first trail drivers crossed the Arkansas River and headed for places like Abilene, Hays, Dodge, and many other hot spots.

Of course, the bootleggers and moonshiners moved in at once. The cattle drives eventually swung west into the higher country where there were not many towns, heading for Fort Lyon, Granada, or Kit Carson to ship their beef or maybe on to Ogallala on the U.P. But it wasn't because of the lack of forty-rod that they swung away from Kansas. There was still plenty to be had. It was that Kansas had become a sod-busting state, with barbed wire blocking the trails and stock inspectors at every county line with palms out, threatening to quarantine the Longhorns for fever ticks.

It was not until the late nineties that Carrie Nation was moved to revive the prohibition cause from its moribund state. Carrie lived in Medicine Lodge when she became aware of her powers as the leader of a cause. She first organized the women to protest the use of strong drink.

Carrie and her followers sang:

> They who tarry at the wine cup,
> They who tarry at the wine cup,
> They who tarry at the wine cup,
> They have sorrow, they have woe.

Soon the ladies became militant and started marching on places where grog was available. At first, Carrie used a hammer to smash windows, but later on the hatchet became her emblem.

The theme song of her organization became *John Brown's Body Lies Mouldering in the Grave.*

Carrie became famous nationwide, so much so that her attentions became welcome by saloonkeepers. When they learned their establishments were to be visited they passed the word around, knowing this assured them a full house for the evening. The word, full, is used advisedly. The cash registers jingled merrily. A few panes of glass were a small price to pay for the rush in trade.

Carrie met her Waterloo in the person of stagecoach driver D. R. "Cannonball" Green, for whom Greensburg, Kansas, is named. Green loved to smoke cigars. He had Carrie as a passenger when he was puffing away at a particularly villainous, black variety of the weed, and enjoying it thoroughly. Carrie was not captivated. Being a woman of instant decision and action, she snatched the offending cigar from Cannonball's lips and hurled it into the roadside dust.

Thereupon Cannonball yanked the horses to a halt, jammed on the brake, lifted the plump Carrie down from the seat she had been occupying, and set her on her feet in the dust with the ruined smoke. Boarding the stage, he drove away, leaving her standing there fuming. U.S. Route 54 in Kansas is still known locally as Cannonball Highway.

## CHAPTER 12

## SUPERMEN AND OTHER PESTS

Barring mechanical devices, such as the jeep, dune buggy, helicopter, etc., the fastest means of travel between two points in rough country is still the horse. It was the only means of rapid transport in the frontier days. Nearly all the male population, and a sizable proportion of the distaff side, thought no more of stepping into the saddle to ride to the mercantile or saloon, than the modern man or wife think of climbing into the family car and heading for the supermarket or the beer joint.

Buggies, buckboards, drays, spring wagons, Pittsburgh and Conestoga schooners, and an endless variety of other vehicles carried their share of persons bound on business or pleasure, of course, but the equestrian was in the majority. He was as commonplace in the West as run-over boot heels.

A man who mentioned feeling a little stove-up after twenty or thirty miles in the saddle caused raised eyebrows, and his wife was secretly advised to see to it that old Charlie take it a little easier, and that it might be as well if he had Doc Sawbones look him over the next time the medic happened by on his rounds.

Next to riding the four-legged steeds, men took the greatest pride in their skill at judging the qualities of the equines in the bargaining rings. Horse trading was an art. It also had aspects of thimblerigging, conmanship, and unadulterated fraud. Nearly every town had its trading days when animals were brought in from near and far to the ring, which was usually in a large open lot off the main drag or a livery stable corral.

Trading day was a time of high entertainment, with jugs passing around, men meeting old friends they hadn't seen in days, and wives resigning themselves to most anything happening—and it often did. Fist fights were commonplace. Sometimes even gunplay. Sharpers who showed up in bib overalls and barefoot, looking like they'd just emerged from a gopher hole, and talking like it, and leading a flea-bitten burro, might trade up into a fine stallion before the day was over, then buy the burro back from the original receiver and depart for the next town and the next group of suckers.

Horses were also raced. At any time and any place, and at the drop of a hat. The Indians, who never believed in gambling in a small way, were known to bet not only their tepees but all its contents, including their wives, on the outcome of a race. Sometimes they won, and went away with the white man's saddle and shirt. Sometimes they lost, and went away nearly naked, but unconcerned.

Ringers were rung in. A knob-kneed, rat-tailed cayuse that apparently hardly had the strength to lean against a post would outrun a jack rabbit when turned loose. The tinhorns would vanish when they lost, leaving the stakeholder with a wad of worthless strips cut from newspapers instead of the greenbacks he believed had been handed him. All these were part of the world of horses.

Riding twelve to fourteen hours a day was routine on cattle ranches. A cowhand rolled out at daybreak, finished a breakfast that often consisted only of black, scalding coffee and a Bull Durham cigarette, roped a cantankerous horse from the corral if they were working out of the home ranch, or from the *remuda* the wrangler hazed in if they were on roundup. He then forced a "candystick," or bit, into the steed's unwilling mouth, cinched down forty pounds of saddle, which was single or double-rigged, according to preference, endured the teeth-jarring, spine-grinding jolts as the bronc registered his daily protest by bucking vigorously for a spell. Then the cowpoke rode off to work with a noon meal of cold biscuits and beans in his possession. At dark, after a day of mending fence, digging postholes, packing salt, doctoring worms, repairing windmills, and a few score of other chores, he unsaddled, ate a dinner of whatever the cook decided for the day, went to bed, and arose at first hint of dawn to go through the same routine.

Work like that hardened a man, especially in certain places. He became part horse, part human. Eugene Ware, as a cavalryman, rode sixty-five miles in a day, campaigning against the Sioux, and, on arriving at Julesburg for the night, found the residents preparing for an evening of dancing. He joined the fun. After midnight, the regular caller being indisposed, he called the squares. At reveille, he was back in the saddle for another day of chasing the wily red man. On another occasion, he rode one hundred miles in a day to attend a court-martial, but that was only commonplace.

Some of the thrilling tales of distance riding come from the short existence of the Pony Express. In those cases, more was at stake than delivering the mail. The riders were gambling with their lives.

The longest and best authenticated ride was that by "Pony Bob" Haslam during the bloody Paiute war in Nevada. Haslam began his iron-man feat at Friday's Station below Lake Tahoe in California. Heading east, by way of Carson City, he found the crew at Buckland's Station in a panic because of the proximity of a war party. The relay rider refused to accept the leg eastward and Haslam continued across the desert to Smith's Creek where he found a rider willing to go on with the mail.

Haslam had covered 190 miles with little rest. He took an eight-hour breather and headed west with the mail. At Cold Springs, where he had changed horses on his eastward leg, he found the station crew massacred. He continued the ride, picking up a companion at one nearly deserted station, and reached Buckland's Station safely, having traveled 380 miles in two days.

Haslam added to his riding feats after the Pony was discontinued. There were other lesser-known Pony routes still in existence. For a year he rode the ten-hour mail route from Friday's Station to Virginia City. Alexander Majors, in his memoirs, says that Haslam later rode a twenty-three mile route from Reno to Virginia City daily in one hour, using relays of fast ponies. He had numerous narrow escapes from Indians. During a stint over the dangerous Salt Lake-Virginia City (Montana) division,

Haslam witnessed the hanging of Joseph Slade by the Vigilantes at the Montana mining camp.

The Pony Express ride attributed to Buffalo Bill Cody at an early age in Wyoming has so many parallel features to Haslam's feat it brings up the question: did Cody actually make such a ride, or was Pony Bob's deed appropriated by Ned Buntline in one of his novels, and became a part of the Cody legend?

Jim Moore, another Pony rider, figured in a similar incident, staying in the saddle for 280 miles to and from the Julesburg station when relay riders had been killed by Indians.

The Pony's greatest long-distance feat was accomplished when news of Abraham Lincoln's election was carried from St. Joseph, Missouri, to the end of the western telegraph line at Fort Churchill, Nevada, in seven days, seventeen hours, a distance of eighteen hundred miles. The Pony's regular schedule over this route varied from eleven to eighteen days, according to season. News of the election was carried from St. Joseph to Denver, six hundred and sixty-five miles in two days, twenty-one hours. The last ten miles were covered in thirty-one minutes by relays of swift horses. All these heroic deeds were not needed again. Less than a year later, the Western Union had spanned the continent with wires, and the Pony was no more.

A feat of horsemanship that is still regarded with awe was performed by one François Xavier Aubrey, a Santa Fe trader. An ox train usually required ten to twelve weeks to make the journey between Independence and Santa Fe. The average good horseman could cover the eight hundred miles in about three weeks, depending on weather and Indian danger.

Aubrey set out on December 22, 1847, to see what he could do. He was accompanied by several others, but they turned back after a few days when Indians stole their pack animals. Despite a two-day delay, Aubrey arrived at Independence inside of two weeks. That only whetted his desire to see what he could *really* do.

He returned to Santa Fe with a caravan, then started for Independence alone on horseback. This time, he made it in eight days, ten hours. He rode three horses and two mules to death, walked forty miles to find fresh mounts, and got what sleep he could in the saddle.

He still wasn't content. He later made the trip in five days, sixteen hours, using relays, although one relay had been killed by Cheyennes at Point of Rocks. He killed six horses on that trip and won a bet of either one thousand or five thousand dollars, according to the differing versions. Aubrey's Crossing on the Arkansas River marks where he forded. He was later slain by a newspaper editor in the La Fonda Hotel in Santa Fe after a dispute.

Travel by stagecoach was never leisurely even on roads that were meant for mere passage and not, essentially, for speed. The thorough-braces on the Concords were rated as springs, but they were made of bands of tough bullhide leather of several thicknesses, and while they cushioned some of the shocks of rough travel, one of their primary functions was to steady the eternal end-for-end motion of the vehicle, particularly on the steep pitches, of which there were many. Passengers who stayed with a mail coach on one of its fast runs, day and night for a long stretch, often had an addled appearance of eyeball and garb when they finally staggered back to terra firma.

A superman, indeed, must have been the newspaperman Waterman Lily Ormsby, Jr., in spite of the middle name his parents hung on him when he was a defenseless baby. As correspondent for the New York *Herald*, he rode the first Butterfield stage from St. Louis to San Francisco. This was a distance of 2,696.5 miles, according to the meticulous Butterfield schedule, and the first run went through in September, October 1858.

The distance mentioned was surveyed at ground level and did not take into account Ormsby's vertical flights and descents during the twenty-three days and twenty hours of his journey. This up-and-down distance must have been considerable, taking into account the fact that his was the *first* journey over a trail that had been hurriedly built. Evidently none of the builders was hardy enough to test their handiwork over the entire distance as did Ormsby. The Butterfield schedule called for an average of four and one half miles an hour over the greater part of the route and a mile less in a few mountain stretches.

Ormsby made little mention of the hardships, dwelling more on the virtues of such speedy transportation. For this, he was accused by rival newspapers of painting too bright a picture in the Butterfield's favor. However, he was one of the few who seemed to have made the entire trip without stopping over in various places for rest and repairs.

There were other iron men in Concords. Ben Holladay bounced over the Overland route in one of his coaches from Salt Lake City to Atchison, 1,255 miles, in less than 7 days. He set up the best horses along the line at the swings, and prepared a special coach for the run at a cost of $2,000. It was worth it. It got newspaper space all over the nation.

Members of a convivial group who also wanted to see their names in the papers induced the Overland into putting them through by coach from Atchison to Denver in four and a half days. On special trips, such as this, the teams were changed in three minutes or somebody got chewed out.

Taking a leaf from Holladay's book, the Santa Fe railroad won an avalanche of publicity for itself back in 1905 by using the iron horse in a similar feat. Incidentally, it also made famous a talkative, publicity-loving desert prospector named Walter Scott, who became better known as Death Valley Scotty.

Scotty, never one to shun the presence of newspapermen, nor to object to being referred to as the "mysterious" Death Valley Scotty, "rented" a special train in California, saying he was in a hurry to get to Chicago to confer with his millionaire partner, who financed Scotty's activities. The train, well stocked with reporters and railroad publicity men, made the run of 2,250 miles in 44 hours, 54 minutes. Scotty became famous. The Santa Fe prospered at a cost of $5,500. Fast freights now make the run in less time. Tourists now rush to view Scotty's Castle in Death Valley, which his rich friend also financed, and many never get around to seeing the natural wonders in that fantastic slot in the earth.

But to get back to the horsebackers. Many men are credited with long, dangerous rides in emergencies. Joe Rankin, a civilian scout, worked his way through Indian lines that besieged four companies of troopers at Milk Creek, Colorado, and rode 160 miles in 27 hours to alert the Army to send help.

Kit Carson made a 500-mile forced ride from the Arkansas River to Taos to prevent ambush of a Mexican wagon train by Texans who sought to avenge defeat of their attempt to invade New Mexico. Kit is said to have been paid $300 for the trip. By whom, is not recorded.

However, despite supermen in the saddles and aboard stage-coaches, nothing on the frontier was faster than a bullet, not even an arrow. One of the most remarkable feats of marksmanship, coming at an extremely dramatic moment, is claimed for Billy Dixon, the buffalo hunter. It is described by his wife, Olive K. Dixon, in her book telling of her husband's career.

It took place during the renowned Dobe Walls fight between plainsmen and more than a thousand warriors of the allied tribes of the southern Plains. The fight began on the morning of June 26, 1874.

Many amazing events were connected with this engagement. The Walls was a trading settlement that catered to hunters who were risking their lives in order to peel hides in the stamping grounds of the Kiowa, Comanches, and prairie Apaches south of the Arkansas River. Dixon, along with Bat Masterson, who was later to win fame as a gunman sheriff at Dodge City, contemporary of Wyatt Earp, had headed to the Walls for safety, as had many other hunters when the situation became increasingly ominous.

There were twenty-nine men and one woman in the strong point. The woman was Mrs. William Olds, wife of one of the hunters. Despite the fact that hunters had been killed in their camps, and that all arrivals had stories of seeing the country alive with hostiles, everyone was sleeping soundly that night, as though they were back in peaceful Illinois, or Kentucky or Tennessee, or from wherever they had originally sprung. Every door was wide open to admit air, for the night was hot and sultry. Dixon remarked that locked doors were unheard of at the Walls. That was hardly the place for thieves. He and his companions were wrong. They had overlooked one point. There were persons around who wanted something they possessed. Their lives.

A remarkable event probably saved them all. After midnight, the cottonwood ridgepole supporting the dirt roof in Jim Hanrahan's saloon cracked with a loud sound that awakened men sleeping on the barroom floor. At least they were sure it was the ridgepole, for they spent a lot of time and effort in bracing it. The activity aroused the entire stockade, so that daybreak came before anyone thought of settling down again.

Someone happened to glance off toward the timber. And that

was it! The horizon was alive with a moving wall of color and ferocity. The Indians came in a screeching charge, hundreds of them. Feathers waving, war paint hideous in the dawn, the world alive with the drumming of the hoofs of their ponies.

But the defenders, all wide awake, had guns, and knew how to use them. These men were all marksmen. The first attack failed under withering fire from the Walls. Two men, who for unknown reasons had chosen to put their blankets down at a distance from the post, were instant casualties. They were slain and mutilated. The Indians of the allied tribes were brave. They charged time and again, taking heavy losses, but never reached the Walls. They finally withdrew, taking their dead and wounded.

The settlement buried its dead, nursed its own few slight wounds, and waited. More hunters came in the next day. Riders were sent to bring help from Fort Dodge. A group of Indians eventually appeared on a rise a long distance off, making rude gestures and evidently jeering the buffalo hunters and daring them to fight. The distance was too great to hear the words.

Dixon, having a reputation as a crack shot, was urged to empty at least one shell in the direction of the blasted redskins. He borrowed a .50 Sharps, his own being out of commission at the moment, and drew a long, slow bead while the bystanders waited in silence.

Boom! Every eye watched the tiny figures in the distance. An incredulous shout arose. One of the Indians had toppled from his pony. The distance was later paced off as measuring 1,538 yards. Dixon conceded that it was a "scratch" shot.

Other remarkable features about this fight: After it was over, nobody could find anything in the least wrong with the saloon ridgepole that was believed to have cracked; William Olds, husband of the only woman among the defenders, was killed accidentally by his own gun while descending a ladder from his place of lookout; Hanrahan and a man named Brown became involved in a dispute over a gun that had been loaned to Bat Masterson, and nearly came to the point of a pistol fight. This created such bad blood that the former defenders split into two factions and left the place jeering at their opposites.

Later on, Dixon was involved in the dramatic Buffalo Wallow fight on the Washita River when he and the famed scout Amos Chapman and four soldiers were besieged by a war party of

Kiowa and Comanches. Dixon finally made his way to Camp Supply and brought help. One soldier was killed. Amos Chapman lost a leg by amputation after the battle.

Luther North has related another "superman" incident that is as grim as it is remarkable. His company, pursuing a party of Spotted Tail's band when he was an officer in his brother's unit of Pawnee scouts, killed the pony of a fleeing Indian. One of the scouts, a half-breed Spanish-Pawnee named Baptist Behale, was armed only with a bow and arrow, preferring this "repeating" weapon to the single-shot Springfields the Army had issued. Behale pursued the Sioux alone and drove an arrow through his quarry's body.

The Sioux seized the projecting arrowhead, pulled the shaft entirely through his body, fitted the shaft to his bow, and fired the arrow back at Behale. It missed. Then the warrior fell dead. Surely, he was a superman. And brave.

There were giants among the cowboys also. Bill Pickett, Negro, who is regarded as perhaps the greatest bulldogger of all time, defeated one of Mexico's best fighting bulls in the arena at Mexico City for a bet of five thousand dollars. *Barehanded!* He was with the Miller Bros. 101 Ranch circus for years. He died in 1932 at the age of seventy. Cause of death: kicked in the head by a horse. Even supermen make mistakes around the wrong end of a cayuse at times.

And, of course, there are the fish stories. The present-day disciple of Izaak Walton is resigned to traveling deeper and deeper into the wilds to find a stream or lake that is not dappled with empty beer cans, used picnic plates, and such, and denuded of fish. Even as far back as 1849, one stampeder, in his diary, remarked bitterly that those ahead of him had fished out a fine mountain stream before he could try his own luck.

On a happier note, General Bisbee, telling of his days as a young officer, said that he and five other soldiers caught eighteen hundred trout in one day while fishing a stream near old Fort Fred Steele in Wyoming. That's right. *Eighteen hundred* trout in one day. Now, that was very good fishing.

Bisbee stated they sat on the bank with barbless hooks and flies and lifted out the fish, which soldiers took off the lines and prepared for the commissary. The fish averaged seven inches in length, few varying much from that size.

Then there is the story of the Oregon-bound stampeder who kept getting strikes that broke his line while attempting to replenish the larder by fishing in Snake River. Exasperated, he finally shaped a hook from heavy wagon iron, attached it to a length of strong rope, baited it with a chunk of meat from a fallen ox, and cast.

He hooked onto something too big for him to land. He tied the end of his fishing "line" to a tree on the bank of the river and hurried to camp to fetch a team of oxen with which to bring ashore his catch. Behold! When he got back to the river, tree, tackle, and a portion of the riverbank were missing.

The tale might not be too farfetched. Pacific sturgeon, running hundreds of pounds in weight, came up the Columbia River system as far as Twin Falls before modern power dams checked their migrations. Some years ago, this writer, bound for Montana, stepped suddenly on the brake as he drove down the principal street of Twin Falls, Idaho. He had glimpsed what seemed to be a side of beef, but resembled a section of a fish, hanging in the window of a meat store. It was a part of a fish. We didn't believe it for a while. That was our first experience with Snake River sturgeon.

On the other hand, there were pests on the Plains in addition to supermen. It is questionable whether it was the long, hard miles, or the mosquitos, buffalo gnats, and ticks that caused the greatest misery on the long trail. They were there in the days of '49, and are on hand today. Stampeders complained of being "teased and severely bitten" by buffalo gnats which swarmed at Ash Hollow during the big rush. Mosquito netting was used by drovers and riders and placed on the heads of oxen, horses, and mules in the Platte Valley, where the pests were in such numbers they formed clouds that glinted in the sun.

The winged pests caused many stampedes by stock along the trail, the poor beasts being driven to frenzy and to running away in search of relief from their tormenters. Human nerves were rubbed to raw edge. Insects were blamed for shortening tempers to the point where many fist and gunfights erupted for no apparent cause.

Then there were the rattlesnakes. Also the hydrophobia skunks and coyotes. General Bisbee told of the killing of seventy-three rattlesnakes in a single hunt around Fort Fred Steele in an attempt to reduce the numbers of the deadly serpents.

Rattlers were a very real hazard on the Santa Fe trail, particularly in the early days of freighting, and took a heavy toll of livestock. This peril lessened after the bullwhackers worked on the reptiles with their blacksmith whips, according to Alexander Majors. The average bullwhip was twelve to fourteen feet long, of plaited leather that was an inch and a half thick at the base, tapering to a wicked cracker, with a stock up to two feet long. A driver who could not break a rattler's neck at nearly twenty feet hung his head in shame.

Buffalo crickets, also called Mormon crickets, were encountered. Though not a menace to humans, they were often met in enormous "armies" that swarmed loathsomely over wide stretches of the trail. They were crushed under wheels and hoofs. They invaded clothing and wagons to the screams of women and children, and the yells of disgust from males.

To this day, migrations of these pests across highways in the Great Basin and Nevada offer hazards as wheels crush insects and the roadway becomes grease-slippery for vehicles. In Salt Lake City stands a monument to the seagulls, which are said to have providentially arrived to alleviate the Saints of this and other pests that were devastating grainfields.

Some travelers called these insects Mormon grasshoppers. The true grasshopper offers a far greater challenge to farmers and ranchers. In trail days they sometimes covered the land in such swarms that caravans detoured for miles, blazing new paths in attempts to avoid them—usually without success. This scourge continues to the present day.

Hydrophobia was, and is, always a hazard to man and beast. Skunks and coyotes are particularly susceptible to the malady. They abounded everywhere and were much feared by cowboys, particularly the trail crews. A cowboy might sleep in his "soogans" (quilts), his head pillowed on his warsack, confident that no rattlesnake would cross the horsehair rope he had laid in a circle around him. Experiments have shown that his confidence was more mental than real, but, at least, he slept peacefully in rattlesnake country. Not so in skunk country, particularly in the so-called "dog days" of August when rabies are supposed to be at their peak.

Until the Louis Pasteur inoculation was perfected in 1885, there was no antidote for the malady, so rabies took their toll despite the use of "mad stones," patent medicine fakes, whisky, and other antidotes that did not antidote. Rabies is an ancient disease. The early trappers feared it.

John Marsh, a doctor who was in trouble with the law in the States, was with a party of trappers in the 1830s when a mad "wolf" invaded the camp at night and bit a young New Yorker, George Holmes. The next night the animal returned. This time it attacked one of the oxen. The oxen developed rabies a few days later and died in agony. Then it was Holmes's turn. He came to such a state he could not endure the sight of water and had to be blindfolded and carried across streams. In the end, he was allowed to walk out of the camp into the wilderness and was not seen again. Some thirty fatal cases of hydrophobia from the bites of skunks were reported in a single summer around Dodge and Hays City.

Then, of course, there were such customers to deal with as tarantulas, scorpions, gila monsters, and centipedes. The venomous power of some of these had been discounted in many quarters, with some experts rating the lowly centipedes, in certain varieties, as the more lethal. We have never cared to experiment.

Then there was the fat little prairie dog. His numbers are greatly diminished now, but he has a long record of bringing disaster to horses and horsemen. His colonies once covered wide areas of prairie and plain, forcing miles of detour around him. The "picket pin" of the Plains won epithets from bull-whackers and cowboys, but he also had a place of affection in their hearts. His shrill whistling helped turn back the silence of the vast land for lonely travelers.

But he was an expense to ranch owners. It is recorded that the Spur Ranch in Texas spent more than $70,000 on poison grain to clear its 440,000 acres of his presence.

Poison! An ugly word. But the fact is that poison has been used liberally from the early days by ranchers in war against what they consider pests, and by hide hunters out to collect bounty on wolves, coyotes, cougars, and bear. And it is still being used.

More modern methods of extermination have been brought into play. A sheep rancher in Wyoming was accused of spending thousands of dollars to have eagles shot from airplanes and helicopters on the grounds that they were preying on young lambs. Hundreds of eagles were slain by this method.

But poison, along with the other inroads of civilization, has been the great destroyer of wild life in the West. Small game and jack rabbits have been so decimated in the western deserts that the surviving coyotes, bobcats, mountain lions, and even rattlesnakes, are often forced to invade settled communities in search of sustenance on rats, mice, cats, and garbage.

But, of them all, the mosquito undoubtedly has been responsible for more misery to man and beast than all the others combined.

## CHAPTER 13

## MAN AGAINST NATURE

Great feats of endurance and daring were, by no means, the prerogative of men on horseback or on the boxes of stage-coaches. Every member of the wagon caravans that made the trip from the Missouri frontier to Oregon or California in the days of the Great Medicine Road, would likely scoff at the deeds sketched in preceding chapters.

Merely getting there—to Oregon or California—was an accomplishment of such proportion that these people considered themselves a class apart. Their descendants regard themselves as a cut above the average run of the population and are prone to look down on the heirs of later arrivals who made it by stage-coach or train, or, pardon the expression, by auto.

Women and children, as a rule, rode at least part of the way during the early stages of the trail. They took to heel-and-toe travel only in the sand or rough going for the first few weeks, but by the time they reached the Raft or Humboldt rivers nearly everyone able to walk was doing so, and putting their shoulders to the wheels to give what help they could to the skin-and-bones oxen.

What is looked upon as one of the greatest, if not the greatest, feat in the history of moving wagons through trackless country took place in 1879. This was the San Juan Mormon migration. The Salt Lake City hierarchy ordered that a settlement be established on the San Juan River south of the mighty Colorado River gorges. The area was so rough that the pioneering party suffered great hardships and endured weeks of travel merely to reach the brink of the two-thousand-foot cliffs near Escalante, Utah.

A "road" was built down the cliffs at the cost of incredible labor and danger. Dugways were carved in living rock. Slits were carved wide enough for a wheel and just deep enough so as not to bind the hubs. The slits were uphill so as to prevent the vehicles from sliding off the precipice. In other places trestles were built on almost sheer walls. Many animals slipped to their deaths, but, after three months of effort, the first wagon was roped down to the river. Others followed. The river was ferried, and eventually Bluff, Utah, was founded. It is still a wide place in the road.

The two most written-about parties of trail days are the Donner and Death Valley caravans. Both parties followed the customary route up the Platte Valley, but it was not until they reached the California mountains that their real troubles began.

The Donners were bound for the mid-California country by way of a dangerous pass in the Sierra Nevadas. It was not the first company to be trapped in that area by snow. A caravan known as the Davis party set out from Council Bluffs in May 1844 and were caught by snow in the mountains in mid-November. They had started with eleven ox wagons, twenty-six men, eight women, and seventeen children.

Two groups from this party went ahead at different times, leaving three men to guard the six wagons that were still with them. Two of these men eventually fought their way over the summit, leaving Moses Schallenberger, about nineteen, alone in a rude shelter.

All survived, reaching Sutter's Fort against heavy odds. Schallenberger was rescued in the spring, having subsisted on the flesh of foxes he caught in traps that had been in one of the wagons. He also caught coyotes and tried to down their cooked flesh. Hungry as he was, he found this impossible.

The Davis party not only won through without loss of life but their ranks actually numbered two more than at the start. A baby had been born far back on the trail while crossing South Pass. A second, Elizabeth Yuba Murphy, arrived while her parents were camped on the headwaters of the Yuba River in California.

The Donner party's fortunes ran to the other extreme. The

members came struggling up the same trail two years later, fording the Platte at the Oregon crossing near where Julesburg now stands. They were members of a large caravan, bound for Oregon. A group headed by George Donner decided to swing toward California instead. Disregarding advice, they split from the main group after crossing South Pass and headed directly for the Salt Lake Basin. They knew they were late in season and knew of the narrow escape of the Davis people.

Maps showed it would be much shorter to cut directly west than to take the known trail by way of Fort Hall and Raft River to the Humboldt. This, of course, was two years before the rush of '49 indelibly marked the trail.

They were influenced in their decision by the eloquence of a young man, twenty-three, named Lansford Hastings. It was for him that the deadly Hastings Cutoff was named. His powers of speech were far greater than his actual knowledge of the route he championed vigorously.

The Donners did not know it at the time, but they lost the race back in the rough canyons of the Wasatch Mountains. They took wrong turns and spent weeks fighting their way clear, when others covered the same distance in days. They literally had to lift the wagons by manpower up and down some of the ridges.

They finally reached the California sierra in October. Ahead lay a mountain pass that is a funnel through which the moisture-laden storms from the Pacific break against the peaks and annually deposit some of the heaviest snow packs on the continent. They were short on food and their oxen were already about finished. However, back of them lay a bleak desert which also had its icy winds and blizzards in winter. They had no choice but to attempt the ascent of the sierra.

And so they set out, twenty-seven men, seventeen women, forty-three children. *Forty-three* children? And the Davis party had included seventeen children with two more arriving on the way. There was no race suicide among the early pioneers.

The party fought its way up the Truckee River. Snow was falling on the pass ahead. An advance party made it as far as the summit, but waist-deep snow drove them back. From then on it was a story of starvation and terror. Finally cannibalism. Eventually, ten men and five women made a try for it, some deserting children and wives or husbands. One man was abandoned in an overnight camp during the trip, and was described as sitting by the campfire smoking his pipe while the other fourteen continued fighting their way onward through the snow.

Of the remaining nine men, only two emerged alive from the mountains. Cannibalism had been practiced as the weaker died. *All five women survived.* The survivors reached an Indian village in such pitiful condition the squaws wept and wailed in sympathy.

Determined, brave men risked their lives to fight their way to the relief of those who remained in the pass. Of the eighty-seven in the original party forty reached Sutter's Fort alive. The diaries that were written recounted stories of great self-sacrifice and bravery, of avarice and selfishness. Many left loved ones to die, others stayed to the end, sacrificing their own lives in vain. Tamsen Donner refused to leave her dying husband and shared his fate in the snows. One man found alive, of four who had been in an isolated cabin, was said to have been in good health and well nourished. Food was stolen from the pots of some. Food? For weeks it consisted mainly of the hides of slain cattle. Some boiled the leather in their shoes.

There were many who shared their last morsel with comrades. One man, attempting to reach Sutter's Fort in the hope of bringing help for his starving wife and children, found in his pack a few scraps of dried ox hide that his wife had hidden there, along with a note saying that at least he might survive, no matter what happened to the rest of his family. Greater love hath no wife.

And greater love hath no man than that of William Lewis Manly and the mysterious John Rogers of the Death Valley party, for they were willing to lay down their lives for those of their comrades.

These two found themselves thrown together by chance during the gold rush. Manly, whose account, written thirty years later, is accepted as the bible of what happened in the Valley of Despair in 1849, had been a trapper in upper Michigan and Wisconsin. John Rogers came from Tennessee, and that seems to be about all Manly knew about him, even though they walked, side by side, in a remarkable saga of devotion to others.

Manly, in the spring of '49, planned to join a wagon party

headed by his friend, Asabel Bennett, but, on reaching the starting point in Missouri, learned that Bennett had gone ahead with a caravan. Manly hired out as driver for the owner of wagons in another outfit, but quit the job on reaching Green River. There he joined six men in repairing an old scow that had been used as a ferry. One of the six was John Rogers.

They blithely floated down the Green, having been told by someone that the stream would carry them to the Pacific Ocean. This was one of the several false prophets they were to encounter. The hardihood of the early pioneers seemed to have only been matched by their naïveté. Too often they were eager to listen to pic-in-the-sky dreamers and out-and-out liars rather than face hard facts.

A chance meeting with a kindly Paiute leader, Chief Walker, saved them. The chief dissuaded them from facing the dangers of the Colorado River canyons and placed them on the trail that led them into the Salt Lake Valley. Two of the seven had more faith in the false prophets than in the Indian chief and continued down the river. They were never heard of again.

Manly met Asabel Bennett and his party by chance near Salt Lake. The season was growing late, and the story of the Donner party's travail two years earlier was well known. Many wagons had halted in the Salt Lake country, trying to decide what to do.

Mormons had traveled to Los Angeles, part of the route being over the old Spanish Trail from Taos and Sante Fe, which had been traversed for years by mountain men and the colorful Spanish traders who carried their wares by mule pack. Few or no wagons had made the journey, but the hazards, and, above all, the water holes were well mapped. But, like the Raft River route to California, this path swung far from the direct line to the gold fields. It crossed the grim Colorado River desert, and finally arrived at a dot on the map which bore the name El Pueblo de Nuestra Señora la Reina de Los Angeles.

That village was hundreds of miles south of their objective. While the same maps showed nothing but the Sierra Nevada range as an obstacle to heading directly west and cutting off those hundreds of miles there was no reason to believe that it could not be done. In fact there were stories that it was level, well-watered country.

A stalwart, experienced desert man, Captain Jefferson Hunt, knew nothing about the unmapped country, but knew enough about the Spanish Trail to agree to guide the caravan through to the pueblo. Price was ten dollars per wagon.

By that time many caravans had arrived and combined. Among them were the Jayhawkers. The Jayhawkers! A colorful name, a name that complemented the bright spirit of the young, adventurous men, who were determined to find yellow, glittering gold. Kansas, the Jayhawker state, was built on the same determination, but these men hailed from the country around Galesburg, Illinois. Any member joining their company had to agree to rigid rules set down by the directors, and go through a noisy initiation that included nipping bits of flesh from his bared leg to see if he possessed the proper fortitude against pain.

There were 36 Jayhawkers in the final assembly of between 105 and 112 wagons that agreed to follow Captain Hunt. Manly set the figure at 107 wagons, and perhaps other researchers added or subtracted a few. He does not number the humans, but says there were about 500 head of stock in camp, an estimate so low it can hardly be believed, for it allowed only an average of five animals to a wagon. Many of these people possessed riding stock as well as milk cows, in addition to the yoke and harness animals.

This unwieldy caravan set out southward, with Hunt guiding the way. Now the false prophets, like Lansford Hastings, began to appear. Manly names the principal one as a Captain Smith. He was said to have been a Mormon, and had a map supposed to have been drawn by a person named Williams. Neither of these persons, as far as Manly was concerned, seemed to have a given name, and that is an indication as to how the stampeders were ready to listen to siren songs.

Williams did have a first name. It was Alexander. He was a Mormon who was being sent to the Sandwich Islands on a mission for the church. The Sandwich Islands and the Hawaiian Islands are one and the same.

The map showed a fine and easy route westward, with good grass and water at regular marching distances apart. Copies were passed from eager hand to hand and sold at a price. Walker, the great pioneer, had traveled that route, had he not? Well, not exactly, although nobody knew that. Walker Pass existed, right enough, but it was many deserts and many valleys away. Many gravestones in the distance. Nobody had heard of the Amargosa

Desert. It wasn't on the map. Nor of Panamint Valley. Least of all had they heard of Death Valley. It had not yet been named.

Jefferson Hunt was a skeptic. "I do not believe any white man has ever gone that way," he told the assembled wagon people. "I agreed only to pilot you to California by the trail that is known. However, if you insist on changing the route, I will do my best to find water, but I have no reason to expect success. But if even one wagon continues by the agreed route, I will guide it."

His doubts were derided and buried under a torrent of words by another man, who, like Lansford Hastings, had a gift for oratory and a talent of swaying people to his views. He proved to be another false prophet. His name was J. W. Brier, and he was a minister of the gospel. He had a wife and two sons, and evidently was about the most impractical man ever to enter Death Valley. That covers quite a field, for the more one delves into the history of the great stampedes the more one marvels at the percentage of visionaries and out-and-out dingalings who took part.

Brier's wife, who left one of the few personal accounts of the journey, aside from Manly's, is credited with having gotten her family through alive. In any event, Reverend Brier, according to P. A. Chalfant, who was a member of the caravan, was instrumental in swaying the stampeders into following the false map.

At the southern rim of the Great Basin, near where the Mountain Meadows massacre of a wagon train occurred eight years later, the caravan, at a general meeting, held a vote. The majority agreed to turn right on what Manly called the Smith trail. Only seven voted to follow Jefferson Hunt down the known road. However, within a few days, those following the will-o'-the-wisp Smith trail found themselves toiling into rugged canyons that were not on the map Smith had shown them. The majority of them turned back and caught up with Hunt's party, which made it to the better known route, and they reached Los Angeles without undue incident.

Asabel Bennett and his friend, J. B. Arcane, decided to continue westward with others who still believed in the Smith map. Bennett was accompanied by his wife, two daughters, and a son. Arcane had a wife and son. For a time they were all a part of the Jayhawker party, whose strength at least protected them from danger of Indian attack.

Then the Jayhawkers held a meeting and laid down new rules.

No women! No children! They were in a hurry to reach the mines and had no intention of being delayed by petticoats and such. The Bennett-Arcane party was no longer welcome. The Briers were equally unwanted, but the minister was not the kind to be snubbed easily and tried to tag along in the dust of the fast-moving Jayhawkers.

From then on, the wagoneers fought their way deeper into a desert that became more pitiless with each mile. Manly did the hunting and the scouting. Each time he climbed to a ridge to peer ahead his heart would sink. More sterile ridges, more vacant desert, more desolation. And the oxen were already failing.

After bitter weeks, bitter miles, what Manly called a snowy peak loomed over lower ridges ahead. This stirred their failing courage enough to travel a little longer ahead. The peak might have been Telescope Peak in the Panamint Mountains. They believed it was in the Sierra Nevada, which, in fact, was still far away.

They finally emerged into full view of a snow-covered range. But at their feet lay a trough between mountains so savage-looking it drove new horror to them. To the south stretched crusted salt flats, cracked by the heat of the fierce summers and the cold of winters. Great sand dunes barred the way to the north. The land and canyons glowed with furnace colors as though the devil was still shaping the inferno.

They could not retrace their steps. Their supplies were about gone, their cattle were bone racks that moaned and wept like children as they struggled ahead.

They descended into this pit. On Christmas Eve. Manly said the situation seemed so hopeless he wished it was not his duty to stand by the women and children. What John Rogers thought was not set down.

They found a run of brackish water amid a stand of the weird desert plant known as arrowweed. The massive Panamint range soared overhead. This is where Bennett eventually made what is known as his long camp.

Meanwhile, the Jayhawkers, who had rushed here and there into box canyons and impassable gorges, had burned their wagons and were finding their way on foot out of the valley over a long, water-less slope, which was to carry them into the next gouge in the earth, almost as brutal as the one from which they were fleeing—Panamint Valley.

Other parties had scattered. Apparently the valley was well populated for a time with wandering wagoneers. The majority of them escaped through the lower end of the valley, found the Spanish Trail, and reached Los Angeles. The Brier party was one of these. Reverend Brier, from the first, had faith everything would come out all right for him. Manly, on a visit to his camp in Death Valley, said he found the minister calmly lecturing his wife and children on the importance of education as a means of getting on in the world. At this moment the Bennett and Arcane children were crying for water in their dreary camp not far away, and the oxen were lying down and refusing to get back on their feet.

Manly and Rogers finally were asked to attempt to escape from the trap and bring help. Then began the saga of devotion. Manly mentioned Rogers only occasionally in his entire account of the trip, but, evidently, they were close friends and pulled together. Being still young and not as weak as the others, they agreed to give it a try.

Bennett gave Manly a rifle to replace his own disabled weapon. Rogers was armed with a double-barreled shotgun. They carried knives. Manly had no coat, Rogers only a thin summer jacket. Despite Death Valley's reputation for heat, it is cold in that locality in winter. Their warmer garments had been given the women and children.

The women had made moccasins of ox hide for them. They carried tin cups and a kettle holding water. For food, Manly said, they had seven eighths of the flesh of a starved ox. The animal had been so thin they carried the meat in their knapsacks along with a few spoonfuls of rice and tea. They took all the money in camp, amounting to less than a hundred dollars.

Remaining in the long camp were the five Bennetts, the three Arcanes, two brothers, a boy named Earhart, and a Captain Culverwell, along with a few others. Eleven adults, in all. A family named Wade preferred to camp apart.

As in the case of the Donner party, there had been food thefts, with the culprits being unnamed. Individual wagons, such as that of the Wades, that were in better condition and better provisioned, avoided the failing companies. No food or help was offered the Bennett camp.

Manly and Rogers, with great toil, made their way through the Panamint Mountains over a route that is still in doubt and emerged into a new country that stretched endlessly ahead—without sign of water. A snow-covered range that must have been the Sierra Nevada was visible far to the west. Manly estimated the distance at two hundred miles although it was actually scarcely half that far away.

They veered south, evidently aware there would be settlements in that direction. They finally sighted a pond of water and rushed to it, only to recoil. It was salt. This bitter experience was repeated several times. This was a land that beckoned them, mocked them. Rippling blue lakes that appeared in the distance proved to be hardpan alkali playas, whose sterile surfaces reflected the blue sky. Their mouths became so dry they could not swallow the tough ox meat.

Rogers, miraculously, located a thin, small panel of ice remaining from the freeze of the previous night, and this carried them a little farther.

They came upon segments of the Jayhawkers, and also two of Bennett's original crew, who had hired out as teamsters, but who had gone their own way in an attempt to reach safety. All were in desperate straits. Manly said he and Rogers shared their scant food with the teamsters. Some of the Jayhawkers gave them messages to be sent to loved ones back east. They had already left several of their party dead on their back trail.

The two found a spring of good water and that carried them into a desert where they came upon weird trees with hairy arms and twisted forms, such as they had never seen before. These were later to be known as Joshua trees, although botanical purists call them tree yuccas. Manly and Rogers followed a trail of bones of animals, many of them those of horses, the cause of whose death they never learned.

They kept going. Far, far behind them now were the Bennett and Arcane women and children. Ahead were mountains that surely must be the last barrier. They were finding no more water. A crow that alighted on brush nearby fell to the shotgun. Its meat was strengthening. Later, they killed a hawk.

They reached greener country. Trees, green grass. Paradise after escaping from the pit. Signs of civilization. They came upon cattle and shot one, jerking its meat.

Finally, human beings! Living in strangely built houses. No hoops or shoes on the women. Sandals on the men. A strange tongue that was Spanish. They could not make themselves understood.

They were led to the Catholic mission at San Fernando where they were furnished with food and shelter for the night. Americans who spoke their language arrived. They were told that the road to the mines was long, by way of Los Angeles, but comparatively easy. At least, compared to what they had been over. They were told stories of great fortunes being dug, of men panning out more gold in a day than he could lift.

And here they were, after all these weary months of privation and toil, their strength restored, young, vigorous men who could be in the mines within a few weeks. They had conquered the desert. They were *alive!*

But more than a week's travel across their fearsome back trail were the Bennett and the Arcane women and children, and the others. Dead, probably, by this time. But were they dead? Manly and Rogers did not speak to each other for a long time as they sat, trying to accustom their stomachs to the tortillas and frijoles that were being placed before them. They were trying to think clearly.

Then, without discussing it openly, they began preparing. They made their own flour at the crude mill their hosts owned. They were given beans and wheat and jerky. For thirty dollars they bought two nondescript horses. Later on, for fifteen dollars, a mule whose owners considered they had got the best of the deal, and a mare.

They headed out. Not for the mines, but back from whence they had come. They traveled alone, two men who owed no real obligation to those for whom they were risking their lives. Their duty was to themselves and their consciences.

They followed the Jayhawker trail as they backtracked, and that led them into trouble. They missed water holes and wandered across miles of loose, shifting desert soil where even greasewood and rabbit brush grew small and sparse. They detoured around wide playas where a man and a horse might break through the crusted surface and sink into bottomless mud.

The three horses gave out and were abandoned. They made the passage of the Panamints once more, the mule proving to be as tough as the two men.

Finally they stumbled out of a draw, and before them lay the fearful valley from which they had once escaped, only to return. They had now been without water for two days, and their condition was far worse, physically, than when they had set out to bring help.

They stumbled toward the distant patch of brush and arrowweed. Then they halted, gazing at a sprawled body that lay on the barren earth ahead. Moving fearfully closer, they found that it was the corpse of Captain Culverwell. Evidently he had tried to escape alone on foot from the valley, but had managed to travel only a mile or so.

They finally came in sight of the long camp. Only four vehicles remained in the dreary place instead of the seven that had been there when they had left. There was no sign of life. No evidence of survivors after they had traveled nearly five hundred miles in an attempt to save them.

Manly fired a shot from his rifle. That sound seemed to be swallowed by the droning wind and the barren distances.

Then, behold! Voices! Asabel Bennett came hurrying from a tent. His family and the Arcanes appeared. They were thin, haggard ghosts. In turn, they gazed, horrified, at the gaunt pair who stood before them—phantoms from the grave whom they had long since given up as dead. They had been awaiting death themselves. They were the only ones. The others had parted from them, believing that Manly and Rogers would never return.

The survivors made saddles for the oxen and shod them with skins from dead animals. They set out on a journey through country that was even worse than any the Bennetts and Arcanes had already seen. Fear and terror had been their greatest burden for weeks. These emotions had almost destroyed their wills to survive. There was now a difference. They knew now there could be an end to this awful ordeal. They were buoyed by that magic word—hope. That carried them through. Nineteen days later they arrived at the mission. All were still alive.

The valley is named Death Valley, but none of the Bennetts or Arcanes died there. Manly and Rogers had returned in time.

The two men made their way to Los Angeles and turned their thoughts back to their original purpose, that of getting to the mines and finding gold. They made it to the mines, but they found no gold.

They drifted apart, these men who had walked side by side

out of the Valley of the Shadow, then had returned to it to help others. Manly saw John Rogers for the last time, by chance, when they waved to each other from the decks of passing ferryboats in San Francisco Bay. Merely a distant salute. Then John Rogers was gone into the oblivion from which he had come. The great adventure was over. Manly died at the age of eighty-three in San Jose in 1903.

Some researchers wonder why Manly mentioned Rogers so few times in his account of their journey together. They also speculate on the possibility that Manly's book, first published in 1894, so long after the feat, might have been rewritten by someone else. But the authenticity of the journey itself is unchallenged.

CHAPTER 14

## THE STEEL THREAD

Nearly a score of years after Manly and Rogers had forded the Platte, a new thread began creeping across The Mighty Land, a thread of steel that was to be far more durable, far more significant in the future of the Plains than even the Great Medicine Road. It was to make obsolete that historic trail. It was to end forever the silence of the vast land, end the myth of "the great American desert." It was the sinew that was to bind the nation together. This was the coming of the railroad, the building of the Union Pacific.

Western Union had spanned the nation in 1861 with its telegraph wires, strung in many areas of the West on wooden insulators nested above square poles. This partly ended the isolation of frontier settlements and brought the coasts closer together, at least as far as news and communication went. The telegraph put an end to the Pony Express. But both had whetted the appetite of those far-flung specks of humanity for even better service. They wanted fast transportation also.

A railroad to the Pacific had been talked of since the mid 1840s, and surveys had shown that it was feasible. The only sticking point was that the majority of the men in Congress considered it sheer insanity to consider throwing money away on building a railroad hundreds of miles through what even the maps listed as a wasteland.

The gold strike in California began to change that viewpoint. Discovery of the Comstock silver lode at Virginia City, Nevada, was the clincher. The Civil War intervened, absorbing the nation's resources, although the Pacific Railway Act was signed by President Lincoln on July 1, 1862.

Ground was broken, however, at Omaha on November 30, 1863. Work had started even sooner in California. There a brilliant young engineer, Theodore D. Judah, had convinced a quartet of ambitious Golden State merchants that a railroad *could* be built over the *impassable* Sierra Nevada—and right past Donner Lake of evil reputation, of all places.

The provisions of the railroad act were tempting. The railroad builders were offered a 400-foot right-of-way from the Missouri River to Sacramento, along with government loans of $16,000 per mile of track on the prairie, $32,000 in the rougher going, and $48,000 in the mountains. Ten square miles of public land was to be granted for each mile of track laid. These provisions were the bait that built the first transcontinental railroad. There were scandals, investigations, graft, ruined political careers, and men elevated from obscurity into national prominence. But the railroad survived.

However, when Appomattox came, only forty miles of rusty, seldom-used track extended west of Omaha. In California, the Central Pacific had built just twenty miles each year toward the mountains. Judah had died of fever, and the work was in the hands of Charles Crocker, Collis P. Huntington, Leland Stanford, and Mark Hopkins. Crocker was head of construction, the others financiers. Between them they saw to it that the Central Pacific was finally built. They were determined men.

They had their counterparts in Thomas C. Durant, the driving force back of the Union Pacific, and his construction chief, General Grenville Dodge. The end of the war had released a flood of unemployed men whose energies needed an outlet. Congress responded by passing the legislation to finance work on the transcontinental.

"I need a million crossties—and right now!" Durant said. "And ten thousand rails and a few other things, for a beginning."

It was impossible, of course. But he got them. They came by steamboat, by wagon, by barge to Omaha. Timber out of which ties could be chopped by ax crews, rails from Pennsylvania, fishplates, bolts, sledges, spikes, and grading tools. Men arrived, first by the hundreds, then by the thousands, the majority of them still clad in the Union blue they had worn at Chickamauga and in the

Wilderness. A heavy percentage were Irish, uneducated, tough, aggressive, and willing. They were not men to follow weak leaders.

They were proud to labor under such as Tom Durant. He had proved his mettle when he personally saved a bargeload of iron after it had broken loose from the levee at Omaha during a flood. Durant, pulling off his boots, plunged into the river, setting an example for others to follow, and the precious load was brought under control, averting a disaster that would have delayed construction for weeks. The veteran soldiers were happy to work under Grenville Dodge also, for he had fought in the war, as they had, and had nearly died from wounds. Sure and he carried the scars.

Ten thousand men eventually swarmed along the right-of-way, aided by ten thousand draft animals, hundreds of wagons, and hundreds of scrapers and bridge builders. The graders worked a hundred miles ahead of the track crews. The rails advanced slowly at first, then reached a pace of a mile a day. Still that was not enough. The task was always being speeded up.

By January 1, 1867, the Union Pacific had reached North Platte, leaving behind it such places as Columbus City, Platte City, Fort Kearney, and Grand Island. By that time the crews were putting down upward of two miles of track a day and the work was still being stepped up. There was always that distant thunder a thousand miles beyond the western horizon—the coming of the Central Pacific. The Central was still laboring in the mountains, beset by sheer cliffs, deep canyons, and torrential streams. Also by the heaviest snowfalls on the continent.

To surmount these difficulties the C.P. was importing Chinese coolies by the hundreds. Men were being lowered on bo's'n chairs down sheer cliffs to begin chipping away at the granite so that a ledge could be formed for the track. This was the infernal Cape Horn job that took lives, took precious time, and wore the nerves of men to the breaking point. A tunnel was necessary at the Cape Horn summit. Men began working at both ends. That was not enough. A shaft was bored down into the center of the survey. Coolies worked inside the mountain in both directions. Even so, despite the four-way attack, a year was required to complete the tunnel's less than half a mile length.

At the same time, the Union Pacific crews were having no picnic. Survey camps and construction crews were being hit by

raiding parties of Cheyennes, Sioux, and Crows, who swept out
of ambush without warning, killing and carrying off captives to be
tortured. However, the men in the U.P. crew were Civil War
veterans who knew which end of a rifle the bullets came from,
and the tribesmen began to pay dearly for their attempts to hold
back the Iron Horse.

The Plains winter brought blizzards and snow so deep that at
times chains of five locomotives were needed to buck a plow
through the drifts. The Central Pacific had the same problem.
In places it built miles of snowsheds.

By the time the U.P. raced up the South Platte into Julesburg,
which was considered the halfway point, the work had been honed
to machinelike precision. The rails were brought to end of steel
from the work train on small light handcars and seized, one-by-one,
by sixteen men working in pairs. They were dropped on the ties
and spiked down by the sledge men, three blows to a spike. The
handcar, when empty, was tipped off the track, and another quota
of rails was rushed into the place, while the empty was returned to
the work train at a pace a horse could gallop. The work train kept
moving up, moving up, moving up, on the freshly laid rails.

Efficiency extended into the bunkhouses and bunk-cars. It is
said that some of the mess bosses nailed tin plates to the tables and
these were filled hastily by helpers sloshing buffalo stew from
steaming pots. As soon one shift of men emptied the plates they
filed out, a mop-up man hurried along, swabbing off the plates
with a mop, and a second shift of hungry construction workers filed
in to take their places.

Construction work in the field was under direction of the famed
Jack Casement, who had been a general in the Civil War. With
the help of his brother Dan, he kept the brawling, rough crews in
hand, and also tamed some of the wild towns along the way. One
of those that needed taming—and received it in a historic incident
—was the little town of Julesburg.

When the clang of steel in the distance awakened the citizens of
Julesburg Number 2 to the realization that, because of grading
problems, the U.P. was going to pass by on the opposite side of
the river, the town moved, bag and baggage, to its third location.
(Later on, when the Denver spur was built, it moved again.)

However, Julesburg Number 3 was born just in time. End of steel
had arrived and "The Wickedest City in the World" was in busi-

ness. The knockdown gambling houses, saloons, and brothels were heaved off flatcars into the sagebrush and set up within an hour.

The most pretentious of these was the "Big Top," which operated under canvas, 100 by 40 feet. Its brass bands blared music that never ceased around the clock. It had a stage where women in tights kicked up their heels, and offered a sawdust-covered dance floor where patrons could cavort with the percentage girls at whatever cost the traffic would bear.

By nightfall the temporary city of fun was going full blast, with hurdy-gurdies tinkling, barkers bellowing the delights of the establishments they represented, thimbleriggers making their pitch at tent-front tables. Torches and reflector lamps fought back the great darkness of the Plains. By morning Julesburg had a king-sized hangover.

The construction crews had made merry under these same canvas roofs on the way up the Platte Valley at way points whose citizens were still recovering from the binge and staring disbelievingly at the trampled terrain where only yesterday the music had been raucous, the painted ladies willing, the gamblers deft.

The Union Pacific had acquired a following it had not anticipated and did not desire. Crooked gamblers, hardcases, outlaws from all over the nation, had joined the entourage. They became so ambitious they began to attempt to take charge of the whole operation. They particularly resented rules that Jack Casement laid down, loose as they were, to protect his terriers from the human buzzards.

They were dealing with the wrong man. When Casement selected choice ground at Julesburg for storage sheds and railroad shops, the gamblers attempted to seize the land for their own purposes. Casement armed one hundred of his terriers and marched into town one evening.

General Dodge arrived in Julesburg a few days later. "Are the gamblers peaceful?" he asked Casement.

"They sure are, General," said Casement. "Go see for yourself. They're out there in the cemetery."

Hell on Wheels moved on, leaving Julesburg smoldering and sputtering out, its day of glory over. Steel reached Cheyenne on November 13, 1867, after a battle with blizzards and more Indian forays. The pace was ever quickening as the line advanced across the high Wyoming plain. The Central Pacific had emerged from its travail in the Sierra, and was laying rails at frenzied speed across the flat Humboldt Desert.

Union Pacific bosses cursed and prodded the crews.

> *Drill, ye terriers, drill,*
> *Drill, ye terriers, drill,*
> *Oh, it's work all day,*
> *No sugar in your tay,*
> *Workin' on the old U.P.*

Four miles a day, now. "Faster, you micks! Faster! Sure, an' you're not goin' to let a lot o' yella-skinned Chinks beat you? They laid nigh onto five miles in the Humboldt yisterday. The Western Union operator just told me. Faster!"

Ties, more ties. Steel, more steel. Bobsleds were used to haul supplies in the frozen Wasatch Mountains of Utah. In places, the rails were laid above frozen snow, with the promise of being replaced on solid ground when spring came. Trains were run over these precarious stretches.

Down Weber Canyon toward the easier going on the flats around Great Salt Lake. Ties were costing upward of five dollars each. Cottonwood and cedar were being hardened by a scorching process and were mixed in with the expensive oak and chestnut that was brought from the East. Debts were mounting. Durant was running excursion parties of eastern moneybags out from Omaha to end of steel to convince them that investment in the U.P. was a good thing. Dodge took them on tours of gambling houses and brothels in the settlements along the way.

Faster! Nearly four hundred twenty-eight foot rails were being laid to a mile, ten spikes to a rail for the first crew. Let the follow-up crews finish the spiking. Trains could move on ten-spike rails if all went well.

Nearing the end of the race, Casement's terriers blazed ahead, laying six miles of track between sunup and sundown—an unprecedented feat. Charles Crocker's Central Pacific Chinese responded on the Humboldt by completing seven and a half miles in the same time. Furthermore, Crocker boasted that he could lay ten miles of rails if there was the proper incentive. Tom Durant, never one to back away from a wager, furnished the incentive in the form of offering to bet ten thousand dollars that the feat was impossible.

Crocker accepted the bet. He picked a crew of brawny Irish terriers to handle the rails and sledges, while coolies laid the ties and took care of the ballast. They handled upward of 4,000 rails weighing 600 pounds each, drove 40,000 spikes, and bolted down some 7,500 fishplates. They rushed the job along so fast they even took an hour off for a noon rest, beer, and chest inflation. They completed ten and six-tenths miles of rails before the sun sank, and Crocker collected the wager.

The U.P. spent a million dollars grading one hundred miles west of Promontory Point, and the C.P. graders were working eighty miles east before Congress forced a compromise and designated the meeting place on the bleak Salt Lake desert.

A great crowd for such an isolated place gathered for the historic event on May 10, 1869. A tie of polished laurel was the last to be laid. Golden spikes from California and silver spikes from Nevada were ready. The golden spikes had been connected to the telegraph line, which was on a nationwide hookup, but the plan failed, and the operator stood ready to tap out the signal.

Speeches, invocations, were uttered. The Army band played selections while the nation waited. Finally, the operator broke the silence on the wire, saying, "We have got done praying. The spike is about to be presented."

Durant swung one of the silver sledges, and Governor Leland Stanford, of California, the other. Both missed. But the operator tapped his key as they swung. The word was flashed across the continent. The railroad to the Pacific was finished. Omaha was 1,085 miles from Promontory Point, Sacramento, 690 miles. Hard-won miles. Miles of desert, mountain, prairie, plain.

Cannon boomed in New York City, in Washington, in Chicago, in a hundred other cities. The Liberty Bell was rung in Philadelphia. Fireworks lighted the skies across the nation, bands played, speeches ran long and windy.

The steel thread stretched endlessly across The Mighty Land. It stretched up the Platte Valley past Kearney, past North Platte, past Julesburg, past Cheyenne. It snaked down the canyons of the Wasatch Range and lay ruler-straight under the sun of the Nevada desert. The Sierra Nevada of California had been conquered. The champagne was flowing in Sacramento, and also in Denver, which soon would claim to be queen of the Plains.

The land lay there, vast, rich, waiting for the millions who would claim it. It is still there. The view of The Mighty Land from the Shining Mountains is still stupendous.

# Bibliography

Allen, Durward. *The Life of Prairie and Plains*. New York: McGraw-Hill, 1967.

Altrocchi, Julia Cooley. *The Old California Trail*. Caldwell, Idaho: Caxton Printers, Ltd., 1945.

Banning, Captain William, and Banning, George Hugh. *Six Horses*. New York: Appleton-Century-Crofts, 1930.

Bell, Major Horace. *On the Old West Coast*. New York: Morrow, 1930.

Bisbee, Brigadier General William H. *Through Four American Wars*. Boston: Meador, 1931.

Bradley, General Omar N. *A Soldier's Story*. New York: Holt, Rinehart & Winston, 1951.

Burchardt, Bill. *Oklahoma Today*.

Caesar, Gene. *King of the Mountain Men*. New York: Dutton, 1961.

Chalfant, W. A. *The Story of Inyo*. California: Bishop, 1933.

Chapman, Arthur. *The Pony Express*. New York: Putnam, 1932.

Custer, Elizabeth B. *Boots and Saddles*. Norman: University of Oklahoma Press, 1962.

Custer, General George A. *My Life on the Plains*. Norman: University of Oklahoma Press, 1962.

Davis, Burke. *To Appomattox*. New York: Holt, Rinehart & Winston, 1959.

Dixon, Olive K. *The Life of Billy Dixon*. Dallas: P. L. Turner, 1914.

Driggs, Howard R. *The Pony Express Goes Through*. New York: Stokes, 1935.

Duffus, R. L. *The Santa Fe Trail*. New York: Longmans, 1930.

Geiger, Vincent, and Wakeman, Bryarly. *Trail to California*. New Haven: Yale University Press, 1945.

Gerson, Noel B. *Kit Carson*. Garden City, N.Y.: Doubleday, 1964.

Glasscock, C. B. *The Big Bonanza*. New York: Bobbs-Merrill, 1933.

Havighurst, Walter. *Annie Oakley of the Wild West*. New York: Macmillan, 1954.

Horan, James D., and Sann, Paul. *Pictorial History of the Wild West*. New York: Crown, 1954.

Hulbert, Archer Butler. *Forty-Niners,* Boston: Little, Brown, 1931.

Hunter, J. Marvin, ed. *The Trail Drivers of Texas.* Nashville, 1925.

Hunter, Vickie, and Hamma, Elizabeth. *Stagecoach Days.* Menlo Park, Calif.: Lane, 1963.

Jackson, Clarence S. *Picture Maker of the Old West.* New York: Scribner, 1947.

Kanas Federal Writers Project. *Kansas, a Guide to the Sunflower State.* New York: Viking, 1939.

Lake, Stuart. *Wyatt Earp, Frontier Marshal.* New York: Houghton-Mifflin, 1931.

Langford, N. P. *Vigilante Days and Ways.* New York, 1912.

Leonard, Elizabeth J., and Cody, Julia. *Buffalo Bill: King of the Old West.* New York: Library Publishers, 1955.

Leonard, Levi A., and Johnson, Jack T. *A Railroad to the Sea.* Iowa City: Midland House, 1939.

Magoffin, Susan Shelby. *Down the Santa Fe Trail and Into Mexico.* New Haven: Yale University Press, 1962.

Majors, Alexander. *70 Years on the Frontier.* Columbus: Long's College Book Co. 1965 reprint of 1893 edition.

Manly, William Lewis, *Death Valley Days in '49.* Los Angeles: Dawson Book Shop, 1929.

Marshall, James. *Santa Fe.* New York: Random House, 1945.

Mattison, Ray M. *Cowboy and Cattlemen.* Montana collections.

Miller, Ronald Dean. *Shady Ladies of the West.* Los Angeles: Westernlore, 1964.

Monaghan, Jay. *Custer.* Boston: Little, Brown, 1959.

Nadeau, Remi. *Fort Laramie.* Englewood Cliffs, N.J.: Prentice-Hall, 1967.

North, Luther. *Man of the Plains.* Lincoln: University of Nebraska Press, 1961.

Ormsby, Waterman Lily. *The Butterfield Overland Mail.* San Marino, Calif.: Huntington Library, 1955.

Paden, Irene D. *Wake of the Prairie Schooner.* New York: Macmillan, 1943.

———— *Prairie Schooner Detours.* New York: Macmillan, 1949.

Page, Elizabeth. *Wagons West.* New York: Farrar & Rinehart, 1930.

Parkhill, Forbes. *The Wildest of the West.* New York: Holt, Rinehart & Winston, 1951.

Parkman, Francis. *The Oregon Trail.* Boston: Ginn & Company, 1910.

Pinkerton, William A. *Address to the International Association of Police Chiefs.* Jamestown, Va., 1907.

Roosevelt, Theodore. *The Winning of the West.* 14 volumes. New York: Putnam, 1893–96.

Rosa, Joseph G. *They Called Him Wild Bill.* Norman: University of Oklahoma Press, 1964.

Russell, Don. *Lives and Legends of Buffalo Bill.* Norman: University of Oklahoma Press, 1960.

Ruxton, George Frederick. *In the Old West.* New York: Outing Publishing, 1915.

Rynning, Captain Thomas. *Gun Notches,* as told to Al Cohn and Joe Chisholm. New York: Stokes, 1931.

Salisbury, Albert and Jane. *Here Rolled the Covered Wagons.* Seattle: Superior, 1948.

Sandoz, Mari. *The Buffalo Hunters.* New York: Hastings House, 1954.

———— *Cheyenne Autumn.* New York: Hastings House, 1959.

Sell, Henry Blackman, and Weybright, Victor. *Buffalo Bill and the Wild West.* New York: Oxford, 1955.

Seymour, Flora Warren. *The Story of the Red Men.* London: Longmans, Green, 1929.

Spring, Agnes Wright. *The Cheyenne and Black Hills Stage and Express Routes.* Lincoln: University of Nebraska Press, 1948.

Stackpole, Edward J. *Sheridan in the Shenandoah.* Harrisburg, Pa.: Stackpole, 1961.

Stevers, Martin D. *Steel Trails.* New York: Putnam, 1933.

Stewart, E. I. *Custer's Luck.* Norman: University of Oklahoma Press, 1955.

Streeter, Floyd B. *Prairie Trails and Cow Towns.* New York: Devin-Adair, 1963.

Twain, Mark. *Roughing It.* New York: Harper Brothers, 1899.

Ulyatt, Kenneth. *North Against the Sioux.* Englewood Cliffs: Prentice-Hall, 1967.

Van de Water, Frederic F. *Glory Hunter.* New York: Bobbs-Merrill, 1934.

Vestal, Stanley. *Kit Carson.* New York: Houghton Mifflin, 1931.

Ware, Captain Eugene F. *The Indian War of 1864.* Lincoln: University of Nebraska Press, 1961.

Webb, W. E. *Buffalo Land.* Philadelphia, 1874.

Webb, Walter Prescott. *The Great Plains.* New York: Grosset & Dunlap, 1931.

Werner, M. R. *Barnum.* Garden City: Doubleday, 1926.

Wetmore, Helen Cody, and Grey, Zane. *Last of the Great Scouts.* New York: 1918.

Wheeler, Colonel Homer B. *Buffalo Days.* New York, 1923–25.

Willison, George F. *Here They Dug the Gold.* New York: Coward-McCann, 1931.

Winther, Oscar Osburn. *Via Western Express & Stagecoach*. Stanford University Press, 1954.

Wood, R. Coke, and Bush, Leon. *California History and Government*. San Francisco: 1962.

Wormser, Richard. *The Yellowlegs*. New York: Doubleday, 1961.

Also special appreciation to many others who aided me in research, particularly Mrs. Guy Dunn of the Fort Sedgwick Historical Society and the other ladies of the Julesburg, Colorado, library. Also my friend, Harry Hill Morgan, whose private library was available to me. I am much indebted to many contributors to the fine magazine *True West*, and its predecessor at Bandera, Texas, *Frontier Times*.

# INDEX